The SAS® Programmer's PROC REPORT Handbook

Basic to Advanced Reporting Techniques

Jane Eslinger

§sas.

support.sas.com/bookstore

The correct bibliographic citation for this manual is as follows: Eslinger, Jane. 2016. *The SAS® Programmer's PROC REPORT Handbook: Basic to Advanced Reporting Techniques.* Cary, NC: SAS Institute Inc.

The SAS® Programmer's PROC REPORT Handbook: Basic to Advanced Reporting Techniques

Contents

About This Book

Purpose

The purpose of this book is to describe every aspect of PROC REPORT. The book reviews options and syntax and how the data set is processed behind the scenes. Most importantly, it provides many examples of the kinds of reports programmers need to create every day. The book explains why specific options and statements are required for certain kinds of reports and provides the most efficient code for generating the desired reports.

Is This Book for You?

This book is meant for SAS programmers of all skill levels in all industries who need to create reports. PROC REPORT can create easy, bland reports, but programmers, no matter the skill level, are rarely tasked with creating such reports. This book will help you increase your skill level and proficiency in generating the reports you need.

Prerequisites

Basic knowledge of SAS programming is necessary to understand the concepts and examples in this book. You should understand data structure and formats. You need a general understanding of what the Macro Facility is and you should know the basic concepts of sending output to Output Delivery System (ODS) destinations.

Scope of This Book

This book is entirely about PROC REPORT. It covers everything there is to know about PROC REPORT.

Although it includes the FORMAT, TRANSPOSE, MEANS, SQL, and DOCUMENT procedures, they are not covered in depth in this book. The syntax of those procedures is described only enough to convey the reason the procedure is needed in conjunction with PROC REPORT. The book also includes use of the Macro Facility.

PROC REPORT is designed specifically for generating reports; therefore, ODS plays a major role in the final appearance of the report. A full description of the syntax and use of ODS is beyond the scope of this book. However, where necessary, the behavior of a certain destination is explained as it pertains to PROC REPORT.

About the Examples

Software Used to Develop the Book's Content

The examples in this book were developed using Base SAS 9.4TS1M3. The examples can be run in 9.4TS1M0-9.4TS1M3, with all available hot fixes installed.

The examples should work in SAS 9.3 as well, but please note: if the example programs are run interactively in 9.3, the NOWD option should be added to the PROC REPORT statement. This book is also compatible with SAS University Edition.

Example Code and Data

The Orion Star data used throughout this book is with the permission of Sean O'Brien and Eric Rossland. The majority of the examples in this book use one data set, ORDERS. The other data sets are either a subset or restructuring of the ORDERS data set. Using just one data set should limit the confusion of having to understand the data structure of multiple data sets.

ORDERS contains purchase order data. The data set is unique at CUSTOMER_ID, ORDER_ID, and PRODUCT_ID level. A customer can have multiple orders and within each unique order, the customer can purchase multiple products.

The QUANTITY variable contains the quantity ordered of a specific product.

The CUSTOMER variable contains one record for each CUSTOMER_NAME value.

The SUMINFO variable was created by running a PROC MEANS step on the ORDERS data set. It contains one record for each CUSTOMER_COUNTRY-CUSTOMER_GROUP combination.

The TRAN_ORDERS variable was created by running a PROC TRANSPOSE step on the ORDERS data set. It contains one record for each CUSTOMER_ID-CUSTOMER_NAME combination and has one variable for each order the customer placed.

The ORDERS_3OBS variable contains three observations and four variables. The variables match those from the ORDERS data set that are used throughout the book.

To use the example programs from the author page, you need to store the five data sets described above in the WORK location. You also need to submit the createfmts.sas program. The program creates two formats, called $cntry and typef, used throughout the book. The formats should be stored in a catalog in the WORK location as well.

You do not have to read this book cover to cover to gain valuable knowledge about PROC REPORT. Each example demonstrates one technique and a specific outcome. However, the examples and chapters do build on each other, so you might find it helpful to read entire sections or chapters in order to fully understand the purpose of each example.

You can access the example code and data for this book by linking to its author page at http://support.sas.com/publishing/authors. Select the name of the author. Then, look for the cover thumbnail of this book, and select Example Code and Data to display the SAS programs that are included in this book.

If you are unable to access the code through the website, send email to saspress@sas.com.

SAS University Edition

If you are using SAS University Edition to access data and run your programs, then please check the SAS University Edition page to ensure that the software contains the product or products that you need to run the code: http://support.sas.com/software/products/university-edition/index.html.

Output and Graphics Used in This Book

The output in this book is sent to many of the ODS destinations, including PDF, HTML, RTF, Tagsets.ExcelXP, and the Excel destination. Most of the output is sent to the PDF destination. When another destination is used, it is noted with the example.

Terminology Used in This Book

The terms *report-item*, variable, and column are used interchangeably throughout the book and the term that is used is determined by the context. The term *report-item* distinguishes the type of compute block or required syntax for a specific statement. Otherwise, the term variable or column is used.

The terms *location* and *target* are italicized to distinguish how variables are used on BREAK, RBREAK, and COMPUTE statements. *Location* controls the placement of the break rows or where a compute block executes. *Target* controls when the execution takes place. This book capitalizes the value of a specific location or target when referred to within text.

The words group, order, and across are capitalized when the context refers to the usage value on the DEFINE statement. All statement names, options, and variable names are capitalized in text.

Additional Help

Although this book illustrates many analyses regularly performed in businesses across industries, questions specific to your aims and issues might arise. To fully support you, SAS Institute and SAS Press offer you the following help resources:

- For questions about topics covered in this book, contact the author through SAS Press:
    - Send questions by email to saspress@sas.com; include the book title in your correspondence.
    - Submit feedback on the author's page at http://support.sas.com/author_feedback.
- For questions about topics in or beyond the scope of this book, post queries to the relevant SAS Support Communities at https://communities.sas.com/welcome.
- SAS Institute maintains a comprehensive website with up-to-date information. One page that is particularly useful to both the novice and the seasoned SAS user is its Knowledge Base. Search for relevant notes in the "Samples and SAS Notes" section of the Knowledge Base at http://support.sas.com/resources.
- Registered SAS users or their organizations can access SAS Customer Support at http://support.sas.com. Here you can pose specific questions to SAS Customer Support; under *Support*, click *Submit a Problem*. You will need to provide an email address to which replies can be sent, identify your organization, and provide a customer site number or license information. This information can be found in your SAS logs.

Recommended Reading

If you enjoy this book, consider reading these SAS Press books next.

Benjamin, William. 2015. *Exchanging Data between SAS® and Microsoft Excel: Tips and Techniques to Transfer and Manage Data More Efficiently*. Cary, NC: SAS Institute Inc.

Burlew, Michele M. 2014. *SAS® Macro Programming Made Easy, Third Edition*. Cary, NC: SAS Institute Inc.

Carpenter, Art. 2007. *Carpenter's Complete Guide to the SAS® REPORT Procedure*. Cary, NC: SAS Institute Inc.

Fine, Lisa. 2013. *PROC REPORT by Example: Techniques for Building Professional Reports Using SAS®*. Cary, NC: SAS Institute Inc.

Smith, Kevin D. 2014. *ODS Techniques: Tips for Enhancing Your SAS® Output*. Cary, NC: SAS Institute Inc.

Keep in Touch

We look forward to hearing from you. We invite questions, comments, and concerns. If you want to contact us about a specific book, please include the book title in your correspondence.

Contact the Author through SAS Press

- By email: saspress@sas.com
- Via the web: http://support.sas.com/author_feedback

About The Author

 Jane Eslinger is a Senior Technical Support Analyst at SAS World Headquarters in Cary, North Carolina. Jane is a SAS Certified Advanced Programmer for SAS(R)9 and a SAS Certified Advanced Visual Business Analyst. She has presented at numerous conferences and users groups, including the 2015 SAS Global Forum conference where she presented a paper on compute blocks in PROC REPORT.

In her day-to-day work, Jane enjoys supporting SAS customers using ODS and Base SAS procedures, with an emphasis on PROC REPORT. Prior to joining SAS, Jane served as a statistician and statistical programmer in the social science and clinical research fields. She has a Bachelor of Science in Statistics from North Carolina State University.

Learn more about this author by visiting her author page at http://support.sas.com/eslinger. There you can download free book excerpts, access example code and data, read the latest reviews, get updates, and more.

Acknowledgments

First I would like to thank Kelly Close, without whose encouragement and support I would never have started writing this book. I would also like to thank Grace Whiteis for her support as I worked on the drafts of this book.

A number of people unwittingly helped me with portions of this book before it took its final shape; for that I am grateful to Bari Lawhorn, Tim Hunter, Jerry Leonard, Chevell Parker, and Marcia Surratt. I am also grateful to all of the technical reviewers of this book, which include Kathryn McLawhorn, Cynthia Zender, and Robin Crumpton.

Preface

With PROC REPORT you can sort and transpose data. You can calculate statistics and create new variables. You can concatenate character variables and multiply numeric variables. No other procedure comes close to this kind of versatility. Because PROC REPORT acts like no other procedure in Base SAS, it might be the hardest to learn and understand. It can be both frustrating and confusing.

In this book I try to show you the power of PROC REPORT and help you imagine all of the things you can do with it. I also try to show you the pitfalls that make you want to throw up your hands in defeat. Programmers are no longer tasked with just calculating a number; you must create output in a certain form and it must be aesthetically pleasing. The output must be suitable for all levels of management and areas of expertise. Therefore, all programmers should learn how to use PROC REPORT because at any time, they might be asked to create a report. I admit it takes time to learn all the nuances, but it is well worth the time spent.

The best advice I can give you about learning PROC REPORT is to just try. Write a piece of code and see if it works. If the code works, build on it. If the code doesn't work, then take one thing out at a time to see where it breaks. The best way to learn PROC REPORT is to use it.

I want to thank you in advance for reading this book. I have attempted to put everything I know about PROC REPORT in this book. I hope the information in these pages will deepen your knowledge and understanding of PROC REPORT and expand your programming skills.

Chapter 1: Syntax – How to Use Statements and Their Options

1.1 Introduction

The REPORT procedure is a powerful tool for generating reports in any industry. PROC REPORT is a versatile procedure that allows you to calculate statistics, create new columns, consolidate, sort, and transpose observations. The goal of this book is to teach you, through examples, how to make PROC REPORT perform each one of these functions and generate the report that you need.

Chapter 1 explains each statement in PROC REPORT and the available options. Chapter 2 discusses important concepts on how PROC REPORT builds a report. Use Chapters 1 and 2 as a reference as you work your way through the examples in Chapters 3, 4, and 5. Those chapters demonstrate how to structure the report that you want. Chapters 6 and 7 provide examples that put the finishing touches on your report by adding style changes and a table of contents. Chapter 8 helps you troubleshoot any errors or warnings that you might encounter along the way.

Learning any procedure in SAS starts with understanding the various statements and options associated with that procedure. PROC REPORT has eight statements to use along with the procedure statement. Each of these statements and their options play a unique role in creating the desired report output.

The statements covered in this chapter are:

1. PROC REPORT – assigns the input and output data sets and controls the general layout of the report.
2. COLUMN – dictates the *report-item*s that will appear in the final report and creates spanning headers.
3. DEFINE – specifies how each *report-item* is used, along with format and style specifications.
4. BREAK – generates summary rows for groups.
5. RBREAK – generates summary rows for the entire report.
6. COMPUTE – begins a compute block, which is where PROC REPORT allows you to create new *report-item*s, generate LINE statements, and apply cell-specific style attributes.
7. ENDCOMP – ends a compute block.
8. CALL DEFINE – sets the value of an attribute for a specific row or column.
9. LINE – writes a row of text to the final report.

Knowing the statements used in PROC REPORT is the first step to successfully creating output. This chapter explains each valid statement within PROC REPORT and its use. The chapter also discusses the options for each statement and how they might, or might not, affect your output. Commentary is provided on the options for each statement to give helpful advice on how the options should be used and when they should not be used.

As it explores each option, this chapter references both the ODS Listing and non-Listing ODS destinations many times. The Listing destination is the traditional, monospace destination that was the default destination prior to SAS 9.3. All other destinations, such as HTML and PDF, fall into the non-Listing destinations category. As you learn to use PROC REPORT you will begin to understand how to apply options that affect the destination where your final report will be sent.

The information in this chapter should be used as a starting point for learning what PROC REPORT can do, but this chapter is not designed to replace or be as thorough as *Base SAS Procedures Guide*, nor does it contain an exhaustive list of options.

1.2 PROC REPORT Statement

The PROC REPORT statement is the only required statement of the entire procedure and none of the options on the statement are required. You could run the entire procedure with just this syntax:

```
proc report;
run;
```

It is highly unlikely that you would want the report produced by this piece of code, but it is important to know the starting point for this procedure. Without any other statements, the output will contain every variable from the input data set, in the order the variables appear in the data set. If the input data set has at least one character variable, the resulting report will be a printout of all variables for all observations. If the input data set has only numeric variables, the report will consist of one row, containing the overall sum of every variable.

Most of the options on the PROC REPORT statement have been available since the early days of SAS. The majority of the options that control the report are designed for and are specific to the ODS Listing destination. We will explore the options that affect every report created by PROC REPORT and touch on the options specific to Listing. As SAS and current business needs have evolved the Listing destination is used less and less; for cleaner code, specifying only the options valid for the open destination is the best practice.

1.2.1 General Options

The options in this section designate the input and output data sets as well as the information that PROC REPORT writes to the log. The section also covers options that affect the overall appearance of the final report.

DATA=
> This option is used to specify the data set you want the procedure to use. It is optional, but it is best programming practice to include this option.

OUT=
> PROC REPORT can create a data set with the results of the procedure. The output data set is used for many types of applications, such as quality control or as an input for another procedure. The data set will contain all of the variables from the COLUMN statement, including variables defined as NOPRINT. It also contains the automatic variable _BREAK_, which indicates whether the row was created by a BREAK or RBREAK statement. The data set does not contain any temporary variables created inside of a compute block. Also, the value of GROUP and ORDER variables will be populated on every row, which is not what you see in the output because those variables' values are included in the output only for the first row of the grouping. In the output data set, columns created by stacking variables under an ACROSS are named in the form _Cn_, where n is the column number. There is no option to change this behavior. To change the variable names, you have to use the RENAME= data set option.

CENTER|NOCENTER

By default, the table created by PROC REPORT is centered on the page of the output destination. Using NOCENTER moves the table as far over to the left as it can go. In paging destinations, such as ODS RTF and ODS PDF, the left margin value determines where the table will start. NOCENTER is helpful when the output is very wide and you want to make sure as many columns as possible will fit on the page. The system option CENTER|NOCENTER does affect the output. PROC REPORT will use the system option value unless you override the system option with this procedure option.

LIST

The LIST option writes to the log portions of the code that PROC REPORT uses to generate the report. The information on the DEFINE statements is the most useful, as it gives the usage keyword, format, width, and label that PROC REPORT will use for each variable. In general, this option is most useful when you are sending the output to Listing; however, it can be used regardless of where you send the output. This option is needed when debugging, such as determining the format and width that is used.

SHOWALL

This option forces all items from the COLUMN statement to be displayed, even when the NOPRINT option is used on the DEFINE statement. This option is a great debugging tool! When all *report-item*s are displayed in the report, it is easy to determine the correct column number. Using this option will help ensure you refer to the correct column number in a compute block when an ACROSS variable is used. With this option all GROUP and ORDER columns are displayed. You will be able to determine when the values of those columns change in relation to all other GROUP/ORDER columns. This information is really helpful in trying to figure out why a value conditioned on a GROUP variable is not changing, as well as why values of other GROUP variables are printed out when you might not expect them to be.

NOHEADER

This option suppresses the printing of all column headers and spanning headers. It is most useful when you are forced to create output with two PROC REPORT steps, but you do not need the headers for the table in the second step.

NOWD

This option prevents the interactive report window from opening. In SAS 9.4 this option is the default behavior. In previous versions of SAS the report window opened automatically in an interactive session unless NOWINDOWS, NOWD, or NOFS was placed on the PROC REPORT statement.

1.2.2 Report Contents Options

The options discussed in this section dictate the inclusion of specific values from the input data set. The options affect the contents of the data within the report.

COMPLETECOLS|NOCOMPLETECOLS

The purpose of this option is to include all possible combinations of ACROSS variables. The default value is COMPLETECOLS. For the majority of reports, you will not need to change this option.

COMPLETEROWS|NOCOMPLETEROWS

The purpose of this option is to include all possible combinations of GROUP variables. The default value is NOCOMPLETEROWS. In some instances, the option COMPLETEROWS needs to be specified so that the report contains all combinations of GROUP variables. The behavior of COMPLETEROWS does not always create the expected output. See Chapter 4 for an in-depth discussion on the behavior of this option and to determine whether you should use it for your report.

MISSING

This option forces PROC REPORT to include observations with a missing value for variables defined as GROUP, ORDER, or ACROSS. By default, PROC REPORT excludes observations from the input data set if the value of one of the variables defined as GROUP, ORDER, or ACROSS is missing. It applies to all variables defined as GROUP, ORDER, or ACROSS. This option should not be used if you consider missing values to be valid for only one of those variables.

NAMED

This option places the name of the variable followed by an equal sign in every column and every row of the report. This option has few practical uses, but can be used for all output destinations.

COLWIDTH=

This option overrides the default values for the number of characters used to write numeric and COMPUTED *report-item*s to output. It is rarely seen or used in most PROC REPORT code but its effects are very important. See Chapter 2 for a discussion of COLWIDTH.

1.2.3 Report Appearance Options

This section discusses the options that change the appearance of the final report. For example, you can change the style attributes to add color to your report or force the data values to wrap to a new line.

CONTENTS=

By default, PROC REPORT generates three nodes in a table of contents. This option controls the second node. This option is designed for destinations that have the ability to generate a table of contents, such as RTF, PDF, HTML, and others. You can specify hardcoded text or a macro variable inside of quotations for this option. #BYVAL and #BYVAR are not resolved. See Chapter 7 for examples of manipulating table of contents values.

SPANROWS

This option creates a single, merged cell for GROUP or ORDER variable values that apply to multiple rows. This option is only valid in non-Listing output destinations. It will also repeat the value of GROUP and ORDER variables when the value spans multiple pages.

Note: This option works differently in the RTF, PDF, and Tagsets.RTF destinations. LINE statements and summary rows can affect the creation of a single cell and the option might not provide the expected functionality.

STYLE<(location(s))>=
> The attributes from this option override the attributes specified in the style template used by the output destination. The default location is REPORT which in general refers to the report as a whole. Location is not required but it is best practice to use a location value. The attributes listed within this option affect only non-Listing output. See Chapter 6 for a discussion regarding the effects of location.

SPLIT=
> This option is a character that forces text onto a new line. In the Listing destination, the split character is honored in both the header text and variable values. In destinations other than Listing, the split character is honored in the header text. To split text in variable values, you must use inline formatting functions to insert a new line. This requires changes to the data value. You can specify only one character as the split character.

BYPAGENO=
> The option allows you to reset the page numbering when a BY variable is used. It behaves very similarly to the system option PAGENO; this BYPAGENO= option resets the page number in the middle of the procedure, whereas PAGENO does it between procedures. This option does affect the value used by the THISPAGE and PAGEOF inline formatting functions; however, it might be of little use if you are including in the output the page numbers in the form of "Page X of Y" because it does not change the Y value.

The following is a list of options that are often included on the PROC REPORT statement, but are only valid in the Listing destination. You can remove these options from your code if you are sending the report to a different destination.

- FORMCHAR=
- LS=
- PS=
- SPACING=
- WRAP
- HEADLINE
- HEADSKIP

1.3 COLUMN Statement

The COLUMN statement is not required for the procedure to create output, but you most likely want a COLUMN statement because it has many important roles.

The most important role of the COLUMN statement is to control the order of the columns in the report. The *report-items* will be displayed in the order that they appear from **left to right** on the COLUMN statement. As part of this role, the COLUMN statement dictates the order of execution, which is discussed in further detail in the next chapter.

All variables that are needed from the input data set must be included in this statement; this includes variables that you do not want to see a column for in the final report but need their value for another purpose. You will get a note in the log that the variable is uninitialized if you reference a variable from the input data set that is not on the COLUMN statement.

PROC REPORT does allow more than one COLUMN statement. PROC REPORT concatenates the list of variables starting with the first COLUMN statement, then the second COLUMN statement, and so on. The most common use of this capability is to specify variables to use based on the value of a macro variable, as demonstrated in Example 1.1.

Example 1.1: Multiple COLUMN statements

```
%let all = Y;
%macro rep;
proc report data=orders;
   column customer_country customer_group;
   %if &all=Y %then %do;
      column customer_age_group customer_gender;
   %end;
   column quantity total_retail_price;
run;
%mend rep;

%rep
```

Another role of the COLUMN statement is to identify the contents of a column. The contents of a column can simply be the value of the variable directly from the input data set. The contents can also be a statistic for an ANALYSIS variable. Example 1.2 shows that a statistic can be "stacked" under an ANALYSIS variable by using a comma (,) between the variable name and the statistic name.

Example 1.2: Stack a Statistic

```
proc report data=orders;
   column quantity,min total_retail_price,max;
run;
```

Output 1.1: Example of Stacking a Statistic

Quantity Ordered	Total Retail Price for This Product
min	max
1	$1,937.20

As you can see, no other statements or options are needed to stack *report-item*s.

Along with stacking variables, the COLUMN statement can be used to group variables under the same heading. The grouping is accomplished by using parentheses around items that need a common header. In Example 1.3, MIN and MAX are stacked under QUANTITY. The parentheses put the values under one heading that contains the label for QUANTITY.

Example 1.3: Multiple Values under One Heading

```
proc report data=orders;
   column quantity,(min max);
run;
```

Output 1.2: Example of Placing Multiple Values Under One Heading

Creating spanning headers is another important role of the COLUMN statement. In the previous example, the label "Quantity Ordered" is placed over multiple columns by default. When you specify the text that is placed over multiple columns, it is called a spanning header. Like the previous example, spanning headers are created by the use of parentheses on the COLUMN statement. The syntax, as seen in Example 1.4, is ('text' var).

Example 1.4: Spanning Header on COLUMN statement

```
proc report data=orders;
   column ('Sales data' quantity total_retail_price);
run;
```

Output 1.3: Example of a Spanning Header

The values of a variable can become column headers with statistics stacked underneath. Example 1.5 demonstrates this behavior. Notice the COLUMN statement contains both a comma and parentheses. This combination dictates that both QUANTITY and TOTAL_RETAIL_PRICE will be stacked underneath CUSTOMER_GENDER.

Example 1.5: Stack Statistics under an ACROSS Variable

```
proc report data=orders;
   column customer_gender,(quantity total_retail_price);
   define customer_gender / across;
run;
```

Output 1.4: Example of Stacking Statistics under an ACROSS Variable

Customer Gender			
F		M	
Quantity Ordered	Total Retail Price for This Product	Quantity Ordered	Total Retail Price for This Product
498	$49,747.43	580	$50,330.04

The terms "stacking" and "across" are used interchangeably in many examples of PROC REPORT, but strictly speaking, they are not the same thing. The examples above demonstrate that you can stack items in one column without having a DEFINE statement. "Stacking" is generally applied to using analysis variables and statistics. "Across" is generally applied when using a categorical variable to create headers with other information in the column.

A comma is not needed on the COLUMN statement every time a variable is defined as ACROSS. By default, PROC REPORT will place frequency counts (the N statistic) in the columns created by an ACROSS variable, as seen in Example 1.6 below.

Example 1.6: N Statistic under an ACROSS Variable

```
proc report data=orders;
   column customer_gender;
   define customer_gender / across;
run;
```

Output 1.5: Example of Placing the N Statistic under an ACROSS Variable

Customer Gender	
F	M
277	340

The COLUMN statement is easier to read and understand when a comma is used, because it is a clear indication that multiple items contribute to the contents of the column.

The ACROSS usage is discussed in the next section. Chapter 4 focuses on reports created with the ACROSS usage.

Base SAS Procedures Guide for the COLUMN statement mentions expanding characters, - = . _ *
+ <> ><. These are characters that PROC REPORT will expand (or repeat) to fill the width of the
column in the Listing destination when they are listed as the first and last character in the spanning
header text. Expanding characters are valid only in the Listing destination; they will be removed
for other ODS destinations. Example 1.7 demonstrates using expanding characters in the spanning
header. Output 1.6 shows the results from the Listing destination.

Example 1.7: Include Expanding Characters in Spanning Header for Listing Destination

```
proc report data=orders;
   column ('-Sales data-' quantity total_retail_price);
run;
```

Output 1.6: A Spanning Header with Expanding Characters in Listing

```
-------Sales data-------
                Total Retail
   Quantity       Price for
    Ordered    This Product
       1078      $100,077.46
```

The other destinations do not have an equivalent behavior. If you want characters to repeat, you
must manually include them in the header text. Also, in other destinations, if your header needs to
include those characters, you must have two at the front and back of the text. The non-Listing ODS
destinations will strip the first and last, but leave the remaining characters as part of the text.
Example 1.8 includes expanding characters as part of a spanning header, in non-Listing
destinations.

Example 1.8: Spanning Header with Expanding Characters for Non-Listing Destinations

```
proc report data=orders;
   column ('--Sales data--' quantity total_retail_price);
run;
```

Output 1.7: Example of a Spanning Header with Expanding Characters

-Sales data-	
Quantity Ordered	Total Retail Price for This Product
1078	$100,077.46

Finally, a variable can be repeated on the COLUMN statement. PROC REPORT will generate one
column for each instance of the variable on the COLUMN statement, but it will generate it exactly
the same way each time. A DEFINE statement is required to change the usage or characteristics,
such as headers or formats. PROC REPORT does not allow more than one DEFINE statement for

a specific *report-item*. A new *report-item* is needed so that a new DEFINE statement can be used. You must create an alias (the new name) on the COLUMN statement. The alias is a copy of the variable it is based on.

The COLUMN statement is the only statement inside of PROC REPORT that has keyword aliases. COLUMN, COLUMNS, COL, and COLS are all acceptable references.

1.4 DEFINE Statement

The DEFINE statement tells PROC REPORT how to use a *report-item* and the desired display characteristics. A DEFINE statement is not required for each *report-item* because PROC REPORT has built-in behaviors for each type of variable. A character variable is simply printed out. A numeric variable is summed. The permanently associated format for a variable is used if present; otherwise, PROC REPORT uses variable length for character variables and nine (9.) for a numeric variable. The effect of the default width is discussed in further detail in the next chapter.

1.4.1 Usage Options

The DEFINE statement specifies how to use a *report-item*. A *report-item* can have only one usage. You should include only one of the following options on a DEFINE statement. If you put more than one usage on a DEFINE statement, PROC REPORT will use the last one, the one closest to the semicolon.

ACROSS

This usage creates columns. The values of a variable defined as ACROSS become column headers. The values within the column are dependent on the syntax of the COLUMN statement. This usage can be applied to both character and numeric variables.

ANALYSIS

This usage specifies that the column will be used to calculate a statistic. Only a numeric variable can be defined as ANALYSIS. All numeric variables default to ANALYSIS, so specifying this option is not required. However, it can be helpful to specify this option in order to clarify what the usage is for a particular variable.

COMPUTED

This usage indicates the *report-item* is not in the input data set, but is on the COLUMN statement and will be part of the report. This option is not required, but it is extremely helpful because it makes it obvious that the *report-item* is being created inside of the PROC REPORT step. A compute block is necessary to populate the values. *Report-item*s of this usage default to numeric unless assigned the character type on the COMPUTE statement.

DISPLAY

A variable defined as DISPLAY is simply printed output. The variable values appear in the report in the same order as they are in the input data set. Character variables default to DISPLAY. Numeric variables can be defined with this option, so the values are written to the report without being summed. This option is not the opposite of NOPRINT.

GROUP
> This option is used to both order the report and consolidate rows from the input data set. This usage can be applied to character and numeric variables. It is common practice to put all GROUP variables at the beginning of the COLUMN statement; however, GROUP variables can be placed anywhere on the COLUMN statement. GROUP variables will always have an impact on the order of the rows no matter where on the COLUMN statement they are placed.

ORDER
> This option is used to order the report. It does not consolidate rows. This usage can be applied to both character and numeric variables. It is common practice to put all ORDER variables at the beginning of the COLUMN statement. However, ORDER variables can be placed anywhere on the COLUMN statement. ORDER variables will always impact the order of the rows no matter where on the COLUMN statement they are placed. ORDER variables cannot be stacked under an ACROSS variable.

1.4.2 Interaction Options

The following options interact with the usage options from the previous section. These options affect the contents of the report when used with a specific usage value. The description specifies the usage value the option interacts with.

Statistic
> A statistical keyword is used with the ANALYSIS usage. Specifying a statistical keyword without specifying ANALYSIS will automatically change the usage of that variable to ANALYSIS. The default statistic for a numeric variable is SUM. See *Base SAS Procedures Guide* for a complete list of statistical keywords available to PROC REPORT.

WEIGHT=
> Specifies a numeric variable from the input data set to use as the weight when calculating the requested statistic for an ANALYSIS variable. The referenced weight variable does not have to be placed on the COLUMN statement, but it does have to exist on the input data set.

MISSING
> This option instructs PROC REPORT to include observations from the input data set that have a value of missing for a GROUP, ORDER, or ACROSS *report-item*. When used on the DEFINE statement this option impacts only missing values for that specific *report-item*. The MISSING option does not affect the inclusion of missing observations for ANALYSIS *report-items*.

ORDER=
> This option can be used to change the default sort order, which is FORMATTED. *Report-items* defined as GROUP, ORDER, or ACROSS automatically sort the values. The other possible sort orders are DATA, FREQ, and INTERNAL. This option has no effect on ANALYSIS, DISPLAY, or COMPUTED *report-items*. See Chapter 2 for an in-depth discussion on the behavior of this option.

DESCENDING
> This option reverses the display order of the GROUP, ORDER, or ACROSS values.

PRELOADFMT

> The PRELOADFMT option uses the values from a format to include groups with values that are not in the input data set or to customize the order of the values. This option can be used only with GROUP or ACROSS variables. Also, it must be used in combination with either ORDER=DATA or EXCLUSIVE. See Chapter 4 for a discussion on how this option interacts with COMPLETEROWS.

EXCLUSIVE

> The EXCLUSIVE option is used to limit the values that appear in the output to only those included in the format. It must be used with PRELOADFMT, which also means it can be used only for GROUP or ACROSS variables.

NOZERO

> This option prevents a column from being included in the report if every row has a value of zero or missing. Columns defined with this option still contribute to the overall column number. It is most often used to suppress columns under ACROSS variables. The column does not have to have all missing or zero value when coming into PROC REPORT. A compute block can be used to assign all rows of a column to missing or zero. Then since NOZERO is one of the last options that PROC REPORT evaluates and enforces, the column will be suppressed.

NOPRINT

> This option is used to suppress the printing of a column. This option can be placed on any DEFINE statement, no matter what the usage for that *report-item*. Columns defined with this option still contribute to the overall column number. It is used most often for a variable that is used to impose a specific sort order. It can also be used for variables from the input data set whose values are needed in compute blocks but whose values do not need to be seen in the final report. This option is not the opposite of DISPLAY.

1.4.3 Appearance Options

Some options on the DEFINE statement affect the appearance of the report. This section describes those options. Some of them have a different effect on the Listing destination than they do on other ODS destinations. Those differences are noted for each option.

SPACING=

> In the Listing destination, this option controls the number of blank spaces between the column it is applied to and the column to its left. This option does not affect the output in other ODS destinations.

WIDTH=

> This option controls the number of spaces the column uses in the Listing destination. Listing uses this option to change the width of the column but other destinations do not. To change the width of the column for other destinations, CELLWIDTH= (or WIDTH=) must be used inside of the STYLE= option on the DEFINE statement. The WIDTH= option is one of the most confusing options on the DEFINE statement because it does not change the width of the column for most destinations, but it can still affect the output. This option is used to override

the COLWIDTH= default value. See Chapter 2 for a discussion of COLWIDTH= and WIDTH=.

FORMAT=
> FORMAT= specifies a format to use when displaying the value of a *report-item*. Applying a format to a *report-item* is very important. Its primary job is to control the displayed value. However, the format interacts with the COLWIDTH= and WIDTH= options, which affect the value of numeric variables. It also is used along with PRELOADFMT, EXCLUSIVE, and COMPLETEROWS to determine which GROUP, ORDER, or ACROSS values should be present in the output. Either a user-defined or SAS format can be applied to the *report-item*.

MLF
> Specifying the MLF option enables PROC REPORT to use a multilabel format created by PROC FORMAT. This option can only be used with GROUP or ACROSS variables.

STYLE<(location(s))>=
> This option specifies style attribute overrides. The attributes change both the column and header if location is not specified.

> The attributes listed within this option affect only non-Listing output. The attributes from this option override the attributes specified in the style template or the PROC REPORT statement. Location is not required, but it is best practice to use a location value. See Chapter 6 for a discussion regarding the effects of location.

In the Listing destination, the following options impact both the header and the data values. In other destinations these options are applied to the data values but not the header. These options are overridden by the corresponding style attributes inside of STYLE=. Best practice is to only use these options for creating Listing output.

- CENTER
- LEFT
- RIGHT

1.4.4 Utility Options

The following options each perform a unique function in PROC REPORT. They can be applied to any *report-item* regardless of usage.

PAGE
> This is used to insert a vertical page (table) break for really wide reports. In other words, the report has too many columns to fit on one page, so a page break is inserted between two sets of columns. The PAGE option produces different results depending on the destination. See Chapter 2 for a discussion of paging.

ID
> This option designates a *report-item* as an ID variable. ID variables will appear on the left side of every page of the report. This option only needs to be specified on one DEFINE statement; all variables to the left of the *report-item* on the COLUMN statement will also be designated as

ID variables. This option is most useful for reports that wrap. See Chapter 2 for a discussion of paging.

CONTENTS=

This option either changes the text for the third node or inserts an additional entry under the third node depending on the use of CONTENTS= on other statements. By default, PROC REPORT generates three node levels in a table of contents. This option has an effect only when the PAGE option is used. You can specify hardcoded text or a macro variable inside of quotations for this option. See Chapter 7 for examples of manipulating table of contents values.

FLOW

It wraps the values of character values inside of the column instead of truncating a value that is longer than the column width. The FLOW option is valid only for the Listing destination. This option is not necessary in other destinations because they wrap the value automatically.

1.5 BREAK Statement

The BREAK statement creates summary rows or table breaks at places in the report determined by the **target** and **location** values. The BREAK statement requires both a *target* and a *location*, as well as a forward slash (/). The statement does not have any required options. However, the BREAK statement will have no effect on the report if no options are specified.

- *target* is a break variable (a variable defined as either GROUP or ORDER). Target controls when execution takes place.
- *location* is either BEFORE or AFTER. Location specifies where the statement executes.

SUMMARIZE

The SUMMARIZE option generates a row in the report that contains summary information. Statistics, ANALYSIS, and COMPUTED values will be populated in the row. *Target* and any GROUP or ORDER variables to its left (on the COLUMN statement) will also be populated.

CONTENTS=

This option either changes the text for the third node or inserts an additional entry under the third node depending on the use of CONTENTS= on other statements. By default, PROC REPORT generates three node levels in a table of contents. This option has an effect only when the PAGE option is used. You can specify hardcoded text or a macro variable inside of quotations for this option. The text will not vary by or reflect the value of *target*. See Chapter 7 for examples of manipulating table of contents values.

PAGE

The PAGE option produces different results depending on the destination. In the Listing destination, this option inserts a horizontal page break. For other destinations, it ends the current table and starts a new table. A horizontal page break will be inserted if the destination and its associated options allow it. See Chapter 2 for a discussion of paging.

STYLE<(location(s))>=

> This option specifies style attribute overrides. The attributes change the summary row created by the BREAK statement. The attributes also change the LINE statements from the associated compute after *target* block if location is not specified.
>
> The attributes listed within this option affect only non-Listing destinations. The attributes from this option override the attributes specified in the style template or the PROC REPORT statement. Location is not required but it is best practice to use a location value. See Chapter 6 for a discussion regarding the effects of location.

SUPPRESS

> This option prevents the value of the break variable from being printed on the summary row. If this option is used, then the value is unavailable inside of compute blocks. Any IF condition that uses the value of the break variable will be evaluated as false.

The following is a list of options that can be included on the BREAK statement. They overline or underline the summary row in the Listing destination. You can remove these options from your code if you are sending the report to a non-Listing destination.

- DOL
- DUL
- OL
- UL
- SKIP

A LINE statement with blank text inside of a compute block is used to mimic the SKIP option for non-Listing destinations.

```
compute after customer_country;
   line ' ';
endcomp;
```

1.6 RBREAK Statement

The RBREAK statement creates a summary row. The summary row contains the overall (grand total) values of ANALYSIS and numeric COMPUTED *report-item*s. When a BY statement is used, the overall summary values will be for each BY group. The RBREAK statement requires a *location* as well as a forward slash (/). The statement does not have any required options; however the RBREAK statement will have no effect on the report if no options are specified.

location is either BEFORE or AFTER. It specifies where the statement executes.

SUMMARIZE

> This option generates a row in the report that contains summary information. Statistics, ANALYSIS, and COMPUTED values will be populated in the row.

CONTENTS=

This option either changes the text for the third node or inserts an additional entry under the third node depending on the use of CONTENTS= on other statements. By default, PROC REPORT generates three node levels in a table of contents. This option has an effect only when the PAGE option is used. You can specify hardcoded text or a macro variable inside of quotations for this option. This option only has an effect when the *location* is BEFORE and the PAGE option is used. See Chapter 7 for examples of manipulating table of contents values.

PAGE

The PAGE option inserts a horizontal page break in the Listing destinations. For other destinations, it ends the current table and starts a new table. A horizontal page break will be inserted if the destination and its associated options allow it. See Chapter 2 for a discussion of paging.

STYLE<(location(s))>=

This option specifies style attribute overrides. The attributes change the summary row created by the RBREAK statement. The attributes also change the LINE statements from the associated compute after block if location is not specified.

The attributes listed within this option affect only non-Listing output. The attributes from this option override the attributes specified in the style template or the PROC REPORT statement. Location is not required but it is best practice to use a location value. See Chapter 6 for a discussion regarding the effects of *location*.

The following is a list of options that can be included on the RBREAK statement. They overline or underline the summary row in the Listing destination. You can remove these options from your code if you are sending the report to a different destination.

- DOL
- DUL
- OL
- UL
- SKIP

A LINE statement with blank text inside of a compute block is used to mimic the SKIP option for non-Listing destinations.

```
compute after;
    line ' ';
endcomp;
```

1.7 COMPUTE Statement

A COMPUTE statement starts what is referred to as a "compute block," which is used to make various changes to the report. It is not a stand-alone statement. The compute block must be closed with an ENDCOMP statement. The COMPUTE statement must have a *report-item* or a *location*. See Chapter 2 for a discussion on compute blocks.

STYLE<(location(s))>=
> This option specifies style attribute overrides. The attributes are applied only to LINE statements within the compute block.

> The attributes listed within this option affect only non-Listing output. The attributes from this option override the attributes specified in the style template or the PROC REPORT statement. Location is not required and is rarely specified on this statement. See Chapter 6 for a discussion regarding the effects of *location*.

1.8 ENDCOMP Statement

The ENDCOMP statement ends a compute block and must be preceded by a COMPUTE statement. It is not a stand-alone statement. The ENDCOMP statement does not have any options. See Chapter 2 for a discussion on compute blocks.

1.9 CALL DEFINE Statement

A CALL DEFINE statement changes attributes for a particular cell or row. CALL DEFINE statements are valid only inside of a compute block. The CALL DEFINE statement has three required arguments. The syntax for the CALL DEFINE statement is as follows:

```
CALL DEFINE (column-ID | _ROW_ , 'attribute-name', value);
```

1.9.1 Argument 1: Column-ID

The first argument in the syntax, column-ID, specifies the part of the report to which you want to apply the attribute. The column-ID argument can be one of the following items:

- A character literal (in quotation marks) that is the column name
- A numeric literal that is the column number
- A numeric expression that resolves to the column number
- The _COL_ automatic variable
- The _ROW_ automatic variable

In general, you follow the same rules to reference *report-item*s in a CALL DEFINE statement as you do to reference *report-item*s in a compute block. An ANALYSIS variable uses a compound name (for example, QUANTITY.SUM). Columns under an ACROSS variable must be referred to by a column number (in the following code, _C6_ is the column number). GROUP, ORDER, or DISPLAY variables must be referred to by name. All of the column references must be enclosed in quotation marks, as shown in the following example:

```
call define('customer_name','style','style=[foreground=green]');

call define('_c6_','style','style=[foreground=blue]');

call define('quantity.sum','style','style=[foreground=yellow]');
```

The _COL_ automatic variable refers to the *report-item* in the COMPUTE statement. You can use _COL_ when the column that you want to change is the same column as is in the COMPUTE statement. If the column that you want to change is not the one in the COMPUTE statement, you need to use one of the other reference techniques (a column name, column number, or a compound name, as mentioned above). Do not place quotation marks around the _COL_ automatic variable.

```
compute customer_name;
    call define(_col_,'style','style=[background=lightblue]');
endcomp;
```

The _ROW_ automatic variable, shown in the example that follows, applies to every column in a specific row. You can use _ROW_ in any compute block. Be aware that you cannot use _ROW_ when FORMAT is the value for the second argument, the attribute-name. If you use _ROW_ with the FORMAT value, an error is generated in the SAS log. Do not place quotation marks around the _ROW_ automatic variable.

```
compute customer_name;
    if customer_name='John' then call
    define(_row_,'style','style=[background=lightblue]');
endcomp;
```

1.9.2 Argument 2: Attribute Name

The CALL DEFINE statement has a number of possible values for the attribute name argument. No matter which attribute name that you use, the name must be enclosed in quotation marks. The most commonly used attributes are FORMAT, STYLE, and URL. FORMAT is used to apply a format. STYLE is used to apply various style attributes. URL is used to add a hyperlink to a specific cell. See *Base SAS Procedures Guide* for a complete list of argument names.

1.9.3 Argument 3: Attribute Value

The third argument is the value of the attribute specified in the second argument. The value can be:

- a format name that is surrounded by quotation marks
- the STYLE= option
- a URL value that is surrounded by quotation marks or a variable that resolves to a URL.

The format name can be a SAS format or a user-defined format.

When you change a style attribute, the third argument to the CALL DEFINE statement has a specific syntax:

```
'STYLE={style-attribute-name=style-attribute-value<. . .style-
attribute-name-n=style-attribute-value-n>}'
```

The STYLE= option must be enclosed in quotation marks. For this argument, you can use either bracket style: [ ] or { }.

1.10 LINE Statement

A LINE statement generates a row of text. The text can include hardcoded text strings, variable values, or statistics. A LINE statement is valid only within a compute block that is associated with a *location* and is used to write text. A LINE statement is executed after all other statements that appear inside of a compute block. In addition, this statement is always executed; you cannot use IF-THEN logic to conditionally execute the LINE statement. See Chapter 3 for an example of conditionally displaying a LINE statement.

PROC REPORT considers multiple LINE statements within one compute block as one long text string. The text is contained in one large, merged cell that spans the width of the report. The attributes of the row can be changed with the STYLE= option in the COMPUTE statement or STYLE(LINES)= on the PROC REPORT statement. Style attributes for multiple LINE statements from one compute block cannot be controlled separately. Inline formatting can be used for different parts of the text but some options, such as JUST= and BACKGROUND= can be applied only via the STYLE option.

LINE statements are very useful for writing out text or summary values that have a general justification. In LISTING output, you can create alignment using pointer controls such as the at-sign (@) and the plus sign (+). In other ODS destinations, pointer controls do not work in a predictable manner because of font face, font size, margins, and other style attribute settings. When alignment is a requirement, it is best to use a BREAK or RBREAK statement rather than a LINE statement. See Chapter 3 for an example of generating multiple summary rows.

A format must be specified for each variable or statistic on the LINE statement. The format can be a SAS format or a user-defined format. For example:

```
compute before customer_age_group;
   line 'This section is for Age Group ' customer_age_group $20.;
endcomp;
```

1.11 Global Statements

PROC REPORT accepts the following global statements. They work just as they do in other procedures.

- BY
- FREQ
- WEIGHT
- LABEL
- FORMAT
- WHERE

The LABEL and FORMAT statements override those attributes from the input data set. A label or format applied on a DEFINE statement override those attributes from the global statements. Finally, a label or format applied via a CALL DEFINE statement overrides the attributes specified on a DEFINE statement.

Chapter 2: Concepts – How PROC REPORT Works Behind the Scenes

2.1 Introduction

This chapter covers the behind-the-scenes mechanics of PROC REPORT. The chapter discusses the very important topics of how compute blocks work and how to reference variables – two concepts that no other procedure has. You have to know how to reference a *report-item* and when that variables' values are available to get the expected values in the final report. Understanding how to use the power of the compute block will help you get there. These concepts are unique to PROC REPORT because it works like no other procedure in Base SAS.

PROC REPORT can create and access values from temporary variables; this chapter explains how to access those values. GROUP and ORDER variables allow you to order and consolidate observations from the input data set. They act similarly to CLASS variables in other procedures but come with a unique set of challenges, which this chapter will explore.

This chapter also examines the default variable widths PROC REPORT sets. Finally, this chapter describes how PROC REPORT handles date variables as well as sorting and paging. These concepts might seem subtle but you need to be aware of what PROC REPORT is doing behind the scenes.

This chapter includes a lot of information. Some of the information can be hard to understand, but it is important to know how PROC REPORT works in order to get the most out of it and create the needed reports.

2.2 General Execution

PROC REPORT completes many of its behind-the-scenes processing steps prior to building the final report that you see in your output destination. The steps are numbered below, but please keep in mind that some of these actions happen simultaneously.

1. As with other procedures, PROC REPORT first does a syntax check. It will issue error messages and stop processing when a syntax error is found.

2. Once PROC REPORT has finished checking for syntax errors, it evaluates the variable usages found on the DEFINE statements, or inferred based on variable type. If any numeric ANALYSIS variables are present, a call to the summary engine is made. The presence of a GROUP or ORDER variable will trigger a call to the summary engine as well. GROUP, ORDER, and ACROSS variables trigger the use of the sort engine.

3. The summary engine calculates the statistics for ANALYSIS variables for the overall report, and for any GROUP/ORDER values. The summary values are held in memory until they are needed during the report-building phase. Because these values are held in memory, their values are available to various compute blocks. See Section 2.3.2 for a discussion of each type of compute block.

4. If a variable with an ACROSS usage is present, the number of levels is determined. Absolute column numbers are determined and the column names are assigned (_c1_, _c2_, and so on).

5. After summary statistics are calculated and observations are consolidated and ordered, PROC REPORT begins to build the report. The first step of this build process is to initialize all of the temporary variables to missing. PROC REPORT then builds one row and one column at a time. At the start of each of the detail rows, it initializes all of the *report-item* variables to missing, and then fills in the values. When a compute block is present for that particular column, the compute block is executed.

6. Summary rows are built when a BREAK or RBREAK statement is present. Those statements are executed. Then PROC REPORT checks for a compute block associated with that row and executes it.

7. PROC REPORT sends each row to the open ODS destination once it finishes building the row. PROC REPORT hands off any style or paging commands. The ODS destination is responsible for applying the style attributes. It is also responsible for page breaks. See Section 2.11 for a discussion on page breaks.

For a more detailed explanation of all of the steps and phases PROC REPORT uses, see Chapters 1 and 7 of Art Carpenter's book *Carpenter's Complete Guide to the SAS REPORT Procedure.*

2.3 Compute Blocks

The REPORT, TABULATE, and PRINT procedures are considered the reporting procedures in Base SAS. PROC REPORT is unique among these procedures because it can manipulate both the incoming data and the outgoing values using a compute block. Compute blocks start with a COMPUTE statement and end with an ENDCOMP statement. Any number of statements can be inside the compute block, including LINE and CALL DEFINE statements. Also, most DATA step statements can be used inside compute blocks, such as assignment, IF/THEN, and ARRAY statements.

PROC REPORT builds the report one row and one column at a time. Compute blocks are executed as the report is built. PROC REPORT does not require compute blocks. Compute blocks are necessary only when you need to create a new *report-item*, change a value, or make some other modification to the final report. They are also necessary for finer control of style attributes, like changing the format or foreground color of just one cell within a column or row.

This section describes how the *report-item*s and options on the COMPUTE statement dictate what the compute block can do. The section also explains the execution order of the compute block types. Finally, each compute block type is discussed.

Compute blocks are used in many examples throughout the book, you should use this section as a reference. This section does not contain example code for each compute block type. Refer to the program Program2_compute.sas (found on the Author's Page) for small examples of each compute block type. As you read through the book refer back to this section to help you understand how the compute block affects the report that is being created in each example.

2.3.1 COMPUTE Statement

The content of a COMPUTE statement is vital to the output that you want to generate. A COMPUTE statement can contain a number of arguments: *report-item*, *location*, *target*, style=, or *type-specification*. You must specify a *location* or a *report-item* on every COMPUTE statement. You can also have a combination of these arguments.

- *report-item* represents either a data set variable, a computed variable, or a statistic.
- *location* is either BEFORE or AFTER. It specifies where the compute block executes.
- *target* is a break variable (a variable defined as either GROUP or ORDER). The target controls when execution takes place. _PAGE_ is a special value of *target*.
- STYLE= allows you to specify style attributes for any LINE statements within the block.
- *type-specification* is the value CHAR and can include LENGTH= . The type specification defines the variable type of a COMPUTED *report-item*.

2.3.2 Execution of Compute Blocks

This section looks at the effects of combining the *report-item*, *location*, and *target* arguments on the COMPUTE statement. The order of execution of compute blocks is based on the arguments from the COMPUTE statement. The arguments also affect the behavior of the compute block.

Be aware that some report cells can be manipulated by more than one compute block. Also, most PROC REPORT steps do not contain every possible compute block type. However, it is very likely that a PROC REPORT step will have more than one compute block of the same type.

In general, compute blocks are executed in the following order:

1. COMPUTE report-item;
2. COMPUTE BEFORE;
3. COMPUTE BEFORE target;
4. COMPUTE BEFORE _PAGE_;
5. COMPUTE AFTER;
6. COMPUTE AFTER target;
7. COMPUTE AFTER _PAGE_;

Table 2.1 describes the behavior of each compute block type. The execution time column explains when that compute block type is executed. The purpose column describes the functions normally performed within that block. The LINE statement column explains the placement of the text in the final report. The temporary variables column describes if temporary variables are normally created in that block and, if so, what values they contain. The rows altered column describes the rows of the final report that can be altered or manipulated within that block type. The notes column provides additional pieces of information about the block type.

Table 2.1: Compute Block Characteristics

Compute Block Type	Execution Time	Purpose	LINE Statements	Temporary Variables	Rows Altered	Notes
compute *report-item*	Every observation	-Assign values to COMPUTED items -Change value of any cell in the report -Change attribute of any cell in the report -Use temporary variables created in other block types	N/A	-Can be created -Value might change on every row	Every row	Multiple blocks of this type execute in the order the *report-item*s appear on COLUMN statement from **left to right**
compute BEFORE	Before the first detail row OR Once for each BY group	-Change values -Change attributes -Output text via a LINE statement -Place summary values of ANALYSIS variables into temporary variables	Placed below the header and above first detail row	Often created, but rarely used in this block type	Row created by RBREAK BEFORE statement	-Associated with RBREAK BEFORE statement but statement not required -Can have only one instance -GROUP/ORDER values not available
compute BEFORE *target*	At top of section when value of *target* changes	-Change values -Change attributes -Output text via a LINE statement -Place subtotal summary values of ANALYSIS variables into temporary variables	Placed above each *target* section	Created to hold subtotal summary values	Row created by BREAK BEFORE *target* statement	-Multiple blocks of this type execute in the order the *target*s appear on COLUMN statement from **left to right** -Associated with BREAK BEFORE *target* statement but statement not required

Compute Block Type	Execution Time	Purpose	LINE Statements	Temporary Variables	Rows Altered	Notes
compute BEFORE _PAGE_	Once per page	Output text via a LINE statement	Placed at top of page above headers		N/A	Any variable on LINE statement takes value from first detail row
compute AFTER	After last detail row OR Once for each BY group	-Change values -Change attributes -Output text via a LINE statement		Usually not created in this block	Row created by RBREAK AFTER statement	-Associated with RBREAK AFTER statement but statement not required -Can have only one instance -GROUP/ ORDER values not available
compute AFTER *target*	At bottom of section when value of *target* changes	-Change values -Change attributes -Output text via a LINE statement -Place subtotal summary values of ANALYSIS variables into temporary variables	Placed below each *target* section	Usually not created in this block	Row created by BREAK AFTER *target* statement	-Multiple blocks of this type execute in the order the *target*s appear on COLUMN statement from **left to right** -Associated with BREAK AFTER *target* statement but statement not required
compute AFTER _PAGE_	Once per page	Output text via a LINE statement	Placed at bottom of page below the table		N/A	-Any variable on LINE statement takes value from last detail row -Exact location varies depending on length of table -Will be placed on last page of table that spans multiple pages

The compute *report-item* block type is used the most often because it is so versatile. It can manipulate every cell in the report. Because this type of compute block is executed prior to the execution of the other compute block types, changes to a row or cell in this block are made first.

The compute *report-item* block type can manipulate summary rows. An IF condition can be used to include or prevent the summary row when changes are made. However, it might be more efficient to change those values in the compute block that controls that row. The other compute block types execute only on a specific type of row, so an IF condition is not necessary. Changing values in the other compute block types prevents PROC REPORT from evaluating every row in the report, which could use a lot of I/O if the report is very large. But it is always good to know there is more than one way of doing something! If it does not work in one compute block, you can check to see whether it works in another compute block.

Within a compute *report-item* block assignment statements will change the value on every row. If you wish to change values on just the summary rows created by either a BREAK or an RBREAK statement, you must use an IF condition to limit the change to those rows based on the value of the automatic variable _BREAK_.

The automatic variable _BREAK_ is very useful inside of many compute blocks. _BREAK_ is blank if the row is not a summary row. The value of _BREAK_ will be the name of the variable on the BREAK statement if that statement created that specific row. The value will be "_RBREAK_" if the row was created by an RBREAK statement. "_RBREAK_" is always capitalized.

The variable name of the break variable matches the case the variable was originally created with, meaning if the variable was created with a mixture of uppercase and lowercase letters, that is how it will look in _BREAK_. When using the automatic variable _BREAK_ in the IF condition, you might want to consider nesting it inside the UPCASE() or LOWCASE() function so that you know your hardcoded value will match.

When using compute blocks associated with _PAGE_, remember, each ODS destination controls where a page break occurs; and the break is dependent upon the type of destination, the margins, the font size, and so on. PROC REPORT does not know where the page break will occur. For all destinations, except Listing, this compute block type is executed only once at the start of a report. To ensure it is executed for each physical page, you will need to control the page (table) breaks. This can be done using the PAGE option on a BREAK statement.

2.4 Referencing *Report-items*

A compute block is used to accomplish multiple tasks in the creation of a report. Inside of a compute block, *report-item*s must be referenced based on their use. You must use the correct *report-item* reference inside all compute blocks and all statements, such as assignment and CALL DEFINE statements. *Report-item*s are referenced in one of four ways:

name
> *Report-item*s that are defined as type GROUP, ORDER, DISPLAY, or COMPUTED are referred to by name. By default, all character *report-item*s have a DISPLAY usage.

In the following example, the compute block is used to change the value of PRODUCT_LINE, which is a DISPLAY variable. Therefore, it is referenced by name.

```
compute product_line;
   product_line = upcase(product_line);
endcomp;
```

compound name

ANALYSIS *report-item*s are referred to by a compound name; the syntax is variable-name.statistic. By default, all numeric variables are ANALYSIS *report-item*s, and the default statistic is SUM. Even if you do not include a statistical keyword in a DEFINE statement, you must use the compound name in the compute block.

In this example, the value of TOTAL_RETAIL_PRICE is increased by 10%. The compound name is used for both references to the *report-item*.

```
compute total_retail_price;
   total_retail_price.sum = total_retail_price.sum * 1.1;
endcomp;
```

If you do not use the correct reference to an ANALYSIS *report-item*, you might see the following note in the log:

```
NOTE: Variable total_retail_price is uninitialized.
```

alias

An alias is a copy of another *report-item* and is created on the COLUMN statement. You must use that alias on the COMPUTE statement and within the compute block.

In this example, the alias PRICE is created on the COLUMN statement. Within the compute block the alias is used on the assignment statement, which increases the value by 10%.

```
column total_retail_price=price;
compute price;
   price = price * 1.1;
endcomp;
```

If you use variable-name.statistic for an aliased column, the following error is generated:

```
ERROR: The variable type of PRICE.SUM is invalid in this context.
```

column number

A *report-item* that appears in the report under an ACROSS variable is referred to by the column number in the form _Cn_, where n is number of the column (from left to right) in the report. You must use column numbers in every statement that refers to one of these columns. An assignment statement or CALL DEFINE statement is needed for every column under an ACROSS that you want to manipulate.

In this example, the value of QUANTITY is in four columns, one for each value of CUSTOMER_AGE_GROUP. The value of QUANTITY is increased by 10% in column 2 only, referred to by _c2_.

```
column customer_age_group, quantity;
define customer_age_group / across;
compute quantity;
    _c2_ = _c2_ * 1.1;
endcomp;
```

Note: Columns that are not printed still count toward the numbering of the columns.

2.5 Left to Right Availability

Sections 2.2 and 2.3 explain that PROC REPORT works **left to right** based on the *report-item*s listed on the COLUMN statement. The concept is straightforward, but it still trips up even the most advanced programmer. This section explores problems caused by various statements inside of a compute block if the *report-item* is unavailable. We also look at a trick for making sure this never happens to you!

Example 2.1 creates a new *report-item*, TOTAL_COST. This *report-item* is defined with a usage of COMPUTED. A computed *report-item* is a variable that does not exist in the input data set, but is a column in the report.

Example 2.1: Create TOTAL_COST as a COMPUTED *Report-item*

```
proc report data=orders;
   column quantity total_cost costprice_per_unit;
   define total_cost / computed 'Total Cost' format=dollar15.2;

   compute total_cost; ❶
      total_cost = costprice_per_unit.sum * quantity.sum; ❷
   endcomp;
run;
```

```
NOTE: Missing values were generated as a result of performing an
operation on missing values. ❸
      Each place is given by: (Number of times) at (Line):(Column).
      1 at 1:38
NOTE: There were 617 observations read from the data set
WORK.ORDERS.
NOTE: PROCEDURE REPORT used (Total process time):
      real time          5.10 seconds
      cpu time           0.42 seconds
```

Output 2.1: COMPUTED *Report-item* **TOTAL_COST** ❹

Quantity Ordered	Total Cost	Cost Price Per Unit
1078	.	$25,806.13

❶ TOTAL_COST is used on the COMPUTE statement, which is the second of three *report-items* listed on the COLUMN statement.

❷ COSTPRICE_PER_UNIT.SUM is used in the assignment statement. However, COSTPRICE_PER_UNIT is the third *report-item* on the COLUMN statements. Its values are not available in a compute block for TOTAL_COST because it is to the right of TOTAL_COST on the COLUMN statement.

❸ Since all three *report-items* in the assignment statement are numeric, the log does indicate that missing values were generated. COSTPRICE_PER_UNIT.SUM is missing on every observation within a compute block for TOTAL_COST.

❹ The value of TOTAL_COST is missing in the final report. In some instances a missing value might be ok but if you do not expect a missing value, you need to check the log, check your syntax, and especially check to see whether you have referenced *report-items* that are to the right of the *report-item* on the COLUMN statement.

The solution for this problem is to change the *report-item* to COSTPRICE_PER_UNIT. It does seem strange to have use COSTPRICE_PER_UNIT on the COMPUTE statement when you are trying to calculate a value for TOTAL_COST. However, as the third *report-item* on the COLUMN statement, the values are available for all three r*eport-items* needed in the assignment statement. When it creates the TOTAL_COST column, PROC REPORT will simply assign its value as missing, the default value, because it has not encountered another value that it should be assigned to. Then when PROC REPORT creates the COSTPRICE_PER_UNIT column, it will execute the compute block associated with that column. Within the compute block, the assignment statement will be evaluated and the missing value for TOTAL_COST will be replaced with the calculated value. Example 2.2 demonstrates the solution code.

Example 2.2: Solution Code: Assign TOTAL_COST Value in a Different Compute Block

```
proc report data=orders;
   column quantity total_cost costprice_per_unit;
   define total_cost / computed 'Total Cost' format=dollar15.2;

   compute costprice_per_unit;
      total_cost = costprice_per_unit.sum * quantity.sum;
   endcomp;
run;
```

Output 2.2: COMPUTED *Report-item* **TOTAL_COST from Solution Code**

Quantity Ordered	Total Cost	Cost Price Per Unit
1078	$27,819,008.14	$25,806.13

Example 2.3 creates a new *report-item*, DEMOG. DEMOG is also a COMPUTED *report-item*, like in the example above, but DEMOG is a character variable. Its value should be the concatenation of CUSTOMER_AGE, CUSTOMER_GENDER, and CUSTOMER_COUNTRY.

Example 2.3: Create DEMOG as a COMPUTED *Report-item*

```
proc report data=orders;
   column customer_name demog customer_age customer_gender
          customer_country customer_type;
   define customer_age / display noprint;
   define customer_gender / noprint;
   define customer_country /noprint;
   define demog / computed;

   compute demog / char length=20; ❶
      demog = cats(customer_age, "/", customer_gender, "/",
            customer_country); ❷
   endcomp;
run;
```

```
NOTE: There were 617 observations read from the data set
WORK.ORDERS. ❸
NOTE: PROCEDURE REPORT used (Total process time):
      real time            0.21 seconds
      cpu time             0.20 seconds
```

Output 2.3: COMPUTED *Report-item* DEMOG (Partial Listing) ❹

Customer Name	demog	Customer Type Name
Kyndal Hooks	.//	Orion Club Gold members high activity
Annmarie Leveille	.//	Orion Club Gold members high activity
Najma Hicks	.//	Orion Club members medium activity
Yan Kozlowski	.//	Orion Club members medium activity
Kyndal Hooks	.//	Orion Club Gold members high activity
Roy Siferd	.//	Orion Club members medium activity
Alvan Goheen	.//	Orion Club members low activity
Alvan Goheen	.//	Orion Club members low activity
Alvan Goheen	.//	Orion Club members low activity
Dericka Pockran	.//	Orion Club members high activity

❶ DEMOG is the *report-item* on the COMPUTE statement. This makes perfect sense, as it is the variable that you are trying to create. You must have a COMPUTE statement with DEMOG on it so that you can assign the variable type as character and give it a length.

❷ The CATS function is concatenating three variables and hardcoded text strings. The issue with this assignment statement is that the three variables are after the *report-item*, DEMOG, on the COLUMN statement.

❸   Notice the log does not indicate that there are any potential problems. Unlike manipulating numeric variables, SAS does not give details about character functions when values are missing.

❹   In this output, it is fairly easy to see that something is not right, because every customer has ".//" as the value. You would not expect every customer to have missing demography information. However, the problem might not be as obvious if we did not also concatenate the forward slashes. Again, it is important that you know your data. No errors were in the log and you have values in the column, so you can be fairly confident in ruling out a syntax error. The first thing you should check is that you have not referenced an unavailable *report-item*. Then, you should check your data to make sure the variables were not missing coming into PROC REPORT.

One solution for this example is to move CUSTOMER_AGE, CUSTOMER_GENDER, and CUSTOMER_COUNTRY before DEMOG on the COLUMN statement. All three of these *report-items* are DISPLAY and have been defined as NOPRINT. Therefore, moving the columns will not adversely affect the final report. Once the *report-items* are listed to the left of DEMOG, their values are available in the compute block that creates its value.

Please keep in mind, for a COMPUTED *report-item* that you want to be character, you can have a compute block without having an assignment statement. You can use the compute block to initialize the variable as a missing character variable. You can then assign its value in another compute block, specifically, a block that has a *report-item* as a variable to the right of the COMPUTED *report-item* on the COLUMN statement. Example 2.4 demonstrates one possible solution.

Example 2.4: Solution Code: Assign DEMOG Value in a Different Compute Block

```
proc report data=orders;
    column customer_name demog customer_age customer_gender
           customer_country customer_type;
    define customer_age / display noprint;
    define customer_gender / noprint;
    define customer_country /noprint;
    define demog / computed;

    compute demog / char length=20; ❶
    endcomp;

    compute customer_type;
        demog = cats(customer_age, "/", customer_gender, "/",
               customer_country); ❷
    endcomp;
run;
```

❶   The compute block initializes the DEMOG *report-item* as a missing character variable.

❷   The CATS function is concatenating three variables and hardcoded text strings. The *report-item*, CUSTOMER_TYPE, is the last variable on the COLUMN statement, so values are present for all three *report-items* in the statement.

Output 2.4: COMPUTED *Report-item* DEMOG from Solution Code (Partial Listing)

Customer Name	demog	Customer Type Name
Kyndal Hooks	43/F/US	Orion Club Gold members high activity
Annmarie Leveille	23/F/US	Orion Club Gold members high activity
Najma Hicks	21/F/US	Orion Club members medium activity
Yan Kozlowski	38/M/US	Orion Club members medium activity
Kyndal Hooks	43/F/US	Orion Club Gold members high activity
Roy Siferd	73/M/US	Orion Club members medium activity
Alvan Goheen	23/M/US	Orion Club members low activity
Alvan Goheen	23/M/US	Orion Club members low activity
Alvan Goheen	23/M/US	Orion Club members low activity
Dericka Pockran	53/F/AU	Orion Club members high activity

Finally, let's look at an example, Example 2.5, where a CALL DEFINE statement is being used to change the background color of one variable based on the value of another variable. CALL DEFINE statements will be discussed in further detail in Chapter 6.

Example 2.5: Use a CALL DEFINE Statement to Change Background Color

```
proc report data=orders;
   column customer_age_group total_retail_price quantity;
   define customer_age_group / group;

   compute total_retail_price; ❶
      if quantity.sum > 250 then ❷
      call define(_col_,'style','style=[background=pink]'); ❸
   endcomp;
run;
```

```
NOTE: There were 617 observations read from the data set
WORK.ORDERS. ❹
NOTE: PROCEDURE REPORT used (Total process time):
      real time           0.02 seconds
      cpu time            0.01 seconds
```

Output 2.5: Set Background Color for TOTAL_RETAIL_PRICE ❺

Customer Age Group	Total Retail Price for This Product	Quantity Ordered
15-30 years	$30,486.50	304
31-45 years	$34,197.50	397
46-60 years	$14,920.55	175
61-75 years	$20,472.92	202

❶ TOTAL_RETAIL_PRICE is the *report-item* on the COMPUTE statement. This makes sense because it is the column that you want to apply the background color to.

❷ The IF condition always evaluates to false. QUANTITY is to the right of TOTAL_RETAIL_PRICE on the COLUMN statement, so its value is not available. Therefore, when the condition is evaluated, QUANTITY.SUM is always missing. Missing is not greater than 250, so the CALL DEFINE is not executed.

❸ The first argument in the CALL DEFINE statement is _col_, which refers to the variable on the COMPUTE statement, TOTAL_RETAIL_PRICE.

❹ Notice that the log does not indicate that there are any potential problems.

❺ The table is created properly, but all cells in the TOTAL_RETAIL_PRICE column have a white background.

The solution to this problem is to change the *report-item* to QUANTITY. The values of QUANTITY will be available inside the compute block, so the IF condition has the possibility of resolving to both true and false. The first argument in the CALL DEFINE statement will need to change from " _col_ " to "total_retail_price.sum" because you want the color applied to that column and not the QUANTITY column. Example 2.6 demonstrates the solution code.

Example 2.6: Solution Code: Place the CALL DEFINE Statement in a Different Compute Block

```
proc report data=orders;
   column customer_age_group total_retail_price quantity;
   define customer_age_group / group;

   compute quantity;
      if quantity.sum > 250 then call define(
        'total_retail_price.sum','style','style=[background=pink]');
   endcomp;
run;
```

Output 2.6: Set Background Color for TOTAL_RETAIL_PRICE from Solution Code

Customer Age Group	Total Retail Price for This Product	Quantity Ordered
15-30 years	$30,486.50	304
31-45 years	$34,197.50	397
46-60 years	$14,920.55	175
61-75 years	$20,472.92	202

When you use multiple *report-item*s from the COLUMN statement inside of a compute block, it is important to pay attention to the order of the *report-item*s in the COLUMN statement, as well as which variable is specified as the *report-item* in the COMPUTE statement. One method for avoiding the problems described in the previous sections is to make sure that you always use the last *report-item* in the COLUMN statement as the *report-item* in the COMPUTE statement. The last variable in the COLUMN statement is the last column that is built for each row, which means that all of the values in that row are available. You can use one compute block for most of the statements that you need for the entire report, including assignment statements and CALL DEFINE statements.

Note: Whether you choose to adopt this technique depends on programmer preference. You must decide what makes sense to you and what is easiest for you to read and modify.

One way to ensure that you always put the correct *report-item* in the COMPUTE statement is to add a dummy, or placeholder, *report-item* at the end of the COLUMN statement. For example, each time you write PROC REPORT code, include the dummy variable _LASTVAR in the COLUMN statement, define it as NOPRINT, and use that *report-item* in the COMPUTE statement. Example 2.7 uses this technique.

Example 2.7: Place a Dummy *Report-item* on the COLUMN Statement

```
proc report data=orders;
   column customer_age_group total_retail_price quantity total_cost
          costprice_per_unit _lastvar;
   define customer_age_group / group;
   define total_cost / computed 'Total Cost' format=dollar15.2;
   define _lastvar / noprint;

   compute _lastvar;
      total_cost = costprice_per_unit.sum * quantity.sum;
      if quantity.sum > 250 then call define(
      'total_retail_price.sum','style','style=[background=pink]');
   endcomp;
run;
```

Output 2.7: Set Background Color for TOTAL_RETAIL_PRICE using _LASTVAR Compute Block

Customer Age Group	Total Retail Price for This Product	Quantity Ordered	Total Cost	Cost Price Per Unit
15-30 years	$30,486.50	304	$2,172,262.40	$7,145.60
31-45 years	$34,197.50	397	$3,727,444.91	$9,389.03
46-60 years	$14,920.55	175	$711,287.50	$4,064.50
61-75 years	$20,472.92	202	$1,051,814.00	$5,207.00

2.6 Repeating GROUP or ORDER Variable Values

In the final report, the value of a GROUP or ORDER variable is not repeated if its value is the same as in the row above it. A value is only placed in a cell when it is the first value within that grouping. For some reports, you might want the value to be repeated on every row. This section demonstrates how to accomplish that goal.

One important thing to keep in mind is that an IF condition that is based on the value of a GROUP or ORDER variable will be true only on the first row of the grouping, because it is the only row that has a value.

2.6.1 Character Variables

Character GROUP/ORDER variable values can be forced to repeat by using a temporary variable. Example 2.8 shows the syntax for creating the needed temporary variable. In a compute block, create a temporary variable to hold the value from the first row of the grouping. Then, for rows where the value is not originally populated, the held value can be inserted.

Example 2.8: Repeat GROUP Variable Value using a Temporary Variable

```
proc report data=orders;
   column customer_group customer_gender quantity;
   define customer_group / group;
   define customer_gender / group;

   compute customer_group;
      if not missing(customer_group) then hold = customer_group;  ❶
      if missing(customer_group) then customer_group = hold;  ❷
   endcomp;
run;
```

❶ Determine if the CUSTOMER_GROUP variable contains a value. If it does, then place the value in the temporary variable called HOLD. The value of HOLD does not change until a new, nonmissing value of CUSTOMER_AGE is encountered.

❷   Determine if CUSTOMER_GROUP has a missing value. If it does, then set the value to the current value of the temporary variable HOLD.

Output 2.8: CUSTOMER_GROUP Value on Every Row

Customer Group Name	Customer Gender	Quantity Ordered
Internet/Catalog Customers	F	42
Internet/Catalog Customers	M	96
Orion Club Gold members	F	214
Orion Club Gold members	M	94
Orion Club members	F	242
Orion Club members	M	390

2.6.2 Numeric Variables

PROC REPORT treats numeric GROUP or ORDER variables differently. It does not allow you to manipulate the values as it does with character variables. For example, it will not let you overwrite a missing value. When the GROUP or ORDER variable is numeric and you need to manipulate its value, you have to create a new *report-item*.

The new *report-item* should be placed to the right of the variable of interest on the COLUMN statement and defined as COMPUTED. In a compute block, its values are assigned based on the GROUP/ORDER variable. The NOPRINT option is added to the DEFINE statement for the numeric GROUP/ORDER variable because you do not need to see two columns of the same values. Example 2.9 shows how to create a copy of a numeric GROUP variable.

Example 2.9: Create a Character Copy of a Numeric GROUP Variable

```
proc report data=orders;
   column customer_age c_age ❶ customer_gender quantity;
   define customer_age / group noprint; ❷
   define c_age / computed 'Customer Age'; ❸
   define customer_gender / group;

   compute c_age; ❹
      if not missing(customer_age) then hold = customer_age; ❺
      c_age = hold; ❻
   endcomp;
run;
```

❶   Add the new *report-item*, C_AGE, to the COLUMN statement to the right of CUSTOMER_AGE. CUSTOMER_AGE is the numeric GROUP variable that needs to be repeated on every row.

❷   Add the NOPRINT option to the DEFINE statement for CUSTOMER_AGE.

❸ Add a DEFINE statement for C_AGE. It should be defined as COMPUTED. Add a label; the label value should match the label for CUSTOMER_AGE because it is replacing that column in the report.

❹ Use C_AGE as the *report-item* on the COMPUTE statement.

❺ Determine if the value of CUSTOMER_AGE is missing. When the value is not missing, assign it to the temporary variable called HOLD. The value of HOLD does not change until a new, nonmissing value of CUSTOMER_AGE is encountered.

❻ Set C_AGE to the value of HOLD.

Output 2.9: Display CUSTOMER_AGE Value on Every Row

Customer Age	Customer Gender	Quantity Ordered
19	F	36
19	M	8
21	F	42
21	M	17
23	F	79
23	M	33
28	F	78
28	M	11
33	F	49
33	M	56
38	F	61
38	M	90
43	F	47
43	M	94
48	F	41
48	M	45
53	F	20
53	M	17
58	M	52
63	M	81
68	M	55
73	F	45
73	M	21

2.6.3 Undesired Repeating Values

For some reports, the value of a GROUP or ORDER variable might repeat when you do not want it to. Remember that PROC REPORT works left to right and groupings are nested inside GROUP/ORDER variables to the left. When the value of a GROUP/ORDER variable at the beginning of the COLUMN statement changes, the value of the GROUP/ORDER variables to its right will be displayed.

Example 2.10 is an example with both CUSTOMER_BIRTHDATE and CUSTOMER_AGE_GROUP defined as GROUP to demonstrate undesired repeating values.

Example 2.10: Demonstrate Undesired Repeating GROUP/ORDER Values

```
proc report data=orders;
   where customer_gender="F";
   column customer_birthdate customer_age_group;
   define customer_birthdate / group format=monyy5. order=internal;
   define customer_age_group / group;
run;
```

Output 2.10: CUSTOMER_AGE_GROUP Value on Every Row (Partial Listing)

Customer Birth Date	Customer Age Group
JUL34	61-75 years
SEP34	61-75 years
JUN54	46-60 years
JUN59	46-60 years
JUL59	46-60 years
AUG59	46-60 years
FEB64	31-45 years
AUG64	31-45 years
APR69	31-45 years
MAY69	31-45 years
JUL69	31-45 years
AUG69	31-45 years
SEP69	31-45 years

Because it is sorted by the birth date, we expected a number of the rows to fall within the same age group. However, you do not need to see the same value of CUSTOMER_AGE_GROUP written out so many times. You want to see the value only when it changes.

Inside of a compute block, the LAG function will return the value from the previous row. If the returned value matches the current value, then CUSTOMER_AGE_GROUP is set to missing. This prevents CUSTOMER_AGE_GROUP from repeating, as demonstrated by Example 2.11.

Example 2.11: Use the LAG Function to Remove Repeated Values

```
proc report data=orders;
   where customer_gender="F";
   column customer_birthdate customer_age_group;
   define customer_birthdate / group format=monyy5. order=internal;
   define customer_age_group / group;

   compute customer_age_group;
      lagcag = lag(customer_age_group);
      if lagcag = customer_age_group then
        customer_age_group = '';
   endcomp;
run;
```

Output 2.11: CUSTOMER_AGE_GROUP Value Only on First Row of Grouping (Partial Listing)

Customer Birth Date	Customer Age Group
JUL34	61-75 years
SEP34	
JUN54	46-60 years
JUN59	
JUL59	
AUG59	
FEB64	31-45 years
AUG64	
APR69	
MAY69	
JUL69	
AUG69	
SEP69	
DEC69	
FEB74	
AUG74	
DEC74	

Undesired repeating frequently occurs when the COLUMN statement contains ORDER variables that are used to order the rows but are not printed in the report.

To demonstrate this behavior, the ORDERS data set was pre-processed to create the SUMINFO data set. The SUMINFO data set contains a variable called ORD, which designates the desired order of the report. In the PROC REPORT step in Example 2.12, the ORD variable is placed first on the COLUMN statement. The output contains the undesired look of repeating group values, CUSTOMER_COUNTRY.

Example 2.12: Use an ORDER Variable to Control the Sort Order

```
proc report data=suminfo;
   column ord customer_country customer_group quantity;
   define ord / order noprint;
   define customer_country / group;
run;
```

Output 2.12: Sort Order Controlled by an ORDER Variable

Customer Country	Customer Group Name	Quantity Ordered
AU	Internet/Catalog Customers	13
AU	Orion Club Gold members	24
AU	Orion Club members	173
CA	Internet/Catalog Customers	5
CA	Orion Club Gold members	30
CA	Orion Club members	70
DE	Internet/Catalog Customers	48
DE	Orion Club Gold members	48
DE	Orion Club members	10
IL	Internet/Catalog Customers	5
IL	Orion Club Gold members	2
IL	Orion Club members	21
TR	Orion Club Gold members	7
TR	Orion Club members	36
US	Internet/Catalog Customers	67
US	Orion Club Gold members	180
US	Orion Club members	292
ZA	Orion Club Gold members	17
ZA	Orion Club members	30

The previous technique of using the LAG function will work here, but there is another method worth trying. The ORD variable can be moved to the end of the COLUMN statement. As an ORDER variable, it is not consolidating rows, so changing its position is less likely to impact the look of the report. However, it still affects the row order. The technique in Example 2.13 prevents CUSTOMER_COUNTRY from repeating without having to add code.

Example 2.13: Place the ORDER Variable and the End of the COLUMN Statement

```
proc report data=suminfo;
   column customer_country customer_group quantity ord;
   define ord / order noprint;
   define customer_country / group;
run;
```

Output 2.13: An ORDER Variable Controls Sorting and its Placement Prevents CUSTOMER_COUNTRY from Repeating

Customer Country	Customer Group Name	Quantity Ordered
AU	Internet/Catalog Customers	13
	Orion Club Gold members	24
	Orion Club members	173
CA	Internet/Catalog Customers	5
	Orion Club Gold members	30
	Orion Club members	70
DE	Internet/Catalog Customers	48
	Orion Club Gold members	48
	Orion Club members	10
IL	Internet/Catalog Customers	5
	Orion Club Gold members	2
	Orion Club members	21
TR	Orion Club Gold members	7
	Orion Club members	36
US	Internet/Catalog Customers	67
	Orion Club Gold members	180
	Orion Club members	292
ZA	Orion Club Gold members	17
	Orion Club members	30

2.7 Column Widths

The previous chapter explained that the WIDTH= option on the DEFINE statement is valid only in the Listing destination. *Base SAS Procedures Guide* also indicates that the COLWIDTH= option on the PROC REPORT statement is only for the Listing destination. The value of COLWIDTH= influences the value for all destinations but changes the display value only in the Listing destination. For some values, the default COLWIDTH value can cause undesired output in non-Listing destinations.

When FORMAT= and WIDTH= are omitted from the DEFINE statement and a variable does not have a permanently assigned format, PROC REPORT defaults to using the variable length for a character variable and nine (9.) for a numeric variable. In most instances, the default width is fine for character variables. However, the default width might not be correct for numeric variables.

Example 2.14 calculates TOTAL_COST, just as Example 2.2 did, but its value will be inflated by 100%, so we can see how the default COLWIDTH= value can affect large numbers.

Example 2.14: Demonstrate the Effect of the Default COLWIDTH Value of .9

```
proc report data=orders;
   column costprice_per_unit quantity total_cost;
   define total_cost / computed 'Total Cost';

   compute total_cost;
      total_cost = costprice_per_unit.sum * quantity.sum * 100;
   endcomp;
run;
```

The true value of TOTAL_COST is 2781900814.00.

Output 2.14: Displaying Large Numbers in Most ODS Destinations

Cost Price Per Unit	Quantity Ordered	Total Cost
$25,806.13	1078	2.7819E9

Output 2.15: Displaying Large Numbers in the Tagsets.ExcelXP Destination

	A	B	C	D
1	Cost Price Per Unit	Quantity Ordered	Total Cost	
2	$25,806.13	1078	2781900000	
3				

PROC REPORT is limiting the width of the value to nine (9.), before displaying the value. A width of nine is not wide enough to hold the value, so it is translated to scientific notation. PROC REPORT displays as many significant digits as possible, but two of the nine characters will be used for the decimal point (.) and the E.

To get the desired output for long numeric values, you must use the FORMAT= option on the DEFINE statement. Be sure to give a width that is wide enough to hold the entire value, including the decimal point and commas or dollar signs, if those are needed. Example 2.15 demonstrates using a format to ensure that the entire value is written in the report.

Example 2.15: Use a Format for the Desired Width

```
proc report data=orders;
   column costprice_per_unit quantity total_cost;
   define total_cost / computed 'Total Cost' format=dollar20.2;

   compute total_cost;
      total_cost = costprice_per_unit.sum * quantity.sum * 100;
   endcomp;
run;
```

Output 2.16: Displaying Large Numbers with a Format in Most ODS Destinations

Cost Price Per Unit	Quantity Ordered	Total Cost
$25,806.13	1078	$2,781,900,814.00

Output 2.17: Displaying Large Numbers with a Format in the Tagsets.ExcelXP Destination

	A	B	C	D
1	Cost Price Per Unit	Quantity Ordered	Total Cost	
2	$25,806.13	1078	$2,781,900,814.00	
3				

2.8 Date Variables

SAS date variables are numeric; they are often formatted so that we can understand the value, but they are still numeric. Date variables are often thought of as their own category, but PROC REPORT simply sees them as numeric and will sum the values by default. Performing calculations on dates, like determining an interval, might be needed in certain reports, but for other reports, summed date values are not logical. A good rule of thumb is to always have a DEFINE statement for date variables. Often date variables are needed as GROUP, ORDER, or ACROSS variables. For other reports, date variables should be defined as DISPLAY. Defining them as DISPLAY serves two purposes:

1. A DISPLAY variable is not populated in summary rows. This will prevent nonsensical date values from being placed on the summary row.
2. Inside of a compute block, you will not need to remember to refer to the variable with the compound name like DATE.SUM.

For reports that have a date variable defined as GROUP/ORDER/ACROSS, the values will be sorted by their formatted value. This most likely will not give you the desired results, because April will be placed before January. Use the ORDER= option and set it to INTERNAL so that the dates will be output in chronological order. Section 2.10 discusses sorting in PROC REPORT.

2.9 Temporary Variables

PROC REPORT allows the creation and use of temporary variables, sometimes called "DATA step variables." You might also see them referred to as "hold variables." These are variables that are not on the input data set nor are they listed on the COLUMN statement. The variables are created and used inside of compute blocks and are not available anywhere else. They are not considered part of the report and therefore are not included in the output data set, if one is created.

Temporary variables behave much the same way that retained variables behave inside of a DATA step. Temporary variables are initialized to a value and maintain that value until reset to another value. They are not re-initialized or set to missing on each row.

Temporary variables can be created in any compute block. However, you must take into account when the compute block executes, a temporary variable created inside of a COMPUTE AFTER _PAGE_; block will not be of any use. A temporary variable's value is available in the compute block where it is created and any compute block executed after it.

These variables are very useful for repeating GROUP values (as already demonstrated) as well as calculating percentages or maintaining a running total.

2.10 Sorting and the ORDER= Option

The input data set is not required to be sorted unless you use a BY statement. PROC REPORT will sort the contents of a report if at least one variable is defined as GROUP, ORDER, or ACROSS. The report cannot be sorted by ANALYSIS, DISPLAY, or COMPUTED *report-items*.

The values of GROUP, ORDER, or ACROSS *report-items* are automatically sorted. The default sort order is FORMATTED, which is different from most other procedures. To match the default sort order of other procedures, you must specify it on the DEFINE statement using the option ORDER=INTERNAL.

Another way to sort the output is to use ORDER=DATA. PROC REPORT establishes a sort order based on the order the values for that variable appear across all observations in the input data set. This will produce the expected output if you have just one variable ordering the PROC REPORT output. For reports that have multiple variables contributing to the order of the report, you might not get the expected output.

A variable defined with ORDER=DATA might be nested inside of another GROUP/ORDER variable or within a BY group, but the ORDER=DATA sort order is created based on that variable alone. The sort order is **not** re-established or changed per grouping or BY value.

The behavior of ORDER=DATA can be difficult to understand. To visualize the behavior, consider the data set in Figure 2.1.

Figure 2.1: VAR2 Values are Sorted within Values of VAR1

	var1	var2
1	A	1
2	A	2
3	A	99
4	B	1
5	B	2
6	B	3
7	B	99

Now let's look at the results of defining both variables as GROUP within a PROC REPORT step. VAR2 is also defined with ORDER=DATA. The code is in Example 2.16 and the output is in Output 2.18.

Example 2.16: Use ORDER=DATA on the DEFINE statement for VAR2

```
proc report data=temp1;
   column var1 var2;
   define var1 / group;
   define var2 / group order=data;
run;
```

Output 2.18: Results of Using ORDER=DATA

var1	var2
A	1
	2
	99
B	1
	2
	99
	3

The A grouping looks fine. The B grouping might not be what you expect. PROC REPORT encountered the value of 99 in the data set before it encountered the value of 3 and uses that as the established sort order. It maintains that order in the report even though 3 came before 99 within the B records.

Let's look at another example of how using ORDER=DATA might not produce the expected output. Consider the data set from Figure 2.2.

Figure 2.2: VAR1 and VAR2 Values Are Not in a Specific Order

	var1	var2
1	A	1
2	A	1
3	B	1
4	B	4
5	B	3
6	A	2
7	A	3

The PROC REPORT code, shown in Example 2.17 defines both variables as GROUP. Again, VAR2 is also defined with ORDER=DATA.

Example 2.17: Use ORDER=DATA on Data with No Specific order

```
proc report data=temp2;
   column var1 var2;
   define var1 / group;
   define var2 / group order=data;
run;
```

Output 2.19: Results of Using ORDER=DATA on Unsorted Data

var1	var2
A	1
	3
	2
B	1
	4
	3

Because the VAR2 values for the A grouping are 1, 3, 2 you might expect the B grouping to be 1, 3, 4. However, PROC REPORT encountered the value of 4 before it encountered 3 in the input data set. The A grouping does not have a value of 4, so it is not written to that part of the output. The B grouping did have 4, so it is inserted at its original position, which is the second in the list.

ORDER=DATA can be used to your advantage, but you need to be aware of how it works so that you are not caught off guard. See Chapter 4 for an example of avoiding this behavior.

It is common practice to put all GROUP and ORDER variables at the beginning of the COLUMN statement. However, these variables can be placed anywhere on the COLUMN statement. GROUP and ORDER variables will always affect the order of the rows regardless of where on the COLUMN statement they are placed. As discussed previously, PROC REPORT executes from left to right. The report will be sorted by the first GROUP/ORDER variable on the COLUMN statement. Then it will sort the values of the second variable within each value of the first variable, and so on.

For some reports, sorting by INTERNAL or FORMATTED does not provide the desired order. It is possible to place GROUP, ORDER, or ACROSS values in a customized order. See Chapters 4 and 5 for an example of using a customized sort order.

2.11 Paging

The Listing destination has an exact number of spaces per row and a specific number of rows per page. These values are set by the system options LINESIZE and PAGESIZE. When sending to the Listing destination, PROC REPORT knows exactly how much of the output will fit on each page. A warning message will be written to the log if the width of a *report-item* exceeds the LINESIZE value. It is also easy to determine how many rows will fit by subtracting the number of titles and footnotes and the number of rows used by the column headers from the PAGESIZE value.

The PAGE option on a DEFINE statement will immediately create a new page and the columns to the right will be printed on this page. The PAGE option on a BREAK statement will automatically trigger a page break and the new page will contain the next section of the report. Page breaks are straightforward in the Listing destination.

Example 2.18 shows using the PAGE option on the DEFINE statement for COL7. The results of this step are sent to the Listing destination and can be seen in Output 2.20a-2.20d. Each picture contains a separate page. You can see that the Listing destination will output all columns for one set of observations (22 in all) and then output all columns for the remaining 18 observations.

Example 2.18: Use PAGE Option on DEFINE Statement

```
ods listing;
options nocenter ls=150 ps=25 pageno=1 number;
title 'Listing Destination with PAGE Option on DEFINE Statement';
proc report data=tran_orders (obs=40);
   column customer_id customer_name col1-col12;
   define customer_name / id;
   define col7 / page;
run;
```

Output 2.20a: Page 1 of Listing Output Using PAGE Option on DEFINE Statement (Obs 1-22, Col1-6)

Listing Destination with PAGE Option on DEFINE Statement

Customer ID	Customer Name	COL1	COL2	COL3	COL4	COL5	COL6
4	James Kvarniq	$16.70	$92.60	$214.00	$58.90	$201.90	$53.00
5	Sandrina Stephano	$52.50	$33.80	$74.20	$136.80	$50.40	$126.80
9	Cornelia Krahl	$16.00	$29.40	$1,542.60	$514.20	$550.20	$39.20
10	Karen Ballinger	$134.00	$60.90	$60.60	$32.60	$52.90	$37.30
11	Elke Wallstab	$78.20	$72.70				
12	David Black	$48.00	$117.60	$68.40	$48.40	$48.40	$96.30
13	Markus Sepke	$165.50	$126.10	$146.80	$14.10	$6.20	$39.20
16	Ulrich Heyde	$125.20	$177.20	$285.80	$115.00	$406.00	$1,103.60
17	Jimmie Evans	$84.10	$110.20	$86.60	$175.90	$119.95	$257.40
18	Tonie Asmussen	$29.40	$197.90	$50.80			
19	Oliver S. Füßling	$133.20	$77.00	$96.70	$283.30	$56.40	$1,200.20
20	Michael Dineley	$206.00	$145.20	$190.50	$175.30	$68.50	$32.00
23	Tulio Devereaux	$178.50	$369.80	$116.70	$110.40	$28.50	$148.50
24	Robyn Klem	$92.00	$145.90	$11.90	$46.10	$70.20	$46.90
27	Cynthia Mccluney	$58.70	$56.30	$90.00	$91.60	$403.50	$78.40
29	Candy Kinsey	$17.40	$35.00	$119.00	$305.80	$32.80	$74.80
31	Cynthia Martinez	$38.60	$50.30	$63.50	$57.30	$120.40	$277.60
34	Alvan Goheen	$43.80	$38.00	$41.60	$101.30	$86.30	$28.60
36	Phenix Hill	$318.20	$25.80	$146.80	$257.00	$27.60	$34.50
39	Alphone Greenwald	$5.10	$21.99				
41	Wendell Summersby	$39.40	$50.40	$134.00	$21.80	$120.20	$17.00
45	Dianne Patchin	$142.40	$73.80	$128.60	$249.60	$398.60	$40.20

Output 2.20b: Page 2 of Listing Output Using PAGE Option on DEFINE Statement (Obs 1-22, Col7-12)

Listing Destination with PAGE Option on DEFINE Statement

Customer ID	Customer Name	COL7	COL8	COL9	COL10	COL11	COL12
4	James Kvarniq	$80.97	$16.90	$47.70			
5	Sandrina Stephano	$446.60	$247.50	$265.60	$86.30	$31.40	$169.70
9	Cornelia Krahl						
10	Karen Ballinger	$11.30	$231.00	$52.50	$19.20	$40.60	$68.40
11	Elke Wallstab						
12	David Black	$91.20	$268.00	$226.20	$56.70	$193.80	$87.20
13	Markus Sepke						
16	Ulrich Heyde	$68.70	$16.80	$66.80	$146.00	$252.20	$138.70
17	Jimmie Evans						
18	Tonie Asmussen						
19	Oliver S. Füßling	$217.00					
20	Michael Dineley						
23	Tulio Devereaux	$127.20	$949.80	$164.40	$35.40	$73.80	
24	Robyn Klem	$195.60					
27	Cynthia Mccluney	$140.70	$174.40				
29	Candy Kinsey	$51.60	$190.40	$79.90	$154.60		
31	Cynthia Martinez	$172.50	$220.20	$16.00	$195.00	$22.70	$41.50
34	Alvan Goheen	$403.00	$239.50	$712.20	$70.80	$38.80	
36	Phenix Hill	$26.40	$525.20	$150.25			
39	Alphone Greenwald						
41	Wendell Summersby	$222.30	$17.60	$154.00	$88.50	$29.40	$17.00
45	Dianne Patchin	$8.00	$78.20	$231.00	$172.60	$849.90	$420.90

Output 2.20c: Page 3 of Listing Output Using PAGE Option on DEFINE Statement (Obs 18-40, Col1-6)

Listing Destination with PAGE Option on DEFINE Statement

Customer ID	Customer Name	COL1	COL2	COL3	COL4	COL5	COL6
49	Annmarie Leveille	$39.00	$6.50	$33.40	$63.90	$6.50	$35.60
50	Gert-Gunter Mendler	$270.00	$566.60	$28.80			
52	Yan Kozlowski	$19.80	$50.00	$27.40	$116.40	$52.20	$62.20
53	Dericka Pockran	$37.80	$97.60	$180.40	$186.80	$102.90	$240.00
56	Roy Siferd	$50.40	$33.00	$97.20	$75.00	$24.40	$13.50
60	Tedi Lanzarone	$211.40	$21.00	$141.70			
61	Carsten Maestrini	$83.00	$345.00	$544.00	$259.60	$103.20	$440.00
63	James Klisurich	$39.40	$16.50	$84.20	$99.90	$46.90	$173.00
65	Ines Deisser	$99.90	$354.00	$351.40			
69	Patricia Bertolozzi	$23.50	$3.20				
71	Viola Folsom	$65.60	$134.50	$132.80	$250.90	$359.10	$265.60
75	Mikel Spetz	$75.20	$7.20	$109.20	$56.00		
79	Najma Hicks	$36.00	$92.00	$39.00	$176.00	$2.60	$3.40
88	Attila Gibbs	$47.90	$38.70	$106.10	$248.20	$83.60	$62.60
89	Wynella Lewis	$29.70	$192.60	$59.40	$78.00	$58.70	$283.40
90	Kyndal Hooks	$69.40	$14.30	$56.80	$33.60	$172.80	$38.60
92	Lendon Celii	$53.70	$84.10	$396.00	$250.80	$160.50	$105.60
111	Karolina Dokter	$105.80	$25.60	$342.80	$30.80	$67.20	$22.20

Output 2.20d: Page 4 of Listing Output Using PAGE Option on DEFINE Statement (Obs 18-40, Col7-12)

```
Listing Destination with PAGE Option on DEFINE Statement                                                    4

Customer ID  Customer Name              COL7         COL8         COL9        COL10        COL11        COL12
        49   Annmarie Leveille       $187.20       $88.40       $26.70       $28.20      $200.20    $1,514.40
        50   Gert-Gunter Mendler           .            .            .            .            .            .
        52   Yan Kozlowski           $213.20      $208.60       $76.00        $8.00       $50.00      $168.20
        53   Dericka Pockran         $336.40      $112.50       $48.30      $200.10      $362.60            .
        56   Roy Siferd                    .            .            .            .            .            .
        60   Tedi Lanzarone                .            .            .            .            .            .
        61   Carsten Maestrini             .            .            .            .            .            .
        63   James Klisurich          $86.30       $48.40      $174.30       $41.70       $21.99            .
        65   Ines Deisser                  .            .            .            .            .            .
        69   Patricia Bertolozzi           .            .            .            .            .            .
        71   Viola Folsom            $111.40    $1,136.20      $219.90       $48.70       $54.10            .
        75   Mikel Spetz                   .            .            .            .            .            .
        79   Najma Hicks             $234.60    $1,796.00       $54.30       $76.80       $24.10            .
        88   Attila Gibbs             $93.80      $419.00    $1,250.40       $34.50            .            .
        89   Wynelia Lewis           $173.20      $251.80      $114.20      $134.60       $22.85       $65.97
        90   Kyndal Hooks            $213.00       $24.80        $8.00       $64.20       $16.40      $192.40
        92   Lendon Celii             $16.90            .            .            .            .            .
       111   Karolina Dokter         $102.00      $140.10      $113.80       $26.10       $35.50      $191.60
```

Page breaks are not straightforward in other destinations. HTML output is designed to be viewed on a screen, and the amount of the report that can be seen is limited only by the size of your monitor. Scroll bars are used to see output that is extremely wide or long. Destinations such as PDF or RTF are true "paging" destinations and are meant to be printed. Printed output is limited to the size of the paper. However, the amount of output that fits on one page is extremely variable. Titles, footnotes, logos, margins, font face, font size, and borders all affect the output.

PROC REPORT does not control the placement of the output. Each destination is responsible for placement. Each destination and the application used to open the output controls the paging. PROC REPORT does not know where a page break will occur in the non-Listing ODS destinations. The PAGE option, both on the DEFINE and BREAK statements, behaves differently for these destinations. PROC REPORT does not automatically insert a page break. Instead, it creates a new table. The destination then determines whether the new table will be placed on a new page.

When the PAGE option is used on a DEFINE statement, a vertical break will occur, that is, a new table is created. However, all observations for the first set of columns will be printed and then all of the observations for the next set of columns will be printed. Any variables designated as ID will also be printed with the second set of columns. For non-Listing destinations, the order of the results from Example 2.18 is:

1. Output 2.20a
2. Output 2.20c
3. Output 2.20b
4. Output 2.20d

This is vastly different from the Listing destination, where the first set of columns will be output for a given number of observations (determined by PAGESIZE) and then the second set of columns will be output for the same observations. This pattern continues for all observations.

For non-Listing destinations, to get interleaved pages, where the first set of columns is on page one and the second set of columns is on page two, you will need to add a variable to the input data set that can be used as a GROUP or ORDER variable. This new variable will set the number of observations for each table. The new variable must be placed on a BREAK statement with the

PAGE option. This forces the destination to keep the observations together. The PAGE option on a DEFINE statement places the second set of columns in a new table. The destination then places each table on its own page. The value of the new variable is arbitrary. It should be populated based on the number of observations that can reasonably fit on a page when taking into consideration margins, font size, and business requirements.

Because PROC REPORT does not know where in the report a page break will be inserted by the destination, it does not know whether all rows for a particular grouping will fit on a page. PROC REPORT will create a new table when the GROUP or ORDER variable on the BREAK statement changes values and the PAGE option is specified. If you want the value of GROUP or ORDER variable to repeat at the top of a page or you want all rows for a group to be on one page, you have to specify the PAGE option on the BREAK.

The only way to truly control where page breaks occur in non-Listing destinations is to have a "paging" variable. This variable, along with the use of the PAGE option dictates the number of observations and columns that you will see on a page. See Chapter 3 for an example of creating a paging variable.

The THISPAGE, LASTPAGE, and PAGEOF inline formatting functions are often used for the PDF and RTF destinations. The destination is responsible for populating the values. PROC REPORT cannot and does not control these values. The only way PROC REPORT has an effect is through the PAGENO option, discussed in Chapter 1. Even using the PAGE option does not guarantee a new page will start or that the page number will be incremented.

Chapter 3: Examples – How to Get the Desired Report

3.1 Introduction

This chapter is the first of three chapters with examples of how to create various kinds of reports. The chapter begins with the standard reports that PROC REPORT can create by default. PROC REPORT can create a simple listing of the data or an ordered listing of the data. A report can also contain variables not present in the original data set. PROC REPORT will consolidate rows from the input data set and provide summary statistics of the analysis variables.

Next is a section on nonstandard reports. These are reports that are commonly asked for, but require a little more programming effort to produce because PROC REPORT does not create the statistic or structure by default. However, the reports can still be produced by PROC REPORT. Inside of the procedure, percentages can be calculated, informational text can be added for certain sections of the report, and additional rows of statistics can be included.

The last section in this chapter demonstrates how to create reports that require special consideration of the data that you have, like really wide reports or missing data categories. When producing a report, you must know your data. Your data might dictate how you write the PROC REPORT step and whether you must have additional code to generate the final report.

In general, this chapter starts with the least complicated examples and builds to the most complicated examples. The programs in each section use variables that best demonstrate the type of report or technique discussed in that section. Some variable combinations are chosen because they produce the shortest amount of output, not because they represent the most desirable combinations. Once you have learned the techniques, you can expand the code for larger data sets with more variables and observations.

3.2 Standard Reports

The word "standard" has been chosen to describe the reports created in this section because PROC REPORT can create them by default without any extra coding. In this context, standard does not mean correct or typical. Standard reports include detail reports and summary reports based on values present in the input data set. Detail reports have one row in the report for each observation in the data set. Summary reports include a row of aggregate values, or summarized values. Summary reports can include one GROUP/ORDER variable or many GROUP/ORDER variables.

This section includes examples of creating basic reports, ordered reports, and grouped reports. The examples demonstrate how to create new variables to be included in the report and how to insert summary rows.

3.2.1 Create a Basic Report

A basic report is one where you let PROC REPORT and the ODS destination do all of the work. You just want to see the data. Therefore, you accept how PROC REPORT handles each variable type, the alignment, the coloring, and so on. You use the COLUMN statement to specify the variables from the input data set that you want and to specify the order in which you want to see them.

In Example 3.1, the report is restricted to the six *report-item*s on the COLUMN statement. Accepting the default behavior means that this report is simply a listing of the data. The first row of data in the report corresponds to the first observation in the data set, and so on. If you were to send Output 3.1 to the RTF or PDF destination, the file would be approximately 17 pages long.

Example 3.1: Basic Report with Six Columns
```
proc report data=orders;
   column customer_id customer_name customer_age customer_gender
          product_name quantity;
run;
```

Output 3.1: A Detail Report of Six Columns and All Observations

Customer ID	Customer Name	Customer Age	Customer Gender	Product Name	Quantity Ordered
90	Kyndal Hooks	43	F	Kids Sweat Round Neck,Large Logo	2
49	Annmarie Leveille	23	F	Sweatshirt Children's O-Neck	1
79	Najma Hicks	21	F	Sunfit Slow Swimming Trunks	2
52	Yan Kozlowski	38	M	Sunfit Stockton Swimming Trunks Jr.	1
90	Kyndal Hooks	43	F	Fleece Cuff Pant Kid'S	1
56	Roy Siferd	73	M	Hsc Dutch Player Shirt Junior	1
34	Alvan Goheen	23	M	Tony's Cut & Sew T-Shirt	2
34	Alvan Goheen	23	M	Kids Baby Edge Max Shoes	1
34	Alvan Goheen	23	M	Tony's Children's Deschutz (Bg) Shoes	1
53	Dericka Pockran	53	F	Children's Mitten	3
12	David Black	38	M	Rain Suit, Plain w/backpack Jacket	2
41	Wendell Summersby	43	M	Bozeman Rain & Storm Set	1
63	James Klisurich	38	M	Bozeman Rain & Storm Set	1
5	Sandrina Stephano	28	F	Teen Profleece w/Zipper	1
41	Wendell Summersby	43	M	Butch T-Shirt with V-Neck	1
10	Karen Ballinger	23	F	Children's Knit Sweater	2
41	Wendell Summersby	43	M	Children's Knit Sweater	2
75	Mikel Spetz	23	M	Gordon Children's Tracking Pants	2
41	Wendell Summersby	43	M	O'my Children's T-Shirt with Logo	1
69	Patricia Bertolozzi	28	F	Strap Pants BBO	1

Without too much effort, you can add spanning headers to the report. Recall a spanning header is created on the COLUMN statement and produces an additional row of header text that groups columns underneath it. Spanning headers are a good way to add clarification to the report without having to change the data. Example 3.2 adds two spanning headers, resulting in Output 3.2.

Example 3.2: Add Spanning Headers

```
proc report data=orders;
    column ("Customer Details" customer_id customer_name customer_age
            customer_gender)
           ("Order Details" product_name quantity);
run;
```

Output 3.2: Spanning Headers Group Sets of Columns

Customer Details				Order Details		
Customer ID	Customer Name	Customer Age	Customer Gender	Product Name	Quantity Ordered	
90	Kyndal Hooks	43	F	Kids Sweat Round Neck,Large Logo	2
49	Annmarie Leveille	23	F	Sweatshirt Children's O-Neck	1
79	Najma Hicks	21	F	Sunfit Slow Swimming Trunks	2
52	Yan Kozlowski	38	M	Sunfit Stockton Swimming Trunks Jr.	1
90	Kyndal Hooks	43	F	Fleece Cuff Pant Kid'S	1
56	Roy Siferd	73	M	Hsc Dutch Player Shirt Junior	1
34	Alvan Goheen	23	M	Tony's Cut & Sew T-Shirt	2
34	Alvan Goheen	23	M	Kids Baby Edge Max Shoes	1
34	Alvan Goheen	23	M	Tony's Children's Deschutz (Bg) Shoes	1
53	Dericka Pockran	53	F	Children's Mitten	3
12	David Black	38	M	Rain Suit, Plain w/backpack Jacket	2
41	Wendell Summersby	43	M	Bozeman Rain & Storm Set	1
63	James Klisurich	38	M	Bozeman Rain & Storm Set	1
5	Sandrina Stephano	28	F	Teen Profleece w/Zipper	1
41	Wendell Summersby	43	M	Butch T-Shirt with V-Neck	1
10	Karen Ballinger	23	F	Children's Knit Sweater	2
41	Wendell Summersby	43	M	Children's Knit Sweater	2
75	Mikel Spetz	23	M	Gordon Children's Tracking Pants	2
41	Wendell Summersby	43	M	O'my Children's T-Shirt with Logo	1
69	Patricia Bertolozzi	28	F	Strap Pants BBO	1

3.2.2 Define a Variable as ORDER

The order of the observations can be changed so that the report appears in a different order than the data set without changing the data or shortening the report. When a variable is defined as ORDER, the report is sorted by that variable.

In Example 3.3, a DEFINE statement is added for the CUSTOMER_ID variable. As seen in the previous example, this variable is numeric and unique to each customer. By defining it as ORDER, the report is sorted by its formatted value, so the customer with the smallest value of CUSTOMER_ID will be listed first. Also, note in Output 3.3 that CUSTOMER_ID is not repeated on every row. ORDER values will not be printed if they are the same as the value above it. In this case, a customer could have more than one purchase, but their ID value does not change. Therefore, it is not repeated.

Example 3.3: Define CUSTOMER_ID as ORDER

```
proc report data=orders;
   column ("Customer Details" customer_id customer_name customer_age
          customer_gender)
          ("Order Details" product_name quantity);
   define customer_id / order;
run;
```

Output 3.3: Report Sorted By an ORDER Variable

Customer Details				Order Details	
Customer ID	Customer Name	Customer Age	Customer Gender	Product Name	Quantity Ordered
4	James Kvarniq	33	M	Essence.baseball Cap	1
	James Kvarniq	33	M	Monster Men's Pants with Zipper	2
	James Kvarniq	33	M	A-team Sweat Round Neck, Small Logo	4
	James Kvarniq	33	M	Men's Sweatshirt w/Hood Big Logo	1
	James Kvarniq	33	M	Force Technical Jacket w/Coolmax	3
	James Kvarniq	33	M	Swim Suit Laurel	1
	James Kvarniq	33	M	Football - Helmet Pro XL	3
	James Kvarniq	33	M	Helmet M	1
	James Kvarniq	33	M	li Pmt,Bone	1
5	Sandrina Stephano	28	F	Teen Profleece w/Zipper	1
	Sandrina Stephano	28	F	Comp. Women's Sleeveless Polo	2
	Sandrina Stephano	28	F	Ottis Pes Men's Pants	2
	Sandrina Stephano	28	F	Pine Sweat with Hood	2

3.2.3 Define a Variable as GROUP

In Example 3.3, the ORDER option ordered the output. Its value is written out only when it does not match the value above it. The GROUP option performs both of these functions and consolidates the rows. Consolidating rows is the key feature for defining a variable as GROUP. Using a variable as GROUP allows observations from the input data set to be combined so that the report is no longer a listing of the data.

PROC REPORT cannot create an aggregate value if any DISPLAY variables are on the COLUMN statement. If the COLUMN statement contains both a GROUP and a DISPLAY variable, PROC REPORT will calculate an aggregate value for all of the ANALYSIS and COMPUTED variables from the COLUMN statement. The report will still be sorted by the GROUP values and summary rows can still be generated, but the report will contain individual values instead of aggregated ones. The GROUP variable will behave like an ORDER variable and the following note will be written to the log to make you aware that PROC REPORT could not perform all of the functions normally associated with a GROUP variable.

```
NOTE: Groups are not created because the usage of XXXX is DISPLAY.
To avoid this note, change all GROUP variables to ORDER variables.
```

Example 3.4 demonstrates the difference between accepting the default usages of DISPLAY for a character variable and defining it as GROUP. The variables CUSTOMER_ID, CUSTOMER_GENDER, and CUSTOMER_AGE were removed in order to simplify the output. Had they been left in, they would have needed to be defined as GROUP to consolidate rows and prevent the issue described above.

Output 3.4 now contains one row for each value of CUSTOMER_NAME. The quantity ordered column now contains a sum of the QUANTITY variable for each name.

Example 3.4: Define CUSTOMER_NAME as GROUP

```
proc report data=orders;
    column customer_name quantity;
    define customer_name / group;
run;
```

Output 3.4: Report Consolidated by CUSTOMER_NAME

Customer Name	Quantity Ordered
Ahmet Canko	9
Alex Santinello	9
Alphone Greenwald	2
Alvan Goheen	22
Andreas Rennie	2
Angel Borwick	11
Annmarie Leveille	20
Attila Gibbs	14
Avinoam Tuvia	2
Avinoam Zweig	19
Avni Argac	13
Avni Umran	7
Bill Cuddy	8
Bulent Urfalioglu	5
Candy Kinsey	13
Carglar Aydemir	2
Carsten Maestrini	13
Colin Byarley	3
Cornelia Krahl	11
Cosi Rimmington	24
Cynthia Martinez	21
Cynthia Mccluney	15
David Black	31
Dericka Pockran	20
Dianne Patchin	47
Duncan Robertshawe	25
Elke Wallstab	3
Eyal Bloch	7
Gert-Gunter Mendler	5

For Example 3.5, the PRODUCT_LINE variable is added to the COLUMN statement and defined as GROUP. The resulting report, Output 3.5, gives the sum of QUANTITY for each product line within each name. Some customers purchased just one kind of product, so the report contains one row for those customers. Other customers purchased multiple product lines, so there is a row for each product line. The SPANROWS option was added to the PROC REPORT statement so that the CUSTOMER_NAME column becomes one big, merged cell when there are multiple rows associated with it, like for Alvan Goheen.

SPANROWS is the only option available to create a merged-cell look in the output. The option applies only to columns for GROUP or ORDER variables. It also forces the value to repeat at the top of a new page if the value spans a page break. However, the SPANROWS option does have drawbacks. Repeating values at the top of a new page occurs only in the ODS PDF and Tagsets.RTF destinations. Also, a summary row breaks the merged column and inserts its own row. The value might not be repeated after the summary row.

Example 3.5: Add PRODUCT_LINE and Define It As GROUP

```
proc report data=orders spanrows;
   column customer_name product_line quantity;
   define customer_name / group;
   define product_line / group;
run;
```

Output 3.5: Report Grouped by PRODUCT_LINE within CUSTOMER_NAME

Customer Name	Product Line	Quantity Ordered
Ahmet Canko	Outdoors	9
Alex Santinello	Sports	9
Alphone Greenwald	Sports	2
Alvan Goheen	Children	4
	Clothes & Shoes	1
	Outdoors	1
	Sports	16
Andreas Rennie	Sports	2
Angel Borwick	Sports	11
Annmarie Leveille	Children	2
	Clothes & Shoes	11
	Sports	7
Attila Gibbs	Children	1
	Clothes & Shoes	7
	Outdoors	1
	Sports	5
Avinoam Tuvia	Clothes & Shoes	2
Avinoam Zweig	Clothes & Shoes	19
Avni Argac	Outdoors	13
Avni Umran	Outdoors	7
Bill Cuddy	Sports	8
Bulent Urfalioglu	Outdoors	5
Candy Kinsey	Clothes & Shoes	8
	Sports	5
Carglar Aydemir	Outdoors	2
Carsten Maestrini	Clothes & Shoes	4
	Outdoors	9
Colin Byarley	Clothes & Shoes	3

Once a variable is defined as GROUP or ORDER, a new set of report possibilities opens up. Summary rows can be added; those will be covered later in this chapter. Compute blocks that specify a location and the break variable can also be used. As discussed in the previous chapter, these compute blocks allow you to control the values and attributes on summary rows and to write out text via a LINE statement.

Example 3.6 adds text via a LINE statement. The LINE statement is a valuable tool for adding commentary and other information to the report. The text can be static or it can change dynamically, based on values within the report.

Example 3.6: Use a LINE Statement Inside Compute Before CUSTOMER_NAME Block

```
proc report data=orders;
   column customer_name product_line quantity;
   define customer_name / group;
   define product_line / group;

   compute before customer_name; ❶
      line 'Section for customer ' customer_name $50.; ❷
   endcomp;
run;
```

❶ The BEFORE location tells PROC REPORT that whatever is done inside the block should be applied to the top of the section for a given value of CUSTOMER_NAME, meaning that the LINE statement text will be before each name grouping.

❷ The LINE statement is used to add text. The text is a combination of the hardcoded string 'Section for customer' and the current value of CUSTOMER_NAME.

Output 3.6: LINE Statement Text Appears at the Top of Each CUSTOMER_NAME Section

Customer Name	Product Line	Quantity Ordered
Section for customer Ahmet Canko		
Ahmet Canko	Outdoors	9
Section for customer Alex Santinello		
Alex Santinello	Sports	9
Section for customer Alphone Greenwald		
Alphone Greenwald	Sports	2
Section for customer Alvan Goheen		
Alvan Goheen	Children	4
	Clothes & Shoes	1
	Outdoors	1
	Sports	16
Section for customer Andreas Rennie		
Andreas Rennie	Sports	2
Section for customer Angel Borwick		
Angel Borwick	Sports	11
Section for customer Annmarie Leveille		
Annmarie Leveille	Children	2
	Clothes & Shoes	11
	Sports	7
Section for customer Attila Gibbs		
Attila Gibbs	Children	1
	Clothes & Shoes	7
	Outdoors	1
	Sports	5
Section for customer Avinoam Tuvia		
Avinoam Tuvia	Clothes & Shoes	2
Section for customer Avinoam Zweig		
Avinoam Zweig	Clothes & Shoes	19

Output 3.6 is a little redundant because the customer's name was part of the text and it is in a column. You can choose to write the customer name with a LINE statement and prevent the column from being printed. This technique is very useful for wide reports, as eliminating one column buys you space for other columns. The technique is shown in Example 3.7. Output 3.7 displays the report with the CUSTOMER_NAME column removed.

Example 3.7: Remove CUSTOMER_NAME Column

```
proc report data=orders;
   column customer_name product_line quantity;
   define customer_name / group noprint; ❶
   define product_line / group;

   compute before customer_name; ❷
      line 'Section for customer ' customer_name $50.; ❸
   endcomp;
run;
```

❶ Add the NOPRINT option to the DEFINE statement for CUSTOMER_NAME to prevent the column from being printed.

❷   The BEFORE location tells PROC REPORT that whatever is done inside the block should be applied to the top of the section for a given value of CUSTOMER_NAME, meaning the LINE statement text will be before each name grouping.

❸   The LINE statement is used to add text. The text is a combination of the hardcoded string 'Section for customer' and the current value of CUSTOMER_NAME.

Output 3.7: Column for CUSTOMER_NAME Removed

Product Line	Quantity Ordered
Section for customer Ahmet Canko	
Outdoors	9
Section for customer Alex Santinello	
Sports	9
Section for customer Alphone Greenwald	
Sports	2
Section for customer Alvan Goheen	
Children	4
Clothes & Shoes	1
Outdoors	1
Sports	16
Section for customer Andreas Rennie	
Sports	2
Section for customer Angel Borwick	
Sports	11
Section for customer Annmarie Leveille	
Children	2
Clothes & Shoes	11
Sports	7
Section for customer Attila Gibbs	
Children	1
Clothes & Shoes	7
Outdoors	1
Sports	5
Section for customer Avinoam Tuvia	
Clothes & Shoes	2
Section for customer Avinoam Zweig	
Clothes & Shoes	19

3.2.4 Create a New *Report-Item*

One of the unique features of PROC REPORT is it allows you to create brand new *report-item*s to place in the report without having to add them to the input data set. Character *report-item*s can be concatenated or abbreviated. Numeric *report-item*s can be multiplied or added together, along with many other numeric functions. PROC REPORT gives you the flexibility to make the changes that you need to make. Remember PROC REPORT works left to right; when creating new columns the *report-item* on the COMPUTE statement is very important. Of all of the *report-item*s used on the assignment statement, the one farthest to the right on the COLUMN statement needs to be used on the COMPUTE statement so that all values are available.

Character *Report-Item*

This section will demonstrate creating new character *report-item*s. COMPUTED *report-item*s default to being numeric unless you specify otherwise. The option CHAR is used on the COMPUTE statement to tell PROC REPORT to create a character *report-item*. Inside of compute blocks, COMPUTED *report-item*s are referenced by name as are any other DISPLAY, GROUP, or ORDER variables, which is demonstrated in Example 3.8 and Output 3.8.

Example 3.8: Create a Character COMPUTED Variable PROD_INFO

```
proc report data=orders ;
   column customer_name product_line product_name prod_info
          quantity; ❶
   define customer_name / group;
   define product_line / noprint; ❷
   define product_name / noprint; ❸
   define prod_info / computed 'Product Line: Product Name'; ❹

   compute prod_info /char length=100; ❺
      prod_info = catx(' : ',product_line, product_name); ❻
   endcomp;
run;
```

❶   The COLUMN statement contains the character variables from the input data set and the name of the *report-item* to be created by PROC REPORT, PROD_INFO.

❷   PRODUCT_LINE will contribute to the new *report-item* but does not need to be in the final report, so the DEFINE statement contains the NOPRINT option.

❸   PRODUCT_NAME will contribute to the new *report-item* but does not need to be in the final report, so the DEFINE statement contains the NOPRINT option.

❹   PROD_INFO is the new *report-item,* so it is defined as COMPUTED and given an appropriate label.

❺   PROD_INFO is the new *report-item* and designated as a character column with a length of 100. This compute block will be executed for every row of the report.

❻   The value of PROD_INFO is the concatenation of the PRODUCT_LINE and PRODUCT_NAME values.

Output 3.8: Report Contains a COMPUTED Column PROD_INFO

Customer Name	Product Line: Product Name	Quantity Ordered
Ahmet Canko	Outdoors : Men's Jacket Caians	2
	Outdoors : X-Large Bottlegreen/Black	3
	Outdoors : Mayday Serious Headband	3
	Outdoors : Family Holiday 6	1
Alex Santinello	Sports : Bretagne Stabilities Tg Men's Golf Shoes	2
	Sports : Grandslam Staff Grip Llh Golf Gloves	2
	Sports : Grandslam Staff Tour Mhl Golf Gloves	2
	Sports : White 90,Top.Flite Strata Tour 3-pack	1
	Sports : Eagle Pants with Cross Pocket	2
Alphone Greenwald	Sports : Baseball White Small	1
	Sports : Basket Ball Pro	1
Alvan Goheen	Children : Tony's Cut & Sew T-Shirt	2
	Children : Kids Baby Edge Max Shoes	1
	Children : Tony's Children's Deschutz (Bg) Shoes	1
	Clothes & Shoes : Big Guy Men's Mid Layer Jacket	1
	Outdoors : Outback Sleeping Bag, Large,Left,Blue/Black	1
	Sports : Victor 76 76mm Optics Blue	1
	Sports : Shirt Termir	2
	Sports : Wyoming Men's T-Shirt with V-Neck	5
	Sports : Rollerskate Roller Skates Sq9 80-76mm/78a	3
	Sports : Armour L	3
	Sports : Helmet XL	2
Andreas Rennie	Sports : Bretagne Stabilities Women's Golf Shoes	2
Angel Borwick	Sports : Bretagne Stabilities Tg Men's Golf Shoes	2
	Sports : Hi-fly Intimidator Ti R80/10	3
	Sports : Proplay Stand Black	2
	Sports : Rubby Men's Golf Shoes w/Goretex Plain Toe	1
	Sports : Eagle Windstopper Knit Neck	3
Annmarie Leveille	Children : Sweatshirt Children's O-Neck	1

Numeric values can also be converted to create new character *report-item*s. The method, seen in Example 3.9 and Output 3.9, is useful for combining counts and percentages or means and standard deviations into one column.

Example 3.9: Use Numeric Variables to Create a Character COMPUTED Column

```
proc report data=orders;
   column customer_name total_retail_price quantity costprice_per_unit
          item; ❶
   define costprice_per_unit / display noprint; ❷
   define quantity / display noprint; ❸
   define total_retail_price / display noprint; ❹
   define item / computed 'Retail v Cost'; ❺
```

```
compute item /char length=20; ❻
    item = cats(put(total_retail_price/quantity,6.2)," / ",
            put(costprice_per_unit,6.2)); ❼
endcomp;
run;
```

❶   The needed variables from the input data set are placed on the COLUMN statement as well as the new *report-item*, ITEM.

❷   COSTPRICE_PER_UNIT is defined as DISPLAY for convenience, so that the variable does not have to be referred to by compound name inside of the compute block. NOPRINT is used to prevent the column from appearing in the final report. Remember, NOPRINT is not the opposite of DISPLAY.

❸   QUANTITY is defined as DISPLAY for convenience so that just its name is required in a compute block. NOPRINT is used to prevent the column from appearing in the final report. Remember, NOPRINT is not the opposite of DISPLAY.

❹   TOTAL_RETAIL_PRICE is defined as DISPLAY for convenience so that just its name is required in a compute block. NOPRINT is used to prevent the column from appearing in the final report. Remember, NOPRINT is not the opposite of DISPLAY.

❺   ITEM is the new *report-item,* so it is defined as COMPUTED and given an appropriate label.

❻   ITEM is the new *report-item* and designated as a character column with a length of 20. This compute block will be executed for every row of the report.

❼   TOTAL_RETAIL_PRICE is divided by QUANTITY and the resulting value is concatenated with the value of COSTPRICE_PER_UNIT. The resulting text is assigned to ITEM.

Output 3.9: Report Contains CHARACTER Computed Column ITEM

Customer Name	Retail v Cost
Kyndal Hooks	34.70/15.50
Annmarie Leveille	39.00/17.35
Najma Hicks	18.00/7.05
Yan Kozlowski	19.80/8.25
Kyndal Hooks	14.30/7.70
Roy Siferd	50.40/25.30
Alvan Goheen	21.90/11.05
Alvan Goheen	38.00/19.10
Alvan Goheen	41.60/20.90
Dericka Pockran	12.60/5.70
David Black	24.00/11.95
Wendell Summersby	39.40/17.80
James Klisurich	39.40/17.80
Sandrina Stephano	52.50/22.25
Wendell Summersby	50.40/22.75
Karen Ballinger	67.00/28.90
Wendell Summersby	67.00/28.90
Mikel Spetz	37.60/17.00
Wendell Summersby	21.80/9.25
Patricia Bertolozzi	23.50/9.20
Najma Hicks	46.00/16.05
Kyndal Hooks	14.20/6.45
Karen Ballinger	20.30/9.30
Najma Hicks	19.50/8.95
Karen Ballinger	30.30/13.50
Annmarie Leveille	6.50/2.30
Wendell Summersby	60.10/26.80
Ramesh Trentholme	41.40/18.85
Attila Gibbs	47.90/20.90
Robert Bowerman	27.70/13.95

Numeric *Report-Item*

Inside of a compute block, the numeric functions, such as SUM, ABS, MIN, and so on, can be used as well as multiplying and dividing. The COMPUTE statement for a COMPUTED numeric column does not require any extra options. Also, inside of compute blocks, referencing a COMPUTED column is still just the name but numeric ANALYSIS variables must be referenced by compound name. Example 3.10 demonstrates creating a COMPUTED *report-item* inside of a compute block. Output 3.10 contains the resulting table.

Example 3.10: Create a Numeric COMPUTED Column

```
proc report data=orders;
    column customer_name quantity total_retail_price
           estprice_per_item; ❶
    define estprice_per_item / computed 'Est. Item Price'
           format=dollar8.2; ❷
    define quantity / mean;
    define total_retail_price / mean 'Mean Price';
```

```
compute estprice_per_item; ❸
    estprice_per_item = total_retail_price.mean / quantity.mean; ❹
endcomp;
run;
```

❶ Add the name of the new *report-item*, ESTPRICE_PER_ITEM, to the COLUMN statement.

❷ The new *report-item* is defined as COMPUTED with an appropriate format and label.

❸ The *report-item* should be the name of the new variable, ESTPRICE_PER_ITEM, or the variable farthest to the right on the COLUMN statement.

❹ The COMPUTED column is referenced by name. The ANALYSIS variables are referenced by compound name. The ANALYSIS variables contain the MEAN statistic for each CUSTOMER_NAME value.

Output 3.10: Report Contains the Numeric COMPUTED Column ESTPRICE_PER_ITEM

Customer Name	Quantity Ordered	Mean Price	Est. Item Price
Kyndal Hooks	2	$69.40	$34.70
Annmarie Leveille	1	$39.00	$39.00
Najma Hicks	2	$36.00	$18.00
Yan Kozlowski	1	$19.80	$19.80
Kyndal Hooks	1	$14.30	$14.30
Roy Siferd	1	$50.40	$50.40
Alvan Goheen	2	$43.80	$21.90
Alvan Goheen	1	$38.00	$38.00
Alvan Goheen	1	$41.60	$41.60
Dericka Pockran	3	$37.80	$12.60
David Black	2	$48.00	$24.00
Wendell Summersby	1	$39.40	$39.40
James Klisurich	1	$39.40	$39.40
Sandrina Stephano	1	$52.50	$52.50
Wendell Summersby	1	$50.40	$50.40
Karen Ballinger	2	$134.00	$67.00
Wendell Summersby	2	$134.00	$67.00
Mikel Spetz	2	$75.20	$37.60
Wendell Summersby	1	$21.80	$21.80
Patricia Bertolozzi	1	$23.50	$23.50
Najma Hicks	2	$92.00	$46.00
Kyndal Hooks	4	$56.80	$14.20
Karen Ballinger	3	$60.90	$20.30
Najma Hicks	2	$39.00	$19.50
Karen Ballinger	2	$60.60	$30.30
Annmarie Leveille	1	$6.50	$6.50
Wendell Summersby	2	$120.20	$60.10
Ramesh Trentholme	3	$124.20	$41.40

3.2.5 Produce Summary Rows

PROC REPORT has the ability to produce rows containing summary values of ANALYSIS and COMPUTED *report-item*s. The summary rows can be inserted at the group level or at the report level. A BREAK statement adds summary rows at the group level. The statement requires the name of either a GROUP or ORDER variable. An RBREAK statement adds summary rows at the report level.

Rows Created with the BREAK Statement

Example 3.11 explores summary rows created with a BREAK statement. A customer can purchase multiple product lines; the corresponding variables are both defined as GROUP in this example. The CUSTOMER_NAME variable is referenced on the BREAK statement, which creates a summary row for each value of CUSTOMER_NAME. The row presents the sum of QUANTITY and TOTAL_RETAIL_PRICE for each name regardless of product. In Output 3.11, a summary row is shown with each customer.

Example 3.11: Create a Summary Row for Each Customer

```
proc report data=orders;
   column customer_name product_line quantity total_retail_price;
   define customer_name / group; ❶
   define product_line / group;
   define total_retail_price / mean 'Mean Price';

   break after customer_name / summarize; ❷
run;
```

❶ CUSTOMER_NAME is defined as GROUP, so the observations from the input data set are consolidated and the variable can be used to generate summary rows.

❷ CUSTOMER_NAME indicates at what level the summary row should be calculated. AFTER indicates where the summary row should be located. The SUMMARIZE option tells PROC REPORT to generate the summary row.

Output 3.11: A Summary Row Is Inserted for Each Customer

Customer Name	Product Line	Quantity Ordered	Mean Price
Ahmet Canko	Outdoors	9	$278.05
Ahmet Canko		*9*	*$278.05*
Alex Santinello	Sports	9	$95.96
Alex Santinello		*9*	*$95.96*
Alphone Greenwald	Sports	2	$13.55
Alphone Greenwald		*2*	*$13.55*
Alvan Goheen	Children	4	$41.13
	Clothes & Shoes	1	$101.30
	Outdoors	1	$86.30
	Sports	16	$248.82
Alvan Goheen		*22*	*$163.99*
Andreas Rennie	Sports	2	$174.40
Andreas Rennie		*2*	*$174.40*
Angel Borwick	Sports	11	$362.58
Angel Borwick		*11*	*$362.58*
Annmarie Leveille	Children	2	$22.75
	Clothes & Shoes	11	$74.46
	Sports	7	$515.87
Annmarie Leveille		*20*	*$161.66*
Attila Gibbs	Children	1	$47.90
	Clothes & Shoes	7	$107.84
	Outdoors	1	$93.80
	Sports	5	$567.97
Attila Gibbs		*14*	*$238.48*
Avinoam Tuvia	Clothes & Shoes	2	$79.30
Avinoam Tuvia		*2*	*$79.30*
Avinoam Zweig	Clothes & Shoes	19	$90.82
Avinoam Zweig		*19*	*$90.82*
Avni Argac	Outdoors	13	$123.47

In Output 3.11, the summary rows are the ones where the name is italicized and the PRODUCT_LINE value is blank. By default, in some ODS destinations, the values on this row are italicized, so it is easier to distinguish from the other rows. You can change the text attributes for summary rows with the STYLE(SUMMARY)= option on the PROC REPORT or BREAK statements.

Some customers purchased from only one PRODUCT_LINE. Therefore, the summary row contains the same values as the row above it. PROC REPORT does not have the ability to remove or delete these summary rows.

As mentioned in Chapter 2, a COMPUTE AFTER *TARGET* block can be used to change the attributes on the row created by the BREAK AFTER *TARGET* statement. In Example 3.12 and Output 3.12, the block is used to add informative text in the PRODUCT_LINE column and to change the format of the TOTAL_RETAIL_PRICE column.

Example 3.12: Add Text to the Summary Row

```
proc report data=orders;
   column customer_name product_line quantity total_retail_price;
   define customer_name / group; ❶
   define product_line / group;
   define total_retail_price / mean 'Mean Price';

   break after customer_name / summarize; ❷

   compute after customer_name; ❸
      product_line = 'All Products'; ❹
      call define('product_line','style','style=[just=r]'); ❺
      call define('total_retail_price.mean','format','dollar10.'); ❻
   endcomp;
run;
```

❶ CUSTOMER_NAME is defined as GROUP.

❷ The BREAK statement with the SUMMARIZE option and *location* of AFTER creates a summary row after each section of CUSTOMER_NAME.

❸ The COMPUTE statement includes the AFTER *location* and the *target* CUSTOMER_NAME. Any code within the block is applied to the row created by the BREAK AFTER CUSTOMER_NAME statement.

❹ Set the value of PRODUCT_LINE to the text value of "All Products". The text will help distinguish the summary row from the other rows and remind the reader that the values are for all products for that customer.

❺ Use a CALL DEFINE statement to right-justify the text "All Products". Again, this helps distinguish the row.

❻ The CALL DEFINE statement changes the format for TOTAL_RETAIL_PRICE on the summary row to be dollar10., which is different from the format for the other rows of the report.

Output 3.12: Informative Text Is Added to the Summary Row

Customer Name	Product Line	Quantity Ordered	Mean Price
Ahmet Canko	Outdoors	9	$278.05
Ahmet Canko	*All Products*	*9*	*$278*
Alex Santinello	Sports	9	$95.96
Alex Santinello	*All Products*	*9*	*$96*
Alphone Greenwald	Sports	2	$13.55
Alphone Greenwald	*All Products*	*2*	*$14*
Alvan Goheen	Children	4	$41.13
	Clothes & Shoes	1	$101.30
	Outdoors	1	$86.30
	Sports	16	$248.82
Alvan Goheen	*All Products*	*22*	*$164*
Andreas Rennie	Sports	2	$174.40
Andreas Rennie	*All Products*	*2*	*$174*
Angel Borwick	Sports	11	$362.58
Angel Borwick	*All Products*	*11*	*$363*
Annmarie Leveille	Children	2	$22.75
	Clothes & Shoes	11	$74.46
	Sports	7	$515.87
Annmarie Leveille	*All Products*	*20*	*$162*
Attila Gibbs	Children	1	$47.90
	Clothes & Shoes	7	$107.84
	Outdoors	1	$93.80
	Sports	5	$567.97
Attila Gibbs	*All Products*	*14*	*$238*
Avinoam Tuvia	Clothes & Shoes	2	$79.30
Avinoam Tuvia	*All Products*	*2*	*$79*
Avinoam Zweig	Clothes & Shoes	19	$90.82
Avinoam Zweig	*All Products*	*19*	*$91*
Avni Argac	Outdoors	13	$123.47

The same report can also be generated with the code in Example 3.13. The code demonstrates changing the format for the TOTAL_RETAIL_PRICE variable within a compute block for that variable. This block is executed on every row, so an IF condition is required to ensure the change in format only occurs on the summary rows. The automatic _BREAK_ variable is populated only for summary rows.

The compute block that you use to change the format is up to you; it is user preference. However, the code that uses COMPUTE AFTER CUSTOMER_NAME might be more efficient because it only executes at the summary row. The COMPUTE TOTAL_RETAIL_PRICE block executes on every row of the report, but the format change is only applied to a fraction of the rows. Example 3.13 applies a format via a *report-item* compute block, with the results in Output 3.13.

Example 3.13: Change TOTAL_RETAIL_PRICE Format in a *Report-Item* Block

```
proc report data=orders;
    column customer_name product_line quantity total_retail_price;
    define customer_name / group; ❶
    define product_line / group;
    define total_retail_price / mean 'Mean Price';

    break after customer_name / summarize; ❷

    compute total_retail_price;❸
        if upcase(_break_) = 'CUSTOMER_NAME' then ❹
          call define('total_retail_price.mean','format','dollar10.'); ❺
    endcomp;

    compute after customer_name; ❻
        product_line = 'All Products'; ❼
        call define('product_line','style','style=[just=r]');
    endcomp;
run;
```

❶ CUSTOMER_NAME is defined as GROUP.

❷ The BREAK statement with the SUMMARIZE option creates a summary row after each section of CUSTOMER_NAME.

❸ The COMPUTE statement references just a *report-item,* so it is executed on every row of the report.

❹ The IF condition uses the automatic variable _BREAK_ to limit the changes to only the summary rows for CUSTOMER_NAME.

❺ The CALL DEFINE statement changes the format for TOTAL_RETAIL_PRICE on the summary row to be dollar10., which is different from the format for the other rows of the report.

❻ The COMPUTE statement includes the AFTER location and the *target* CUSTOMER_NAME. Any code within the block is applied to the row created by the BREAK AFTER CUSTOMER_NAME statement.

❼ Set the value of PRODUCT_LINE to the text value of "All Products". The text will help distinguish the summary row from the other rows and remind the reader that the values are for all products for that customer. Use a CALL DEFINE statement to right-justify the text "All Products". Again, this helps distinguish the row.

Output 3.13: Format for TOTAL_RETAIL_PRICE Changed on the Summary Row

Customer Name	Product Line	Quantity Ordered	Mean Price
Ahmet Canko	Outdoors	9	$278.05
Ahmet Canko	All Products	*9*	*$278*
Alex Santinello	Sports	9	$95.96
Alex Santinello	All Products	*9*	*$96*
Alphone Greenwald	Sports	2	$13.55
Alphone Greenwald	All Products	*2*	*$14*
Alvan Goheen	Children	4	$41.13
	Clothes & Shoes	1	$101.30
	Outdoors	1	$86.30
	Sports	16	$248.82
Alvan Goheen	All Products	*22*	*$164*
Andreas Rennie	Sports	2	$174.40
Andreas Rennie	All Products	*2*	*$174*
Angel Borwick	Sports	11	$362.58
Angel Borwick	All Products	*11*	*$363*
Annmarie Leveille	Children	2	$22.75
	Clothes & Shoes	11	$74.46
	Sports	7	$515.87
Annmarie Leveille	All Products	*20*	*$162*
Attila Gibbs	Children	1	$47.90
	Clothes & Shoes	7	$107.84
	Outdoors	1	$93.80
	Sports	5	$567.97
Attila Gibbs	All Products	*14*	*$238*
Avinoam Tuvia	Clothes & Shoes	2	$79.30
Avinoam Tuvia	All Products	*2*	*$79*
Avinoam Zweig	Clothes & Shoes	19	$90.82
Avinoam Zweig	All Products	*19*	*$91*
Avni Argac	Outdoors	13	$123.47

Rows Created with the RBREAK Statement

An RBREAK statement creates summary rows at the report level. The *location* value on the
statement dictates whether the row will be placed at the top (BEFORE) or at the bottom (AFTER)
of the report. You can place a summary row at both locations. Also, you can include both a
BREAK and RBREAK statement; they are not mutually exclusive. Example 3.14 adds a summary
row at the top of the report, shown in Output 3.14.

Example 3.14: Add an Overall Summary Row

```
proc report data=orders;
   column customer_name product_line quantity total_retail_price;
   define customer_name / group; ❶
   define product_line / group;

   break after customer_name / summarize; ❷
   rbreak before / summarize; ❸
run;
```

❶   CUSTOMER_NAME is defined as GROUP.

❷   The BREAK statement with the SUMMARIZE option and *location* of AFTER creates a summary row after each section of CUSTOMER_NAME.

❸   The RBREAK statement with the SUMMARIZE option and BEFORE *location* creates an overall summary row at the top of the report.

Output 3.14: An Overall Summary Row Is at Top of Report

Customer Name	Product Line	Quantity Ordered	Total Retail Price for This Product
		1078	$100,077.47
Ahmet Canko	Outdoors	9	$1,112.20
Ahmet Canko		9	$1,112.20
Alex Santinello	Sports	9	$479.80
Alex Santinello		9	$479.80
Alphone Greenwald	Sports	2	$27.09
Alphone Greenwald		2	$27.09
Alvan Goheen	Children	4	$123.40
	Clothes & Shoes	1	$101.30
	Outdoors	1	$86.30
	Sports	16	$1,492.90
Alvan Goheen		22	$1,803.90
Andreas Rennie	Sports	2	$174.40
Andreas Rennie		2	$174.40
Angel Borwick	Sports	11	$1,812.90
Angel Borwick		11	$1,812.90
Annmarie Leveille	Children	2	$45.50
	Clothes & Shoes	11	$670.10
	Sports	7	$1,547.60
Annmarie Leveille		20	$2,263.20
Attila Gibbs	Children	1	$47.90
	Clothes & Shoes	7	$539.20
	Outdoors	1	$93.80
	Sports	5	$1,703.90
Attila Gibbs		14	$2,384.80
Avinoam Tuvia	Clothes & Shoes	2	$158.60
Avinoam Tuvia		2	$158.60

Values and attributes on the row created by the RBREAK statement can be changed. A COMPUTE BEFORE block controls the row from an RBREAK BEFORE statement. A COMPUTE AFTER block controls the row from an RBREAK AFTER statement. Example 3.15 uses a COMPUTE BEFORE block to change the value of CUSTOMER_NAME on the overall summary row, shown in Output 3.15. Be sure that any text assigned to a character variable in a compute block is less than or equal to the length of the character; otherwise, the text will be truncated in the final report. You might need to change the length of the variable in a DATA step to ensure it is long enough for text output via PROC REPORT.

Example 3.15: Change a Value on an RBREAK Summary Row

```
proc report data=orders;
   column customer_name product_line quantity total_retail_price;
   define customer_name / group; ❶
   define product_line / group;

   break after customer_name / summarize; ❷
   rbreak before / summarize; ❸

   compute before; ❹
      customer_name = 'ALL CUSTOMERS'; ❺
   endcomp;
run;
```

❶ CUSTOMER_NAME is defined as GROUP.

❷ The BREAK statement with the SUMMARIZE option and *location* of AFTER creates a summary row after each section of CUSTOMER_NAME.

❸ The RBREAK statement with the SUMMARIZE option and BEFORE *location* creates an overall summary row at the top of the report.

❹ The BEFORE *location* without a *target* means that this block executes once at the top of the report. Any statements inside of the block control the row created by the RBREAK BEFORE statement.

❺ Set the value of CUSTOMER_NAME to the text value of "ALL CUSTOMERS". The text will help distinguish the summary row from the other rows and remind the reader that the values are for all customers in the report.

Output 3.15: Text Added to the Overall Summary Row

Customer Name	Product Line	Quantity Ordered	Total Retail Price for This Product
ALL CUSTOMERS		1078	$100,077.47
Ahmet Canko	Outdoors	9	$1,112.20
Ahmet Canko		9	$1,112.20
Alex Santinello	Sports	9	$479.80
Alex Santinello		9	$479.80
Alphone Greenwald	Sports	2	$27.09
Alphone Greenwald		2	$27.09
Alvan Goheen	Children	4	$123.40
	Clothes & Shoes	1	$101.30
	Outdoors	1	$86.30
	Sports	16	$1,492.90
Alvan Goheen		22	$1,803.90
Andreas Rennie	Sports	2	$174.40
Andreas Rennie		2	$174.40
Angel Borwick	Sports	11	$1,812.90
Angel Borwick		11	$1,812.90
Annmarie Leveille	Children	2	$45.50
	Clothes & Shoes	11	$670.10
	Sports	7	$1,547.60
Annmarie Leveille		20	$2,263.20
Attila Gibbs	Children	1	$47.90
	Clothes & Shoes	7	$539.20
	Outdoors	1	$93.80
	Sports	5	$1,703.90
Attila Gibbs		14	$2,384.80
Avinoam Tuvia	Clothes & Shoes	2	$158.60
Avinoam Tuvia		2	$158.60

The RBREAK row is a summary for a given report. When a BY variable is used, it creates a separate report for each by group. Therefore, the values on the RBREAK summary row change for each BY group.

In Example 3.16, a BY statement is included. In Output 3.16, the QUANTITY summary value at the top changes from 1,078 to 210, which is the total for Australia.

Example 3.16: Use CUSTOMER_COUNTRY as a BY Variable

```
proc sort data=orders;
   by customer_country;

proc report data=orders;
   by customer_country;  ❶
   column customer_name product_line quantity total_retail_price;
   define customer_name / group;
   define product_line / group;

   rbreak before / summarize;  ❷
```

```
    compute before;  ❸
      customer_name = 'ALL CUSTOMERS FOR THIS COUNTRY';  ❹
    endcomp;
run;
```

❶ Include a BY statement to create one report for each value of CUSTOMER_COUNTRY.

❷ The RBREAK statement with the SUMMARIZE option and BEFORE *location* creates an overall summary row at the top of the report.

❸ The BEFORE *location* without a *target* means that this block executes once at the top of the report. Any statements inside of the block control the row created by the RBREAK BEFORE statement.

❹ Set the value of CUSTOMER_NAME to the text value of "ALL CUSTOMERS FOR THIS COUNTRY". The text will help distinguish the summary row from the other rows and remind the reader that the values are just the customers for one country.

Output 3.16: Report for Australia with an Overall Summary Row

Customer Country=AU

Customer Name	Product Line	Quantity Ordered	Total Retail Price for This Product
ALL CUSTOMERS FOR THIS COUNTRY		210	$17,321.49
Candy Kinsey	Clothes & Shoes	8	$584.80
	Sports	5	$476.50
Cosi Rimmington	Clothes & Shoes	2	$408.80
	Outdoors	13	$1,658.70
	Sports	9	$1,080.20
Dericka Pockran	Children	3	$37.80
	Clothes & Shoes	8	$807.70
	Outdoors	5	$448.90
	Sports	4	$611.00
Duncan Robertshawe	Clothes & Shoes	5	$298.50
	Outdoors	2	$142.50
	Sports	18	$2,613.00
Karolina Dokter	Clothes & Shoes	19	$950.30
	Outdoors	2	$61.60
	Sports	14	$1,447.80
Ramesh Trentholme	Children	3	$124.20
	Clothes & Shoes	3	$170.70
	Outdoors	6	$338.70
	Sports	12	$911.90
Robert Bowerman	Clothes & Shoes	18	$880.69
	Outdoors	6	$296.20
	Sports	13	$1,387.70

3.3 Nonstandard Reports

As you saw in the previous section, PROC REPORT can easily create reports that are a listing of the data or summary reports that contain aggregate values of ANALYSIS or COMPUTED variables. Your data or the desired report arrangement might not conform to those standard reports. This section looks at common nonstandard reports. These reports include percentages, a customized sort order, non-default summary rows, and values not present in the input data set. Again, the term nonstandard does not imply atypical. PROC REPORT can create the layout that you need, but it might require more code and additional variables from the input data set.

3.3.1 Calculate Percentages within Groups

Percentages, ratios, and proportions are key figures for explaining data. Percentages are found in a wide range of reports. Unfortunately, percentages are not as straightforward in PROC REPORT as one would hope. PROC REPORT does honor the PCTN and PCTSUM keywords. These statistics are calculated based on the whole report, that is, all of the data. There is not a keyword for calculating percentages within groups. You must do the work yourself. In other words, you have to create a variable that holds the denominator and have an assignment statement for the calculation of the percent.

The first example, Example 3.17 and Output 3.17, shows the values calculated by the PCTSUM keyword. PCTSUM uses the sum of the ANALYSIS variable for a specific row as the numerator and the total sum of the ANALYSIS variable as the denominator.

Example 3.17: Use the PCTSUM Statistical Keyword

```
proc report data=orders;
   column customer_country order_type total_retail_price
          total_retail_price=trp2; ❶
   define customer_country / group format=$cntry.;
   define order_type / group format=typef.;
   define total_retail_price / 'Total Retail Price';
   define trp2 / pctsum format=percent8.1 'Percent Retail Price'; ❷
run;
```

❶ The alias, TRP2, is created for TOTAL_RETAIL_PRICE.

❷ The aliased variable is assigned the statistic PCTSUM with an appropriate format and label.

Output 3.17: The Last Column Contains the PCTSUM Statistic

Customer Country	Order Type	Total Retail Price	Percent Retail Price
Australia	Catalog Sale	$1,679.40	1.7%
	Internet Sale	$613.90	0.6%
	Retail Sale	$15,028.19	15.0%
Canada	Catalog Sale	$5,422.38	5.4%
	Internet Sale	$6,528.70	6.5%
Germany	Catalog Sale	$10,034.40	10.0%
	Internet Sale	$5,360.20	5.4%
Israel	Catalog Sale	$1,316.10	1.3%
	Internet Sale	$243.40	0.2%
South Africa	Catalog Sale	$3,161.70	3.2%
	Internet Sale	$1,988.20	2.0%
Turkey	Catalog Sale	$4,690.20	4.7%
	Internet Sale	$485.60	0.5%
United States	Catalog Sale	$7,627.17	7.6%
	Internet Sale	$6,271.55	6.3%
	Retail Sale	$29,626.38	29.6%

If you add the percentages from every row in the table, they sum to 100. For some reports, you want the percentages within a group to add to 100. Example 3.18 calculates the percentages for TOTAL_RETAIL_PRICE within each country. For this behavior, you have to create a temporary denominator variable and include an assignment statement, as demonstrated below.

Example 3.18: Calculate Percentages within Country

```
proc report data=orders;
   column customer_country order_type total_retail_price pct;  ❶
   define customer_country / group format=$cntry.;
   define order_type / group format=typef.;
   define total_retail_price / 'Total Retail Price';
   define pct / computed format=percent8.1 'Percent Retail Price';  ❷

   compute before customer_country;  ❸
     den = total_retail_price.sum;  ❹
   endcomp;

   compute pct;  ❺
     if den > 0 then pct = total_retail_price.sum / den;  ❻
   endcomp;
run;
```

❶ A new *report-item*, PCT, is added to the COLUMN statement.

❷ PCT is defined as COMPUTED because it is a brand new *report-item* and not a statistic. An appropriate format and label are also applied.

❸ We are interested in values within CUSTOMER_COUNTRY. This compute block is executed at the top of each country value.

❹ Within this block the subtotal value of TOTAL_RETAIL_PRICE for country is available. The value is assigned to DEN, which will change for each country.

❺ PCT is the variable of interest, so it is specified as the *report-item* on the COMPUTE statement. This block will execute on every row.

❻ The current value of TOTAL_RETAIL_PRICE is divided by DEN and assigned to the PCT *report-item*.

Output 3.18: Percentages Are Calculated Within Each Country

Customer Country	Order Type	Total Retail Price	Percent Retail Price
Australia	Catalog Sale	$1,679.40	9.7%
	Internet Sale	$613.90	3.5%
	Retail Sale	$15,028.19	86.8%
Canada	Catalog Sale	$5,422.38	45.4%
	Internet Sale	$6,528.70	54.6%
Germany	Catalog Sale	$10,034.40	65.2%
	Internet Sale	$5,360.20	34.8%
Israel	Catalog Sale	$1,316.10	84.4%
	Internet Sale	$243.40	15.6%
South Africa	Catalog Sale	$3,161.70	61.4%
	Internet Sale	$1,988.20	38.6%
Turkey	Catalog Sale	$4,690.20	90.6%
	Internet Sale	$485.60	9.4%
United States	Catalog Sale	$7,627.17	17.5%
	Internet Sale	$6,271.55	14.4%
	Retail Sale	$29,626.38	68.1%

Example 3.18 shows code for just one ANALYSIS variable. However, the steps can be expanded to any and all other ANALYSIS variables for which a percent is desired. For each ANALYSIS variable, a temporary denominator variable and an assignment statement is needed.

3.3.2 Customized Sort Order

By default, GROUP and ACROSS variables in PROC REPORT are ordered by their formatted values. (Most other procedures sort by the internal value by default.) If no format is applied, the BEST12. format is used for numeric variables. Alternatives to the default of ORDER=FORMATTED can be specified in the ORDER= option in the DEFINE statements. When none of the alternatives provide the desired order, you can create a customized order with a user-defined format.

- The format must be created with the NOTSORTED option. The values in the PROC FORMAT step need to be placed in the order in which you want them to appear.
- The DEFINE statement must include ORDER=DATA, FORMAT=fmtname., and PRELOADFMT.

Note that the PRELOADFMT option applies only to GROUP and ACROSS variables.

Example 3.19 changes the order of the country values in Output 3.19. In the final report, the United States needs to appear first because it is of the most interest for the readers of the report. It is followed by other countries, also ordered by interest level.

Example 3.19: Customize the Order of the Country Value

```
proc format;
    value $cntryOrd (notsorted) ❶
        'US' = 'United States' ❷
        'AU' = 'Australia'
        'CA' = 'Canada'
        'DE' = 'Germany'
        'IL' = 'Israel'
        'TR' = 'Turkey'
        'ZA' = 'South Africa'
        ;
run;

proc report data=orders;
    column customer_country order_type total_retail_price ;
    define customer_country / group format=$cntryOrd. preloadfmt
            order=data;❸
    define order_type / group format=typef.;
    define total_retail_price / 'Total Retail Price';
run;
```

❶ The NOTSORTED option tells PROC FORMAT to store the values in the order in which you define them.

❷ The United States value is the most important value, so it is listed first, followed by the desired order for the other countries.

❸ The newly created format $cntryOrd is referenced by the FORMAT= option. The PRELOADFMT option tells PROC REPORT to include all of the values from the format. ORDER=DATA forces PROC REPORT to maintain the order from the format.

Output 3.19: Report Sorted in a Customized Order

Customer Country	Order Type	Total Retail Price
United States	Catalog Sale	$7,627.17
	Internet Sale	$6,271.55
	Retail Sale	$29,626.38
Australia	Catalog Sale	$1,679.40
	Internet Sale	$613.90
	Retail Sale	$15,028.19
Canada	Catalog Sale	$5,422.38
	Internet Sale	$6,528.70
Germany	Catalog Sale	$10,034.40
	Internet Sale	$5,360.20
Israel	Catalog Sale	$1,316.10
	Internet Sale	$243.40
Turkey	Catalog Sale	$4,690.20
	Internet Sale	$485.60
South Africa	Catalog Sale	$3,161.70
	Internet Sale	$1,988.20

3.3.3 Multiple Summary Rows at One Location

As discussed previously, summary rows are created by BREAK and RBREAK statements. The placement of the rows in the report is dictated by the *location* value, BEFORE or AFTER. Every GROUP or ORDER variable can have two summary rows, one at each *location*. The report can also have a row at the top and bottom. PROC REPORT will not let you place two summary rows at the same *location*. In other words, you cannot have two BREAK or RBREAK statements that look exactly alike. PROC REPORT will produce only one row.

This section demonstrates how to produce a report that looks like it has multiple summary rows at the same *location*. The "trick" is that the rows are actually not at the same *location*; they are produced by different variables that happen to start and end at the same place. Therefore, the summary rows appear at the same place in the final report.

In this section, the summary rows are written to output using the AFTER *location*. Therefore, they appear in the order the variables appear on the COLUMN statement from right to left. The variable farthest right writes the top row. The variable farthest left writes the bottom row.

Producing a report with extra summary rows requires a fairly large amount of code. You have to create additional variables, include DEFINE and BREAK statements for the variables, and create assignment statements for every summary row and column.

Include Statistics Not in Detail Rows

A common report type displays one type of statistic, like SUM, on the detail rows of a report, and then includes summary rows that contain other statistics, like MEAN, MIN, and MAX. The secondary statistics are important, but you do not want them presented in their own columns at the detail level. You just need them at the overall level.

This report type requires additional grouping variables. The grouping variables are not displayed, but they are used on BREAK statements to create summary rows. One grouping variable is required for each additional statistic.

The value of the grouping (dummy) variable and whether it changes depends on where you want the additional row to go. When you want the rows at the very top or the very bottom of the report, the dummy variable can be assigned just one value. This way, PROC REPORT treats the entire data set as a group. When you want additional rows at other places in the report, the dummy variable changes values accordingly. For example, if you want a second summary row where CUSTOMER_GROUP changes, you should set your dummy variable to the same value as CUSTOMER_GROUP, so that they change at the same place.

For Example 3.20, the final report has four summary rows at the end, one for each statistic: SUM, MEAN, MIN, MAX. One of the statistics can be handled with an RBREAK statement. The other three must be handled with a BREAK statement, which requires three dummy grouping variables.

The statistics themselves can be calculated by PROC REPORT with aliased variables. Alias columns will not be printed but their overall values will be assigned to the additional summary rows, demonstrated in Example 3.20 and Output 3.20.

Example 3.20: Include Three Additional Summary Rows

```
data orders2;
   set orders;  ❶
   dummy1 = 1;
   dummy2 = 1;
   dummy3 = 1;
run;

options missing='';
proc report data=orders2;
   column dummy1 dummy2 dummy3 ❷ customer_group order_type
      total_retail_price total_retail_price=trp1
      total_retail_price=trp2 total_retail_price=trp3
      quantity quantity=qnt1 quantity=qnt2 quantity=qnt3
      discount discount=dis1 discount=dis2 discount=dis3;  ❸

      ❹
   define dummy1 / group noprint;
   define dummy2 / group noprint;
   define dummy3 / group noprint;
   define customer_group / group ;
   define order_type / group format=typef.;
```

❺
```
define trp1 / max noprint;
define trp2 / min noprint;
define trp3 / mean noprint;
define qnt1 / max noprint;
define qnt2 / min noprint;
define qnt3 / mean noprint;
define dis1 / max noprint;
define dis2 / min noprint;
define dis3 / mean noprint;
```

❻
```
break after dummy1 /summarize;
break after dummy2 /summarize;
break after dummy3 /summarize;

rbreak after / summarize; ❼
```

❽
```
compute after dummy3;
    customer_group = "Mean: ";
    total_retail_price.sum = trp3;
    quantity.sum = qnt3;
    discount.sum = dis3;
endcomp;
compute after dummy2;
    customer_group = "Min: ";
    total_retail_price.sum = trp2;
    quantity.sum = qnt2;
    discount.sum = dis2;
endcomp;
compute after dummy1;
    customer_group = "Max: ";
    total_retail_price.sum = trp1;
    quantity.sum = qnt1;
    discount.sum = dis1;
endcomp;
```

❾
```
compute after;
    customer_group = "Sum: ";
endcomp;
run;
```

❶ A dummy variable is created for each additional statistic, with the same value for all observations.

❷ The dummy variables are placed at the front of the COLUMN statement, so PROC REPORT will treat all observations as one group.

❸ Each ANALYSIS variable is placed on the COLUMN statement and an alias is created for each additional statistic.

❹   The dummy variables are defined as GROUP and NOPRINT.

❺   The alias variables are defined with the appropriate statistic and NOPRINT.

❻   A BREAK statement with the SUMMARIZE option is needed for each dummy variable. All of the summary rows will be added to the end of the report. Technically they are all at different locations because each is at the bottom of one of the variables.

❼   The RBREAK statement with the SUMMARIZE option adds the fourth desired summary row.

❽   For each additional summary row, assign an appropriate value to the CUSTOMER_GROUP variable. Assign each ANALYSIS variable to the appropriate alias variable. The top row is produced by the farthest right grouping variable.

❾   The last row is created by the RBREAK statement and controlled by the COMPUTE AFTER block. Its values will contain the default SUM statistic. Only a label within CUSTOMER_GROUP is needed.

Output 3.20: The Bottom of the Report Has Four Summary Rows

Customer Group Name	Order Type	Total Retail Price for This Product	Quantity Ordered	Discount in percent of Normal Total Retail Price
Internet/Catalog Customers	Catalog Sale	$11,216.30	99	
	Internet Sale	$2,964.15	39	
Orion Club Gold members	Retail Sale	$13,710.45	169	40%
	Catalog Sale	$6,836.47	58	
	Internet Sale	$11,234.10	81	
Orion Club members	Retail Sale	$30,944.12	390	30%
	Catalog Sale	$15,878.58	136	30%
	Internet Sale	$7,293.30	106	
Mean:		$162.20	1.7471637	33%
Min:		$2.60	1	30%
Max:		$1,937.20	6	40%
Sum:		$100,077.47	1078	100%

Example 3.20 demonstrates the technique for writing multiple summary rows for multiple ANALYSIS variables to the report. The technique requires multiple aliases and compute blocks. The summary values for the DISCOUNT variable are valid values but might not make sense in the report. You must consider the ANALYSIS variables that you are using and decide whether they should have summary values in the new summary rows. If they do not make sense, the variable DISCOUNT.SUM can be set to missing for those rows.

Show Summary Values for Nested Groups

You can request summary rows using a BREAK statement for any variable that you have defined as GROUP or ORDER. However, because PROC REPORT works left to right, when you request a summary row for nested, or "inside" groups, the values are subtotals within the "outside" groups. The values are not for the report as a whole.

PROC REPORT can produce the overall summary values for a nested group, but it requires a lot of code. As mentioned previously, PROC REPORT cannot create two summary rows at the same *location*. Therefore, you have to create a dummy grouping variable so that you can write an additional row at a given place in the report. For each additional row desired, a grouping variable is required. Again, the value of the dummy variable and whether it changes depends on where you want the additional row to be placed.

Output 3.21 has three summary rows at the end, one for each value of ORDER_TYPE. All of the rows will be created with a BREAK statement. Three dummy grouping variables are needed.

The overall totals have to be calculated with temporary variables. One temporary variable is needed for each ORDER_TYPE value. The temporary variables will be incremented each time a detail row is generated. The final tally will be assigned to the ANALYSIS variable on the summary rows.

Note: In the Example 3.21 code below, the IF condition is concerned only with the value of ORDER_TYPE. In reports that contain summary rows throughout the report, another clause might be needed to ensure that only detail rows are tallied. The value of _BREAK_ is blank for detail rows.

Example 3.21: Include Summary Rows for Nested GROUP Variables

```
data orders2;
   set orders;
   dummy1 = 1;  ❶
   dummy2 = 1;
   dummy3 = 1;
run;

options missing='';
proc report data=orders2;
   column dummy1 dummy2 dummy3 ❷ customer_group order_type
          total_retail_price quantity discount;

   ❸
   define dummy1 / group noprint;
   define dummy2 / group noprint;
   define dummy3 / group noprint;

   define customer_group / group;
   define order_type / group format=typef. order=internal;

   ❹
   break after dummy1 /summarize;
   break after dummy2 /summarize;
   break after dummy3 /summarize;
```

❺
```
compute discount;
   if order_type = 1 then do;
      trp1 + total_retail_price.sum;
      qnt1 + quantity.sum;
      dis1 + discount.sum;
   end;
   else if order_type = 2 then do;
      trp2 + total_retail_price.sum;
      qnt2 + quantity.sum;
      dis2 + discount.sum;
   end;
   else if order_type = 3 then do;
      trp3 + total_retail_price.sum;
      qnt3 + quantity.sum;
      dis3 + discount.sum;
   end;
endcomp;
```

❻
```
compute after dummy3;
   customer_group = put(1,typef.);
   total_retail_price.sum = trp1;
   quantity.sum = qnt1;
   discount.sum = dis1;
endcomp;
compute after dummy2;
   customer_group = put(2,typef.);
   total_retail_price.sum = trp2;
   quantity.sum = qnt2;
   discount.sum = dis2;
endcomp;
compute after dummy1;
   customer_group = put(3,typef.);
   total_retail_price.sum = trp3;
   quantity.sum = qnt3;
   discount.sum = dis3;
endcomp;
run;
```

❶   A dummy variable is created for each value of ORDER_TYPE, with the same value for all observations.

❷   The dummy variables are placed at the front of the COLUMN statement, so PROC REPORT will treat all observations as one group.

❸   The dummy variables are defined as GROUP and NOPRINT.

❹   A BREAK statement with the SUMMARIZE option is needed for each dummy variable. All of the summary rows will be added to the end of the report. Technically they are all at different locations because each is at the bottom of one of the variables.

❺ Use the last variable from the COLUMN statement as the *report-item* in the COMPUTE statement, so all values are available. A temporary variable is created for each value of ORDER_TYPE. Increment the temporary variable only on rows of the corresponding type.

❻ For each additional summary row, assign the value of ORDER_TYPE to the CUSTOMER_GROUP variable. Assign each ANALYSIS variable to the appropriate temporary variable. The top row is produced by the farthest right grouping variable.

Output 3.21: Report Has Summary Row for Nested GROUP Variable ORDER_TYPE

Customer Group Name	Order Type	Total Retail Price for This Product	Quantity Ordered	Discount in percent of Normal Total Retail Price
Internet/Catalog Customers	Catalog Sale	$11,216.30	99	
	Internet Sale	$2,964.15	39	
Orion Club Gold members	Retail Sale	$13,710.45	169	40%
	Catalog Sale	$6,836.47	58	
	Internet Sale	$11,234.10	81	
Orion Club members	Retail Sale	$30,944.12	390	30%
	Catalog Sale	$15,878.58	136	30%
	Internet Sale	$7,293.30	106	
Retail Sale		*$44,654.57*	*559*	*70%*
Catalog Sale		*$33,931.35*	*293*	*30%*
Internet Sale		*$21,491.55*	*226*	*0%*

3.3.4 Rows Created with a LINE Statement Versus a BREAK Statement

LINE statements are very useful for writing out text or summary values that have a general justification. In the examples in the previous sections, the text was center-justified or left-justified across the entire table. However, LINE statements are not as useful when you need to align the text or summary values under specific columns. In LISTING output, you can create alignment using pointer controls such as the at-sign (@) and the plus sign (+). In other ODS destinations, pointer controls do not work in a predictable manner because of font face, font size, margins, and other style attributes.

Recall that LINE statements create one large, merged cell. Alignment is best achieved by creating a row with columns that match the detail rows above it. In terms of cell creation, a row that is created with a BREAK or RBREAK statement looks just like a detail row. When alignment is a requirement, it is best to use a BREAK or RBREAK statement rather than a LINE statement.

It is important to consider where you want the new row to appear in the report. If you require multiple rows, one for each section, you should use a BREAK statement. If you require only one row at the top or bottom of the report, an RBREAK statement will work. Depending on the situation, you might need to create a new variable in a DATA step to use as a break variable, as described in Section 3.3.3.

3.3.5 Conditionally Display a LINE Statement

A LINE is used to write text. The text can include hardcoded text strings, variable values, or statistics. A LINE statement is executed after all other statements that appear inside of a compute block. In addition, this statement is always executed; you cannot use IF-THEN logic to conditionally execute the LINE statement. However, you can trick PROC REPORT into conditionally **displaying** a LINE statement.

Recall from Chapter 1 that a format must be specified for each variable or statistic on the LINE statement. The $VARYINGw. format writes character data of varying length. The $VARYINGw. format is followed by a *length-variable*, which is a numeric variable that specifies the desired length of the string. The *length-variable* can be set to zero. Associating the $VARYINGw. format with a length of zero to a variable will prevent text from a LINE statement from being displayed.

Hardcoded text does not require a format. Any text that you wish to write to the report via a LINE statement can assigned to a variable just as easily as it can be hardcoded on the LINE statement. By choosing to assign the text to a variable, you can harness the capabilities of the $VARYINGw. format.

The "conditional" part of displaying a LINE statement is conditionally assigning the *length-variable* to zero for sections of the report where you do not want to see the text from a LINE statement.

The goal of Example 3.22 is to write a row of text that indicates that Australia did not meet its goal of 200 retail sale orders. Since the text applies only to Australia, we do not want text to be written out for the other countries in the report. Inside of the compute block, two variables are created: one variable holds the text string and the other variable holds the desired numeric length. The results are shown in Output 3.22.

Example 3.22: Conditionally Display a LINE Statement for Australia

```
proc report data=orders;
   column customer_country order_type quantity total_retail_price;
   define customer_country / group format=$cntry.;
   define order_type / group format=typef.;

   compute after customer_country;
      length string_text $100; ❶
      if customer_country = 'AU' then do; ❷
         string_text = 'Australia did not meet the Retail goal of
         200!'; ❸
         string_num = 100; ❹
      end;
```

```
            else do;  ❺
               string_num = 0;  ❻
            end;

            line string_text $varying. string_num;  ❼
        endcomp;
    run;
```

❶ You might have multiple conditions, each with a different text length. It is a good idea to have a LENGTH statement for the text variable that you are creating so that the text is not truncated.

❷ Remember the conditional part is assigning the text strings and *length-variable* value. For this example, Australia is the country of interest, so the IF condition is based on CUSTOMER_COUNTRY.

❸ Assign the appropriate text to the variable STRING_TEXT.

❹ Assign a nonzero value to the *length-variable*, STRING_NUM. The value is normally the same as the length associated with the text variable.

❺ The ELSE DO loop captures all of the other countries for which you do not want to display text.

❻ The most important part of this loop is assigning STRING_NUM to zero, which will prevent text from being displayed. You can also assign STRING_TEXT to a null value in this loop, but technically speaking, it is not necessary since the LENGTH statement initializes the variable to blank.

❼ On the LINE statement, place the STRING_TEXT variable containing the text. Follow the text variable by the format, which is required. The format, $VARYING., is followed by the variable STRING_NUM. STRING_NUM will have a value of 100 or 0 depending on the current value of CUSTOMER_COUNTRY.

Output 3.22: LINE Statement Text Is Written Only for Australia

Customer Country	Order Type	Quantity Ordered	Total Retail Price for This Product
Australia	Catalog Sale	26	$1,679.40
	Internet Sale	13	$613.90
	Retail Sale	171	$15,028.19
Australia did not meet the Retail goal of 200!			
Canada	Catalog Sale	32	$5,422.38
	Internet Sale	73	$6,528.70
Germany	Catalog Sale	76	$10,034.40
	Internet Sale	30	$5,360.20
Israel	Catalog Sale	22	$1,316.10
	Internet Sale	6	$243.40
South Africa	Catalog Sale	27	$3,161.70
	Internet Sale	20	$1,988.20
Turkey	Catalog Sale	39	$4,690.20
	Internet Sale	4	$485.60
United States	Catalog Sale	71	$7,627.17
	Internet Sale	80	$6,271.55
	Retail Sale	388	$29,626.38

Using the $VARYINGw. format successfully prevents text from being displayed for any other country.

3.4 Special Data Consideration Reports

Knowing your data is paramount to writing efficient code and producing reports. The contents of your data greatly affect PROC REPORT output. You need to be aware of your data so that you can make the proper adjustments to the PROC REPORT code. You need to know whether you have a large set of variables to write to output. You need to know the order of the data and if any categories are not present. This section shows coding techniques for handling these types of issues.

3.4.1 Wide Tables

Data set TRAN_ORDERS contains a transposed version of the ORDERS data set created just for this example. It contains one record per customer and one variable for each purchase the customer placed. The variables containing the purchase retail price value are COL1-COL32; the example will use only COL1-COL20.

In PROC REPORT, you can use the PAGE option on a DEFINE statement to insert a table break just before printing the first column containing values of the *report-item*. However, when sending to an ODS destination such as PDF or RTF, all observations for the first set of columns will be printed and then all of the observations for the next set of columns will be printed.

To generate a report with interleaved pages, where column set one is on page one and column set two is on page two, you have to have both a vertical and horizontal table break. This requires that you create a paging variable to break on.

The goal of Example 3.23 is to create one table that contains rows 1-25 and columns 1-10 (not including the ID variables), and then to create another table that contains rows 1-25 and columns 11-20. Then the process starts all over again with rows 26-50, and so on.

Example 3.23 inserts a vertical table break with the PAGE option on a DEFINE statement. A horizontal table break is inserted with the PAGE option on the BREAK statement. The result of both types of table breaks creates interleaved pages. Output 3.23a shows columns 1-10. Output 3.23b shows columns 11-20.

Example 3.23: Insert Table Breaks in a Wide Report

```
data tran_orders2;
   set tran_orders;
      if _n_ <= 25 then pageit=1;  ❶
      else if 25 < _n_ <= 50 then pageit=2;
      else if 50 < _n_ <= 75 then pageit=3;
      else pageit=4;
run;

options missing='';

proc report data=tran_orders2;
   column pageit ❷ customer_id customer_name col1-col20;
   define pageit / order noprint;  ❸
   define customer_name / id;  ❹
   define col11 / page;  ❺

   break after pageit / page;  ❻
run;
```

❶ Assign sets of rows to the same value of the paging variable, PAGEIT.

❷ Place the paging variable at the front of the COLUMN statement so that it is the first level of grouping within the report.

❸ Define the PAGEIT variable as ORDER and NOPRINT.

❹ Use the ID option on the farthest right *report-item* that you want repeated on subsequent pages. All *report-item*s to its left are also repeated.

❺ Add the PAGE option to the DEFINE statement for the first column that should appear on another page. In non-Listing destinations, the PAGE option actually creates a new table. Each table is placed on its own page.

❻ Add a BREAK statement with the PAGE option for PAGEIT, the paging variable. In non-Listing destinations, the PAGE option actually creates a new table. Each table is placed on its own page.

Output 3.23a: Top of Page 1

Customer ID	Customer Name	COL1	COL2	COL3	COL4	COL5	COL6	COL7	COL8	COL9	COL10
4	James Kvarniq	$16.70	$92.60	$214.00	$58.90	$201.90	$53.00	$80.97	$16.90	$47.70	
5	Sandrina Stephano	$52.50	$33.80	$74.20	$136.80	$50.40	$126.80	$446.60	$247.50	$265.60	$86.30
9	Cornelia Krahl	$16.00	$29.40	$1,542.60	$514.20	$550.20	$39.20				
10	Karen Ballinger	$134.00	$60.90	$60.60	$32.60	$52.90	$37.30	$11.30	$231.60	$52.50	$19.20
11	Elke Wallstab	$78.20	$72.70								

Output 3.23b: Top of Page 2

Customer ID	Customer Name	COL11	COL12	COL13	COL14	COL15	COL16	COL17	COL18	COL19	COL20
4	James Kvarniq										
5	Sandrina Stephano	$31.40	$168.70	$3.00	$43.40	$353.60	$421.20	$87.20	$138.00	$43.98	
9	Cornelia Krahl										
10	Karen Ballinger	$40.60	$68.40	$32.30	$199.20	$256.20	$12.20	$252.20	$471.20	$86.60	$35.50
11	Elke Wallstab										

The number of rows contributing to the value of PAGEIT is arbitrary. It is based on what the author thought could fit on a page. You will have to consider your needs and settings to determine how many rows might fit on a page. There is not a formula or an automatic way to determine this for you.

There is an alternative method for getting interleaved pages. The method requires use of macro code. One PROC REPORT step must be placed inside of the macro program for each set of columns that need to be grouped together. Then the macro program is run for a subset of data, that is, the number of rows that should appear on each page. The code in Example 3.23 is more efficient in that it requires far less code than a macro program.

3.4.2 Using ORDER=DATA

The possible values of the ORDER= option on the DEFINE statement are discussed in Chapter 2. The section demonstrates how using ORDER=DATA does not always produce the expected results because PROC REPORT bases the sort order on the entire data set. It does not look within BY groups or other groupings.

As demonstrated in Chapter 2, some data values that are expected in the middle of the report are placed at the end of the report. In other reports, data values are expected at the end of the report but are placed in the middle.

In the ORDERS data set, the values of CUSTOMER_COUNTRY appear in this order:

US, AU, IL, CA, DE, TR, ZA.

Example 3.24 uses ORDER=DATA for CUSTOMER_COUNTRY. Note, CUSTOMER_COUNTRY is grouped within values of CUSTOMER_GENDER. The results are shown in Output 3.24.

Example 3.24: Demonstrate ORDER=DATA for a Nested GROUP

```
proc report data=orders;
  column customer_gender customer_country;
  define customer_gender /group;
  define customer_country / group order=data;
run;
```

Output 3.24: CUSTOMER_COUNTRY Sort Order Dictated by ORDER=DATA

Customer Gender	Customer Country
F	US
	AU
	CA
	DE
	ZA
M	US
	AU
	IL
	CA
	DE
	TR
	ZA

The results might not be as desired. In the male section, IL is above CA. For some reports, the desired order for male would be US, AU, CA, DE, ZA, IL, TR. This order puts new values at the end.

There are multiple methods for getting the desired sort order. One method is to create a numeric variable in the data set whose value corresponds to the desired order. This variable will be placed before CUSTOMER_COUNTRY on the COLUMN statement. It is also defined with ORDER=INTERNAL, which sorts the data by increasing numeric value. Example 3.25 uses this method, and the results are shown in Output 3.25.

Example 3.25: Use a Numeric Variable with ORDER=INTERNAL

```
data orders2;
   set orders;

   if customer_country='US' then cord=1;
   else if customer_country='AU' then cord=2;
   else if customer_country='CA' then cord=3;
   else if customer_country='DE' then cord=4;
   else if customer_country='ZA' then cord=5;
   else if customer_country='IL' then cord=6;
   else if customer_country='TR' then cord=7;
run;
```

```
proc report data=orders2;
 column customer_gender cord customer_country; ❶
 define customer_gender /group;
 define cord / group order=internal noprint; ❷
 define customer_country / group; ❸
run;
```

❶ CORD is added to the COLUMN statement after CUSTOMER_GENDER so that CUSTOMER_GENDER orders the report first. CORD is added before CUSTOMER_COUNTRY, so its values enforce the desired order within gender.

❷ CORD is defined as GROUP, so it will consolidate rows just like the previous version of the code. NOPRINT suppresses the column from the output. ORDER=INTERNAL forces PROC REPORT to order the report based on the increasing numeric value of CORD.

❸ Notice ORDER=DATA has been removed from the DEFINE statement for CUSTOMER_COUNTRY. ORDER=DATA causes undesired output, so it needs to be removed.

Output 3.25: A Hidden Numeric Variable Dictates the Order of CUSTOMER_COUNTRY

Customer Gender	Customer Country
F	US
	AU
	CA
	DE
	ZA
M	US
	AU
	CA
	DE
	ZA
	IL
	TR

Another method for getting the desired sort order is to use a format and the technique described in Section 3.3.2, Customize Sort Order. The method that you choose is your preference. You might prefer the format method because it does not require changing the input data set.

3.4.3 Using the COMPLETEROWS Option

Show All Group Combinations

In the ORDERS data set, not every country has all three types of orders. When a report is created with CUSTOMER_COUNTRY and ORDER_TYPE as GROUP variables, the number of rows for each country differs, which can be a little confusing. Also, the report might appear incomplete. In this situation, the COMPLETEROWS option is a useful tool. One use of the COMPLETEROWS option on the PROC REPORT statement is to ensure all possible combinations of GROUP variables appear in the report. Example 3.26 demonstrates using the COMPLETEROWS option to show all values of ORDER_TYPE. The results are shown in Output 3.26.

Example 3.26: Use the COMPLETEROWS Option

```
options missing='0';
proc report data=orders completerows;
   column customer_country order_type quantity total_retail_price;
   define customer_country / group format=$cntry. ;
   define order_type / group format=typef.;
run;
```

Output 3.26: COMPLETEROWS Option Inserts Rows Containing Zeros

Customer Country	Order Type	Quantity Ordered	Total Retail Price for This Product
Australia	Catalog Sale	26	$1,679.40
	Internet Sale	13	$613.90
	Retail Sale	171	$15,028.19
Canada	Catalog Sale	32	$5,422.38
	Internet Sale	73	$6,528.70
	Retail Sale	0	0
Germany	Catalog Sale	76	$10,034.40
	Internet Sale	30	$5,360.20
	Retail Sale	0	0
Israel	Catalog Sale	22	$1,316.10
	Internet Sale	6	$243.40
	Retail Sale	0	0
South Africa	Catalog Sale	27	$3,161.70
	Internet Sale	20	$1,988.20
	Retail Sale	0	0
Turkey	Catalog Sale	39	$4,690.20
	Internet Sale	4	$485.60
	Retail Sale	0	0
United States	Catalog Sale	71	$7,627.17
	Internet Sale	80	$6,271.55
	Retail Sale	388	$29,626.38

Without the COMPLETEROWS option, the Retail Sale rows would not appear for Canada, Germany, Israel, South Africa, or Turkey. The value of zero (0) is the result of the system option MISSING, which is included before the PROC REPORT statement.

Include Groups Not Present in the Data

Example 3.26 works exactly as expected because each value of ORDER_TYPE appears somewhere in the input data set. But what if a certain value is not present in the input data set? The COMPLETEROWS option can also be used to insert values into the report that are not in the data. For this use, COMPLETEROWS must be used in conjunction with the PRELOADFMT option on the DEFINE statement for the grouping variable for which you want to see all possible values. In turn, using PRELOADFMT means that you must also have a format associated with the variable.

In this example, Mexico should be part of the report, but data for Mexico has not yet been received. You have to take additional steps to ensure a row for Mexico is included, shown in Example 3.27. Again, the MISSING system option is used to populate the cells with a value of zero (0).

Example 3.27: Include a Country Value Not in the Data

```
proc format;
    value $cntryAll
        'AU' = 'Australia'
        'CA' = 'Canada'
        'DE' = 'Germany'
        'IL' = 'Israel'
        'MX' = 'Mexico' ❶
        'TR' = 'Turkey'
        'US' = 'United States'
        'ZA' = 'South Africa'
        ;
run;

options missing='0';
proc report data=orders completerows; ❷
    column customer_country order_type quantity total_retail_price;
    define customer_country / group format=$cntryAll. preloadfmt; ❸
    define order_type / group format=typef.;
run;
```

❶ The format used for CUSTOMER_COUNTRY should include an entry for every value that you want to see in the report. In this step the value of MX was added for Mexico.

❷ The COMPLETEROWS option is needed on the PROC REPORT to ensure all desired rows will appear.

❸ The PRELOADFMT option loads all of the values from the $cntryAll. format. COMPLETEROWS uses these values when ensuring that all rows are included in the report.

Output 3.27: Mexico Is Present in Final Report

Customer Country	Order Type	Quantity Ordered	Total Retail Price for This Product
Australia	Catalog Sale	26	$1,679.40
	Internet Sale	13	$613.90
	Retail Sale	171	$15,028.19
Canada	Catalog Sale	32	$5,422.38
	Internet Sale	73	$6,528.70
	Retail Sale	0	0
Germany	Catalog Sale	76	$10,034.40
	Internet Sale	30	$5,360.20
	Retail Sale	0	0
Israel	Catalog Sale	22	$1,316.10
	Internet Sale	6	$243.40
	Retail Sale	0	0
Mexico	Catalog Sale	0	0
	Internet Sale	0	0
	Retail Sale	0	0
South Africa	Catalog Sale	27	$3,161.70
	Internet Sale	20	$1,988.20
	Retail Sale	0	0
Turkey	Catalog Sale	39	$4,690.20
	Internet Sale	4	$485.60
	Retail Sale	0	0
United States	Catalog Sale	71	$7,627.17
	Internet Sale	80	$6,271.55
	Retail Sale	388	$29,626.38

Beware of Unexpected Rows

You must be careful using the COMPLETEROWS option because it can also create unexpected or undesired rows. The above example works well because it has only two GROUP variables. Showing all three ORDER_TYPE values for each country makes sense. However, a third GROUP variable might produce a large number of blank rows or rows for combinations that do not make sense for your data.

Example 3.28 adds PRODUCT_LINE between CUSTOMER_COUNTRY and ORDER_TYPE. Again, COMPLETEROWS is used, so all ORDER_TYPE values appear for the country-product combinations. The drawback is that Output 3.28 contains rows where a specific product was not sold for a given country.

Example 3.28: Use COMPLETEROWS with Three GROUP Variables

```
options missing='0';
proc report data=orders completerows;
   column customer_country product_line order_type quantity
          total_retail_price;
   define customer_country / group format=$cntryAll. preloadfmt;
   define order_type / group format=typef.;
   define product_line  / group;
run;
```

Output 3.28: Report Contains Rows for Products Not Sold in Each Country (Partial Listing)

Customer Country	Product Line	Order Type	Quantity Ordered	Total Retail Price for This Product
Australia	Children	Catalog Sale	2	$120.20
		Internet Sale	4	$59.60
		Retail Sale	7	$348.00
	Clothes & Shoes	Catalog Sale	17	$1,065.70
		Internet Sale	8	$444.40
		Retail Sale	42	$2,830.69
	Outdoors	Catalog Sale	0	0
		Internet Sale	0	0
		Retail Sale	38	$3,206.70
	Sports	Catalog Sale	7	$493.50
		Internet Sale	1	$109.90
		Retail Sale	84	$8,642.80
Canada	Children	Catalog Sale	0	0
		Internet Sale	0	0
		Retail Sale	0	0
	Clothes & Shoes	Catalog Sale	3	$81.80
		Internet Sale	3	$173.70
		Retail Sale	0	0
	Outdoors	Catalog Sale	0	0
		Internet Sale	0	0
		Retail Sale	0	0
	Sports	Catalog Sale	29	$5,340.58
		Internet Sale	70	$6,355.00
		Retail Sale	0	0
Germany	Children	Catalog Sale	0	0
		Internet Sale	0	0
		Retail Sale	0	0

Output 3.28 contains unwanted rows for the combination of Canada and the Children product line. Generating the desired report requires pre-processing the data. See Chapter 5 for an example with the needed steps.

COMPLETEROWS might also have unintended consequences if an ACROSS variable is used. Chapter 5 explores the behavior when both options are used.

3.4.4 Output a Table with No Data

Like most procedures, PROC REPORT will not produce output when the data set has no observations, either because it is empty or does not meet sub-setting conditions. In the context of a large set of tables, if one table is missing, the reader of the report might not realize the table is missing. Some form of output needs to be generated even when no data exists for the table. Generating some sort of output will complete the report and let the reader know that nothing was overlooked.

Normally, the following PROC REPORT step in Example 3.29 would not generate output because the ORDERS data set does not contain any records for Mexico, CUSTOMER_COUNTRY='MX'.

Example 3.29: Subset Report to Just Mexico

```
proc report data=orders;
   where customer_country = 'MX';
   column customer_country order_type product_line quantity
          total_retail_price;
   define customer_country / group format=$cntry.;
   define order_type / group format=typef.;
   define product_line / group;
run;
```

The two sections below examine two methods for generating text to indicate that the ORDERS data set does not contain data for Mexico.

Output Plain Text

In some circumstances, the space for an empty table can be filled with plain text to indicate that no data fits the criteria. The text can be generated via an ODS TEXT= statement, PROC ODSTEXT, or with a PUT statement inside of a DATA step. An ODS TEXT= statement does not generate a bookmark in the table of contents. Therefore, this section will use a PUT statement within a DATA step.

You must determine whether the data set is empty or does not meet sub-setting conditions prior to the PROC REPORT step. Then, you conditionally execute either the PROC REPORT step or the DATA step depending on the number of observations. To conditionally execute these steps, place them inside of a macro program.

An in-depth explanation of macro processing is beyond the scope of this book. You can learn more about the Macro Facility in *SAS 9.4 Macro Language: Reference*. The general macro logic needed to conditionally execute either procedure code or a DATA step is explained in this section.

There are a number of different ways to determine the number of observations in a data set and put that value inside of a macro variable. The macro variable can be created either inside or outside of the macro program. For brevity, Example 3.30 creates the macro variable outside of the macro program using PROC SQL. The results are shown in Output 3.29.

Example 3.30: Check Number of Observations from Sub-setting Conditions

```
proc sql noprint;
    select count(*) into: numobs ❶
    from orders
    where customer_country='MX'; ❷
quit;

%macro reports;
    /* If the data set contains observations execute PROC REPORT */
    %if &numobs ge 0 %then %do; ❸
        proc report data=orders; ❹
            where customer_country = 'MX';
            column customer_country order_type product_line quantity
                    total_retail_price;
            define customer_country / group format=$cntry.;
            define order_type / group format=typef.;
            define product_line / group;
        run;
    %end;

    /* Otherwise execute a DATA step */
    %else %do; ❺
        data _null_; ❻
            file print;
            put "The ORDERS data set does not have data for Mexico"; ❼
        run;
    %end;
%mend reports;

%reports ❽
```

❶ The SELECT and INTO clauses count the number of observations from the data set and put the count into the macro variable NUMOBS.

❷ To get a correct observation count, make sure that the WHERE clause contains the sub-setting conditions.

❸ A %IF condition is the macro program equivalent of a DATA step IF condition. The NUMOBS value is checked to determine whether it is greater than or equal to zero. When the %IF condition is true, the code within the %DO loop executes.

❹ PROC REPORT code is executed when the data set contains observations.

❺ When the %IF condition is not true this loop will execute with alternative code.

❻ In this situation, the alternative code is a DATA _NULL_ step, which does not create a data set but can generate output along with the FILE PRINT statement.

❼ The PUT statement outputs the text that indicates no data fits the criteria.

❽ The macro program %REPORTS is called and executed.

Output 3.29: Text Output Based on Sub-setting Conditions

```
The ORDERS data set does not have data for Mexico
```

The text string from the DATA step will be placed at the top of the output page under any titles that might be in effect. The text font and size can be changed if desired.

Output Text Inside of the Table Structure

In other circumstances, the header of the table needs to be created and text needs to be placed inside the table structure. This method is much harder than the previous method because PROC REPORT requires at least one observation in the data set in order to execute, create headers, and build a table structure. A blank, or dummy, observation must be added to the data set just to get PROC REPORT to execute. A LINE statement inside of a compute block displays the text to indicate that no data fits the criteria. Example 3.31 writes text inside of the PROC REPORT table structure, shown in Output 3.30.

Example 3.31: Create TOTAL_COST as a COMPUTED Variable

```
%macro reports;
   /* If the data set contains observations execute PROC REPORT */
   %if &numobs ge 0 %then %do;
      proc report data=orders;
         where customer_country = 'MX';
         column customer_country order_type product_line quantity
                total_retail_price;
         define customer_country / group format=$cntry.;
         define order_type / group format=typef.;
         define product_line / group;
      run;
   %end;

   /* Otherwise execute a DATA step */
   %else %do;
      data dummy;  ❶
         dummy = 1;
      run;

      data orders2;
         merge orders(where=(customer_country = 'MX'))
               dummy;  ❷
      run;

      options missing=' ';
      proc report data=orders2 missing;  ❸
         column customer_country order_type product_line quantity
                total_retail_price;
```

```
        define customer_country / group format=$cntry.;
        define order_type / group format=typef.;
        define product_line / group;

        compute before;  ❹
            line "The ORDERS data set does not have data for Mexico";
        endcomp;
    run;
  %end;
%mend reports;

%reports
```

❶ Create a dummy data set that has only one record.

❷ Merge the DUMMY data set with the ORDERS data set. Because the DUMMY data set has one record, the resulting data set, ORDERS2, will also have one record. It will also contain all of the variables from both data sets, most importantly, the variables from ORDERS.

❸ The new data set ORDERS2 has missing values for all of the variables that are defined as GROUP. Add the MISSING option to the PROC REPORT statement, so that the blank record will be used and tables will be generated.

❹ The compute block and its LINE statement produce the text to indicate no records meet the table and report criteria.

Output 3.30: Output Text Within the Table Structure

Customer Country	Order Type	Product Line	Quantity Ordered	Total Retail Price for This Product
The ORDERS data set does not have data for Mexico				

The placement of the text in Output 3.30 might not look exactly like you want. You can control the look to a certain extent by removing the borders for the blank table row. However, unless you are sending the output to the Tagsets.ExcelXP or Excel destination, you cannot remove or hide the blank row. See Chapter 6 for examples of changing borders.

The text string can be moved down so that there is a space between the headers and the text. One LINE statement can be used to assign a null text string and a second LINE statement can be assigned the desired text. Also, the Example 3.31 code uses a COMPUTE BEFORE statement. This can be changed to COMPUTE AFTER, as shown in Example 3.32, which will generate Output 3.31.

Example 3.32: Output Text at the Bottom of the Table Structure

```
        compute after;
            line "The ORDERS data set does not have data for Mexico";
        endcomp;
```

Output 3.31: Output Text within the Table Structure

Customer Country	Order Type	Product Line	Quantity Ordered	Total Retail Price for This Product
The ORDERS data set does not have data for Mexico				

The TAGATTR style attribute allows you to insert text strings that the ODS destination interprets as special instructions. In the Tagsets.ExcelXP destination, you can use a special instruction to hide a specific row. The row still exists in the table but is hidden from view. Inside of a compute block, you can instruct Tagsets.ExcelXP to hide the blank row of data, as demonstrated in Example 3.33 and Output 3.32.

Example 3.33: Use TAGATTR to Hide the Blank Row

```
compute customer_country;
   if customer_country = ' ' then call define(
     _row_,"style","style={tagattr=""hidden:yes""}");
endcomp;
```

Output 3.32: The Blank Row Is Hidden in Tagsets.ExcelXP Output

	A	B	C	D	E	F
1	Customer Country	Order Type	Product Line	Quantity Ordered	Total Retail Price for This Product	
3	The ORDERS data set does not have data for Mexico					
4						

In the new ODS destination for EXCEL, you do not have to use special TAGATTR instructions. The destination has an option for hiding rows. You can hide single rows or a range of rows. The destination option will produce the same table as shown in Output 3.32.

```
ods excel options(HIDDEN_ROWS='2');
```

3.4.5 Dynamically Assign Spanning Header Text

Spanning header text is assigned on the COLUMN statement. Its value is generally hardcoded. A macro variable can be specified within double quotation marks as the text, but its value is set at the first pass through the code. The text of the spanning header cannot be changed within one PROC REPORT step. To dynamically assign the spanning header text, you must place the PROC REPORT step inside of a macro program, and execute the macro program for each value of the text that you want displayed.

A final report might require the value of a BY variable to be in a spanning header. #BYVAR is not honored inside of PROC REPORT. Therefore, you need to place the PROC REPORT step inside of a macro program and run the macro program once for each value of the BY variable. A macro variable reference to the BY variable can be placed as a spanning header on the COLUMN statement.

In Example 3.34, CUSTOMER_AGE_GROUP is the BY variable, so one table is created for each value. The BY value becomes a spanning header. The result is shown in Output 3.33.

Example 3.34: Assign Spanning Header Text Using a Macro Variable

```
proc sort data=orders;
   by customer_age_group;
run;

%macro rep(byvar);
   proc report data=orders style(column)=[width=1in];
      where customer_age_group = "&byvar"; ❶
      column ("&byvar Age Group" ❷ customer_name customer_age
              customer_gender);
   run;
%mend rep;

data _null_;
   set orders;
   by customer_age_group;
   if first.customer_age_group then call execute(cats(
     '%nrstr(%rep(',customer_age_group,'))')); ❸
run;
```

❶ Subset the data used by PROC REPORT to the current value of &BYVAR. The macro variable name is BYVAR but notice a BY statement is no longer needed, because the macro program is being run for each CUSTOMER_AGE_GROUP value. Each time PROC REPORT is executed, a new table is created, just as it would be with a BY statement.

❷ Place the macro variable within double quotation marks as a spanning header. The text will change each time the macro program is executed.

❸ Use a CALL EXECUTE statement to execute the macro program for each value of CUSTOMER_AGE_GROUP.

Output 3.33: Spanning Header Text Changes for Each Table

15-30 years Age Group		
Customer Name	Customer Age	Customer Gender
Annmarie Leveille	23	F
Najma Hicks	21	F
Alvan Goheen	23	M
Alvan Goheen	23	M

31-45 years Age Group		
Customer Name	Customer Age	Customer Gender
Kyndal Hooks	43	F
Yan Kozlowski	38	M
Kyndal Hooks	43	F
David Black	38	M

46-60 years Age Group		
Customer Name	Customer Age	Customer Gender
Dericka Pockran	53	F
Ramesh Trentholme	58	M
Attila Gibbs	48	M
Dericka Pockran	53	F

61-75 years Age Group		
Customer Name	Customer Age	Customer Gender
Roy Siferd	73	M
Candy Kinsey	73	F
Wynella Lewis	73	F
Wynella Lewis	73	F

Chapter 4: Examples – How to Use ACROSS Variables

4.1 Introduction

As mentioned in Chapter 1, you can stack statistics or put one variable over another with the ACROSS usage. ACROSS variables transpose your data without changing the data set. The topic of PROC REPORT code using ACROSS variables is often handled as a separate category in the procedure documentation and in other samples, and this book is no different. Reports that use ACROSS variables deserve their own chapter because ACROSS variables can drastically change the code.

Using ACROSS variables changes how you have to think about the report, how you reference variables, and how you have to code the PROC REPORT step. Simply said, these kinds of reports are different. As you read through this chapter, keep in mind that each of column of an ACROSS variable is created entirely independent of the other columns.

This chapter starts by demonstrating standard reports showing how to construct the COLUMN statement and how to refer to columns in compute blocks. Calculating percentages is also covered. The key to percentages is defining the denominator because the value changes based on what you are trying to convey.

Along with understanding how to construct the COLUMN statement and reference columns in a compute block, you must also understand how an ACROSS variable alters the header section of the report. The chapter describes how the header section is built with ACROSS variables and how to manipulate header text.

Formats play an important role in ordering the ACROSS variable values and inserting columns for subtotals. This chapter demonstrates hiding columns and inserting vertical table (page) breaks. The chapter ends with examples of using macro processing to apply changes to columns under an ACROSS variable.

4.2 Standard Reports

This section of the chapter demonstrates various ways multiple pieces of information share a column. You can stack statistics under one column heading. You can also define a variable as ACROSS and put a statistic or another variable underneath it. New *report-item*s can be created and percentages calculated.

4.2.1 Stack a Statistic

PROC REPORT allows you to stack multiple statistics for an ANALYSIS variable under one heading. The syntax on the COLUMN statement is key to this behavior. The ANALYSIS variable is followed by a comma and the name of the statistic. Multiple statistics can be placed inside of parentheses. A DEFINE statement is not necessary for this kind of report. Example 4.1 shows the syntax, and Output 4.1 shows the result.

Example 4.1: Stack Statistics under ANALYSIS Variables
```
proc report data=orders;
   column quantity,(min max sum) total_retail_price,(n mean sum);❶
run;
```

❶ The COLUMN statement has two analysis variables, QUANTITY and TOTAL_RETAIL_PRICE. Each one is followed with a comma and the desired statistics inside of parentheses.

Output 4.1: Multiple Statistics Appear under Each ANALYSIS Variable Header

Quantity Ordered			Total Retail Price for This Product		
min	max	sum	n	mean	sum
1	6	1078	$617.00	$162.20	100077.46

In Output 4.1 each statistic inherited the format of the ANALYSIS variable. The N statistic for TOTAL_RETAIL_PRICE is formatted with a dollar sign because of this behavior. The format can be controlled by using a DEFINE statement for the N statistic and specifying a different format.

You can define categorical variables as an ACROSS without having to specify anything else on the COLUMN statement. PROC REPORT will automatically insert the N statistic, giving you a count for each category, as seen in Example 4.2 and Output 4.2.

Example 4.2: Define a Variable as ACROSS

```
proc report data=orders;
   column customer_age_group;
   define customer_age_group / across;
run;
```

Output 4.2: The N Statistic Is under the ACROSS Variable

Customer Age Group			
15-30 years	31-45 years	46-60 years	61-75 years
172	233	105	107

4.2.2 Multiple Variables under an ACROSS Variable

As nice as those simple reports are, you probably want more. The other method for putting multiple variables in the same column is to use the comma on the COLUMN statement, as we have seen, and put *report-items* after the comma. One of the *report-items*, usually the one preceding the comma, is defined as ACROSS. Recall that when a variable is defined as ACROSS, its values become column headers. Under each of the ACROSS variable values are columns created by other *report-items*. The other *report-items* can be defined as GROUP, DISPLAY, ANALYSIS, or COMPUTED.

In Example 4.3, the values of CUSTOMER_AGE_GROUP become column headers. The summed values for TOTAL_RETAIL_PRICE and QUANTITY are below each new header in Output 4.3.

Example 4.3: Place ANALYSIS Variables under an ACROSS Variable

```
proc report data=orders;
   column customer_age_group, (total_retail_price quantity);  ❶
   define customer_age_group / across;  ❷
run;
```

❶ On the COLUMN statement the *report-item* that is to become the header values is listed first, CUSTOMER_AGE_GROUP. It is followed by a comma and parentheses around the two ANALYSIS variables.

❷ CUSTOMER_AGE_GROUP must be defined as ACROSS.

Output 4.3: Two ANALYSIS Variables Are under CUSTOMER_AGE_GROUP Categories

Customer Age Group							
15-30 years		31-45 years		46-60 years		61-75 years	
Total Retail Price for This Product	Quantity Ordered	Total Retail Price for This Product	Quantity Ordered	Total Retail Price for This Product	Quantity Ordered	Total Retail Price for This Product	Quantity Ordered
$30,486.50	304	$34,197.50	397	$14,920.55	175	$20,472.92	202

Most reports are a combination of *report-item* usages. The restrictions for creating a report with an ACROSS variable are that a statistic must be present and an ORDER variable cannot be placed under the ACROSS. Example 4.4 contains a GROUP, ACROSS, and ANALYSIS variable. Output 4.4 shows the results.

Example 4.4: Combine GROUP, ACROSS, and ANALYSIS Usages

```
proc report data=orders;
    column customer_gender customer_age_group,
           (total_retail_price quantity);❶
    define customer_gender / group; ❷
    define customer_age_group / across; ❸
run;
```

❶ The COLUMN statement lists all of the desired *report-item*s.

❷ CUSTOMER_GENDER is defined as GROUP, so it consolidates the observations from the input data set.

❸ Again, CUSTOMER_AGE_GROUP is defined as ACROSS, so its values become headers. Based on the COLUMN statement, TOTAL_RETAIL_PRICE and QUANTITY will be underneath the new headers.

Output 4.4: Output Grouped by Gender with Age Group across the Top

	Customer Age Group							
	15-30 years		31-45 years		46-60 years		61-75 years	
Customer Gender	Total Retail Price for This Product	Quantity Ordered	Total Retail Price for This Product	Quantity Ordered	Total Retail Price for This Product	Quantity Ordered	Total Retail Price for This Product	Quantity Ordered
F	$25,005.51	235	$16,360.00	157	$5,365.80	61	$3,016.12	45
M	$5,480.99	69	$17,837.50	240	$9,554.75	114	$17,456.80	157

Remember you can use a *report-item* as many times as you need, as long as it has the same usage each time. In Example 4.4 the values of TOTAL_RETAIL_PRICE and QUANTITY are displayed within values of CUSTOMER_AGE_GROUP. Those variables can be used again at the end of the COLUMN statement to give the overall totals for each gender, regardless of age group, as shown in Example 4.5 and Output 4.5.

Example 4.5: Include Total Columns after the ACROSS

```
proc report data=orders;
   column customer_gender customer_age_group,
          (total_retail_price quantity)
          ('Totals' total_retail_price quantity); ❶
   define customer_gender / group;
   define customer_age_group / across;
run;
```

❶ Use the TOTAL_RETAIL_PRICE AND QUANTITY variables twice. The second instance is not under the ACROSS variable. Therefore, it gives the overall total within each value of CUSTOMER_GENDER.

Output 4.5: Total Columns Are Included After the CUSTOMER_AGE_GROUP Columns

Customer Gender	Customer Age Group									Totals	
	15-30 years		31-45 years		46-60 years		61-75 years				
	Total Retail Price for This Product	Quantity Ordered	Total Retail Price for This Product	Quantity Ordered	Total Retail Price for This Product	Quantity Ordered	Total Retail Price for This Product	Quantity Ordered	Total Retail Price for This Product	Quantity Ordered
F	$25,005.51	235	$16,360.00	157	$5,365.80	61	$3,016.12	45	$49,747.43	498
M	$5,480.99	69	$17,837.50	240	$9,554.75	114	$17,456.80	157	$50,330.04	580

4.2.3 A DISPLAY Variable under an ACROSS Variable

Using a DISPLAY variable under ACROSS is common. However, the input data is usually in a concise format. In this context, concise means no repeating values, so that each row is unique, or already summarized data.

You can put a DISPLAY variable under an ACROSS, but a statistic must be included somewhere in the report. In this context, a statistic is either a statistical keyword, like N, or a COMPUTED variable. The presence of an ANALYSIS variable does not eliminate the requirement for a statistic. You can have a statistic under the ACROSS with the DISPLAY variable or outside of the ACROSS, but you have to have a statistic. The statistic column does not have to be displayed in the final report. A COMPUTED *report-item* does not have to be displayed in the final report and does not even have to be given a value.

For the purposes of demonstrating reports that have DISPLAY variables under an ACROSS, a new data set was created from ORDERS. CUSTOMER contains one record for each CUSTOMER_NAME value. The other variables are TOTALR, TOTALQ, SPENDER, and VOLUME. TOTALR is the sum of TOTAL_RETAIL_PRICE. TOTALQ is the sum of QUANTITY. SPENDER and VOLUME are character variables that indicate whether the customer spends and purchases a lot. Example 4.6 uses the CUSTOMER data set and defines VOLUME as DISPLAY. The results are shown in Output 4.6.

Example 4.6: Put a DISPLAY Variable under an ACROSS Variable

```
options missing='0';
proc report data=customer;
   column customer_name order_type,(totalq volume n ❶);
   define customer_name / group;
   define order_type / across format=typef.;
   define totalq / analysis 'Total Quantity'; ❷
   define volume / display 'Large Volume?'; ❸
   define N / noprint; ❹
run;
```

❶ Three items are stacked under ORDER_TYPE. The third item, N, will create a column containing the count.

❷ TOTALQ is defined as ANALYSIS. Its values will be summed. However, its presence does not eliminate the need for a statistic to be associated with the DISPLAY variable.

❸ VOLUME is defined as DISPLAY because we want its value written out for each combination of CUSTOMER_NAME and ORDER_TYPE.

❹ A statistic is required to use DISPLAY under ACROSS. However, it does not have to be shown in the final report, so it is defined with NOPRINT.

Output 4.6: The VOLUME Variable Is Defined As DISPLAY

Customer Name	Order Type					
	Catalog Sale		Internet Sale		Retail Sale	
	Total Quantity	Large Volume?	Total Quantity	Large Volume?	Total Quantity	Large Volume?
Ahmet Canko	9	Y	0		0	
Alex Santinello	0		9	Y	0	
Alphone Greenwald	1	N	0		1	N
Alvan Goheen	0		7	Y	15	Y
Andreas Rennie	2	N	0		0	
Angel Borwick	0		11	Y	0	
Annmarie Leveille	0		0		20	Y
Attila Gibbs	3	Y	0		11	Y
Avinoam Tuvia	2	N	0		0	
Avinoam Zweig	13	Y	6	Y	0	
Avni Argac	13	Y	0		0	
Avni Umran	7	Y	0		0	
Bill Cuddy	0		8	Y	0	
Bulent Urfalioglu	5	Y	0		0	
Candy Kinsey	13	Y	0		0	
Carglar Aydemir	2	N	0		0	
Carsten Maestrini	13	Y	0		0	
Colin Byarley	0		3	Y	0	
Cornelia Krahl	0		11	Y	0	
Cosi Rimmington	0		0		24	Y
Cynthia Martinez	0		5	Y	16	Y
Cynthia Mccluney	0		15	Y	0	
David Black	0		0		31	Y
Dericka Pockran	1	N	5	Y	14	Y
Dianne Patchin	6	Y	0		41	Y
Duncan Robertshawe	0		0		25	Y
Elke Wallstab	0		3	Y	0	

Example 4.7 demonstrates the method of using a COMPUTED *report-item* instead of the N statistic.

Example 4.7: Use a COMPUTED Column to Generate the Same Output

```
proc report data=customer;
   column customer_name order_type,(totalq volume) dummy; ❶
   define customer_name / group;
   define order_type / across format=typef.;
   define totalq / analysis 'Total Quantity'; ❷
   define volume / display 'Large Volume?'; ❸
   define dummy / computed noprint; ❹
run;
```

❶ Add a new *report-item* to the end of the COLUMN statement. Do not place it under ORDER_TYPE.

❷ TOTALQ is defined as ANALYSIS. Its values will be summed. However, its presence does not eliminate the need for a statistic to be associated with the DISPLAY variable.

❸ VOLUME is defined as DISPLAY because we want its value written out for each combination of CUSTOMER_NAME and ORDER_TYPE.

❹ Define the new column as COMPUTED and NOPRINT. Notice a compute block is not necessary. PROC REPORT assigns the value to missing, but because you are not displaying the value, it does not matter what the value is.

The output is the same as Output 4.6.

4.2.4 A GROUP Variable under an ACROSS Variable

An alternative to creating an unseen statistic column is to change the usage from DISPLAY to GROUP. PROC REPORT does not require a statistic when a GROUP is under an ACROSS, as demonstrated in Example 4.8.

Example 4.8: Place a GROUP Variable Under the ACROSS Variable

```
proc report data=customer;
   column customer_name order_type,(totalq volume); ❶
   define customer_name / group;
   define order_type / across format=typef.;
   define totalq / 'Total Quantity';
   define volume / group 'Large Volume?'; ❷
run;
```

❶ The COLUMN statement includes just the *report-item*s of interest, with TOTALQ and VOLUME stacked under ORDER_TYPE.

❷ Define the usage of VOLUME as GROUP.

The output is the same as Output 4.6, produced by both Example 4.6 and 4.7.

The above example created the desired output because the CUSTOMER data set had only one record for each CUSTOMER_NAME-ORDER_TYPE combination and therefore only one value for VOLUME. Trying to consolidate variable values from the input data set and placing them under an ACROSS is tricky. The process is described in Chapter 5.

4.2.5 Create New *Report-Items*

The last chapter demonstrated the unique ability of PROC REPORT to create *report-item*s not in the input data set. New *report-item*s can also be created and placed under ACROSS variables. The difference in the two scenarios is how the report columns have to be referenced inside of the compute blocks that create them. Remember from Chapter 2 that columns created by an ACROSS variable must be referenced in the form _cn_, where N is the absolute column number. Also, an assignment statement is required for each of the new columns under the ACROSS.

In Example 4.9, QUANTITY and TOTAL_RETAIL_PRICE are under the ACROSS variable CUSTOMER_AGE_GROUP with the addition of ESTPRICE_PER_ITEM. ESTPRICE_PER_ITEM is a new *report-item* that needs to be calculated as the

TOTAL_RETAIL_PRICE value divided by the QUANTITY value for each age group. The results are shown in Output 4.7.

Example 4.9: Create a New *Report-item* Called ESTPRICE_PER_ITEM

```
proc report data=orders;
   column customer_age_group, (quantity total_retail_price
        estprice_per_item); ❶
   define customer_age_group / across; ❷
   define estprice_per_item / computed 'Est. Item Price'
      format=dollar8.2; ❸

   compute estprice_per_item; ❹
      _c3_ = _c2_ / _c1_; ❺
      _c6_ = _c5_ / _c4_;
      _c9_ = _c8_ / _c7_;
      _c12_ = _c11_ / _c10_;
   endcomp;
run;
```

❶ Add the new *report-item*, ESTPRICE_PER_ITEM, to the appropriate place on the COLUMN statement. The new item needs a column for each value of CUSTOMER_AGE_GROUP, so ESTPRICE_PER_ITEM is placed inside of the parentheses after the comma.

❷ CUSTOMER_AGE_GROUP is defined as ACROSS.

❸ ESTPRICE_PER_ITEM is defined as COMPUTED with an appropriate format and label.

❹ ESTPRICE_PER_ITEM is the *report-item* because it is the column of interest. The name is used on the COMPUTE statement, but within the compute block, the columns must be referenced as _cn_. This compute block executes on every row.

❺ An assignment statement is needed for each column of ESTPRICE_PER_ITEM. All twelve columns used in the calculations must be referred to in the form _cn_.

Output 4.7: Est. Item Price Is a New *Report-item* under the ACROSS

Customer Age Group											
15-30 years			31-45 years			46-60 years			61-75 years		
Quantity Ordered	Total Retail Price for This Product	Est. Item Price	Quantity Ordered	Total Retail Price for This Product	Est. Item Price	Quantity Ordered	Total Retail Price for This Product	Est. Item Price	Quantity Ordered	Total Retail Price for This Product	Est. Item Price
304	$30,486.50	$100.28	397	$34,197.50	$86.14	175	$14,920.55	$85.26	202	$20,472.92	$101.35

In Chapter 3, new columns could be created with just one assignment statement. As you can see, this is not possible when an ACROSS is involved. The variable name ESTPRICE_PER_ITEM is no longer valid because PROC REPORT immediately changes the name to an absolute column number reference. One name is now insufficient, because you no longer have one column; you have four.

4.2.6 Percentages

Percentages are just as important for reports with ACROSS variables as they are for other reports, but they might require more code to calculate and a little more forethought in determining what value should be used as the denominator.

Default Percentages

Example 4.10 places a second aliased *report-item*, TRP2, under the ACROSS to hold the percent value. The value will be calculated using the PCTSUM statistical keyword to demonstrate what PROC REPORT calculates by default. The results are shown in Output 4.8.

Example 4.10: Use the PCTSUM Statistical Keyword

```
options missing='';
proc report data=orders;
   column customer_country order_type customer_gender,
          (total_retail_price total_retail_price=trp2); ❶
   define customer_country / group format=$cntry.;
   define order_type / group format=typef.;
   define customer_gender / across; ❷
   define total_retail_price / 'Total Retail Price';
   define trp2 / pctsum format=percent8.1 'Percent Retail Price'; ❸
run;
```

❶ TRP2 is an alias and inherits the TOTAL_RETAIL_PRICE value. It will hold the percent value.

❷ CUSTOMER_GENDER is defined as ACROSS, so its values become headers.

❸ TRP2 is defined with PCTSUM. The denominator is the sum of TOTAL_RETAIL_PRICE for the corresponding value of CUSTOMER_AGE_GROUP. In other words, TRP2 is the column percentage.

Output 4.8: Percentages Are Generated Using the PCTSUM Keyword

Customer Country	Order Type	Customer Gender			
		F		M	
		Total Retail Price	Percent Retail Price	Total Retail Price	Percent Retail Price
Australia	Catalog Sale	$1,542.20	3.1%	$137.20	0.3%
	Internet Sale	$218.20	0.4%	$395.70	0.8%
	Retail Sale	$3,666.00	7.4%	$11,362.19	22.6%
Canada	Catalog Sale	$5,074.88	10.2%	$347.50	0.7%
	Internet Sale	$4,317.80	8.7%	$2,210.90	4.4%
Germany	Catalog Sale	$351.40	0.7%	$9,683.00	19.2%
	Internet Sale	$3,296.40	6.6%	$2,063.80	4.1%
Israel	Catalog Sale			$1,316.10	2.6%
	Internet Sale			$243.40	0.5%
South Africa	Catalog Sale	$3,161.70	6.4%		
	Internet Sale	$1,695.60	3.4%	$292.60	0.6%
Turkey	Catalog Sale			$4,690.20	9.3%
	Internet Sale			$485.60	1.0%
United States	Catalog Sale	$4,003.38	8.0%	$3,623.79	7.2%
	Internet Sale	$3,108.50	6.2%	$3,163.05	6.3%
	Retail Sale	$19,311.37	38.8%	$10,315.01	20.5%

Row Percentages

ACROSS variables automatically create columns that can be compared and contrasted. A certain variable takes either 'value a' or 'value b'. Therefore, row percentages are a natural fit for these kinds of reports. The denominator is the total value for a particular row. The numerator is the value for a specific value of the ACROSS variable.

In Example 4.11, the percentage for each gender is calculated for each order type within a country, shown in Output 4.9.

Example 4.11: Calculate Percent For Gender Within Country

```
options missing='';
proc report data=orders;
   column customer_country order_type customer_gender,
          (total_retail_price pct); ❶
   define customer_country / group format=$cntry.;
   define order_type / group format=typef.;
   define customer_gender / across; ❷
   define total_retail_price / 'Total Retail Price';
   define pct / computed format=percent8.1 'Percent Retail Price'; ❸
```

```
        compute pct; ❹
           _c4_ = _c3_ / sum(_c3_,_c5_); ❺
           _c6_ = _c5_ / sum(_c3_,_c5_);
        endcomp;
run;
```

❶ CUSTOMER_COUNTRY and ORDER_TYPE will be the first column. CUSTOMER_GENDER is followed by and comma and TOTAL_RETAIL_PRICE and PCT with parentheses, so they will be under gender.

❷ CUSTOMER_GENDER is defined as ACROSS.

❸ PCT is defined as COMPUTED because it is not in the input data set. It is also given an appropriate label and format.

❹ The *report-item* on the COMPUTE statement is PCT. It is the report column that needs to be calculated and it is the last *report-item* on the COLUMN statement.

❺ An assignment statement is needed for each of the percent columns under gender. Though PCT is on the COMPUTE statement, it cannot be used inside of the compute block, the columns are referenced as _cn_. This compute block is executed for each row in the report, so the denominator changes for each row. The denominator is the total TOTAL_RETAIL_PRICE value for that combination of CUSTOMER_COUNTY and ORDER_TYPE.

Output 4.9: Displayed Percentages Are for Each Gender Within Country and Order Type

| | | Customer Gender | | | |
| | | F | | M | |
Customer Country	Order Type	Total Retail Price	Percent Retail Price	Total Retail Price	Percent Retail Price
Australia	Catalog Sale	$1,542.20	91.8%	$137.20	8.2%
	Internet Sale	$218.20	35.5%	$395.70	64.5%
	Retail Sale	$3,666.00	24.4%	$11,362.19	75.6%
Canada	Catalog Sale	$5,074.88	93.6%	$347.50	6.4%
	Internet Sale	$4,317.80	66.1%	$2,210.90	33.9%
Germany	Catalog Sale	$351.40	3.5%	$9,683.00	96.5%
	Internet Sale	$3,296.40	61.5%	$2,063.80	38.5%
Israel	Catalog Sale			$1,316.10	100.0%
	Internet Sale			$243.40	100.0%
South Africa	Catalog Sale	$3,161.70	100.0%		
	Internet Sale	$1,695.60	85.3%	$292.60	14.7%
Turkey	Catalog Sale			$4,690.20	100.0%
	Internet Sale			$485.60	100.0%
United States	Catalog Sale	$4,003.38	52.5%	$3,623.79	47.5%
	Internet Sale	$3,108.50	49.6%	$3,163.05	50.4%
	Retail Sale	$19,311.37	65.2%	$10,315.01	34.8%

Example 4.11 demonstrated calculating the denominators by summing other columns under the ACROSS, but it does not have to be done that way. PROC REPORT will let you place a single variable on the COLUMN statement multiple times. You can take advantage of this and reuse TOTAL_RETAIL_PRICE. When TOTAL_RETAIL_PRICE is not under CUSTOMER_GENDER, its value is the total for that country and order type.

The difficult part is the placement of the second occurrence of TOTAL_RETAIL_PRICE. You can place it before CUSTOMER_GENDER or at the end of the COLUMN statement. Both require changes to the code above.

When TOT, the alias of TOTAL_RETAIL_PRICE, is placed before CUSTOMER_GENDER, the column numbers change. Example 4.12 moves the *report-item* on the COLUMN statement and changes the column numbers in the compute block.

Example 4.12: Calculate Percentages Using an Alias

```
proc report data=orders ;
   column customer_country order_type total_retail_price=tot
          customer_gender,(total_retail_price pct);
   define customer_country / group format=$cntry.;
   define order_type / group format=typef.;
   define customer_gender / across;
   define total_retail_price / 'Total Retail Price';
   define pct / computed format=percent8.1 'Percent Retail Price';
   define tot / noprint;

   compute pct;
      _c5_ = _c4_ / tot;
      _c7_ = _c6_ / tot;
   endcomp;
run;
```

The output is the same as Output 4.9.

When TOT, the alias of TOTAL_RETAIL_PRICE, is placed at the end of the COLUMN statement, the *report-item* on the COMPUTE statement has to change. It needs to be TOT so that its values are available. This is demonstrated in Example 4.13.

Example 4.13: Calculate Percentages Using an Alias

```
proc report data=orders;
   column customer_country order_type customer_gender,
          (total_retail_price pct) total_retail_price=tot;
   define customer_country / group format=$cntry.;
   define order_type / group format=typef.;
   define customer_gender / across;
   define total_retail_price / 'Total Retail Price';
   define pct / computed format=percent8.1 'Percent Retail Price';
   define tot / noprint;
```

```
    compute tot;
       _c4_ = _c3_ / tot;
       _c6_ = _c5_ / tot;
    endcomp;
run;
```

The output is the same as Output 4.9, produced by both Example 4.11 and 4.12.

Using TOTAL_RETAIL_PRICE on the COLUMN statement twice is very helpful when you have a large number of columns. It prevents you from having to enter as much in the assignment statement or in the SUM function.

Column Percentages within Groups

Percentages can also be calculated within groups. The denominator is more finely defined. In Example 4.14, the denominator is the sum of TOTAL_RETAIL_PRICE for a specific value of gender within country. The sum of TOTAL_RETAIL_PRICE for females in Australia is $5,426.20. For males in Australia, the sum is $11,895.09. Then $9,392.68 is the sum for females in Canada, and so on. The numerator is the value of TOTAL_RETAIL_PRICE for each gender, country, and order type combination. The results are displayed in Output 4.10.

Example 4.14: Calculate Percentages within CUSTOMER_COUNTRY

```
proc report data=orders;
   column customer_country order_type customer_gender,
          (total_retail_price pct); ❶
   define customer_country / group format=$cntry.;
   define order_type / group format=typef.;
   define customer_gender / across; ❷
   define total_retail_price / 'Total Retail Price';
   define pct / computed format=percent8.1 'Percent Retail Price'; ❸

   compute before customer_country; ❹
      denF = _c3_;
      denM = _c5_;
   endcomp;

   compute pct; ❺
      if denF > 0 then _c4_ = _c3_ / denF; ❻
      if denM > 0 then _c6_ = _c5_ / denM;
   endcomp;
run;
```

❶ PCT, along with TOTAL_RETAIL_PRICE, is placed under CUSTOMER_GENDER.

❷ CUSTOMER_GENDER is defined as ACROSS.

❸ PCT is not on the input data set and is not a keyword, it is defined as COMPUTED. An appropriate format and label are assigned.

❹ CUSTOMER_COUNTRY is a contributing factor to the denominator. At the top of each country section denominators must be populated. A temporary variable is needed for each CUSTOMER_GENDER value.

❺ PCT is the *report-item* on the COMPUTE statement because it represents the columns that need to be calculated under every unique value of CUSTOMER_GENDER.

❻ Assignment statements are needed for each column containing a percentage. The percentage column numbers are 4 and 6, which are used in the form _cn_. The appropriate denominator is specified in each assignment statement.

Output 4.10: Displayed Percentages Are for Order Type within Gender and Country

Customer Country	Order Type	Customer Gender			
		F		M	
		Total Retail Price	Percent Retail Price	Total Retail Price	Percent Retail Price
Australia	Catalog Sale	$1,542.20	28.4%	$137.20	1.2%
	Internet Sale	$218.20	4.0%	$395.70	3.3%
	Retail Sale	$3,666.00	67.6%	$11,362.19	95.5%
Canada	Catalog Sale	$5,074.88	54.0%	$347.50	13.6%
	Internet Sale	$4,317.80	46.0%	$2,210.90	86.4%
Germany	Catalog Sale	$351.40	9.6%	$9,683.00	82.4%
	Internet Sale	$3,296.40	90.4%	$2,063.80	17.6%
Israel	Catalog Sale			$1,316.10	84.4%
	Internet Sale			$243.40	15.6%
South Africa	Catalog Sale	$3,161.70	65.1%		
	Internet Sale	$1,695.60	34.9%	$292.60	100.0%
Turkey	Catalog Sale			$4,690.20	90.6%
	Internet Sale			$485.60	9.4%
United States	Catalog Sale	$4,003.38	15.2%	$3,623.79	21.2%
	Internet Sale	$3,108.50	11.8%	$3,163.05	18.5%
	Retail Sale	$19,311.37	73.1%	$10,315.01	60.3%

4.3 Header Section Rows

The above section shows how ACROSS variables affect how columns are created. They also have a big effect on the header section of the report. ACROSS variables can add a number of rows to the header section. They also affect the placement of spanning headers over other columns. All of the rows can be overwhelming and confusing. This section explains the rows that are created and how to change and move header text when an ACROSS variable is present.

4.3.1 Default Header Section Created with ACROSS

By default, the header section has one row containing the column headers. When a variable is defined as ACROSS, two additional rows are added to the header. One row contains the ACROSS variable label, which spans all of the columns created by the variable. Another row contains the ACROSS variable values. Each value will span the columns of the *report-items* listed under the

ACROSS. Example 4.15 creates a report with the header rows created by an ACROSS variable, shown in Output 4.11.

Example 4.15: Default Headers Created by ACROSS

```
options missing='0';
proc report data=orders;
    column product_line customer_age_group customer_gender,
           (quantity total_retail_price); ❶
    define product_line / group "Product"; ❷
    define customer_age_group / group "Age Group"; ❸
    define customer_gender / across "Gender"; ❹
run;
```

❶ PRODUCT_LINE and CUSTOMER_AGE_GROUP are the first listed variables and will be placed before the columns created by CUSTOMER_GENDER.

❷ The label "Product" is assigned to the PRODUCT_LINE variable.

❸ The label "Age Group" is assigned to the CUSTOMER_AGE_GROUP variable.

❹ CUSTOMER_GENDER is given the ACROSS usage and a label. Its values become spanning headers over the QUANTITY and TOTAL_RETAIL_PRICE labels. The label "Gender" will be placed over the values of F and M.

Output 4.11: ACROSS Variable Generates Two Additional Header Rows

| | | Gender | | | |
| | | F | | M | |
Product	Age Group	Quantity Ordered	Total Retail Price for This Product	Quantity Ordered	Total Retail Price for This Product
Children	15-30 years	17	$544.00	6	$198.60
	31-45 years	7	$140.50	11	$473.00
	46-60 years	3	$37.80	4	$172.10
	61-75 years	0	0	1	$50.40
Clothes & Shoes	15-30 years	52	$2,496.90	4	$425.40
	31-45 years	43	$2,256.80	69	$3,484.19
	46-60 years	22	$2,046.00	35	$2,299.20
	61-75 years	15	$1,003.20	35	$2,733.00
Outdoors	15-30 years	37	$4,200.70	16	$2,022.00
	31-45 years	31	$5,602.50	66	$6,115.20
	46-60 years	10	$671.80	15	$1,359.60
	61-75 years	4	$456.60	61	$9,433.60
Sports	15-30 years	129	$17,763.91	43	$2,834.99
	31-45 years	76	$8,360.20	94	$7,765.11
	46-60 years	26	$2,610.20	60	$5,723.85
	61-75 years	26	$1,556.32	60	$5,239.80

4.3.2 Place a Spanning Header beside ACROSS Values

Let's take the code from Example 4.15 and modify it to place spanning headers beside the CUSTOMER_GENDER values. For Example 4.16, the "Product" and "Age Group" labels are moved from the DEFINE statement to the COLUMN statement as spanning headers. The spanning header text is placed immediately beside the variable name within parentheses. The result is that the "Product" and "Age Group" labels are moved up one level and will be beside the ACROSS variable values of F and M, shown in Output 4.12.

Example 4.16: Place Spanning Headers Beside ACROSS Values

```
options missing='0';
proc report data=orders;
   column ("Product" product_line) ❶
          ("Age Group" customer_age_group) ❷
          customer_gender,(quantity total_retail_price);
   define product_line / group ""; ❸
   define customer_age_group / group ""; ❹
   define customer_gender / across "Gender"; ❺
run;
```

❶   "Product" is specified as a spanning header over the PRODUCT_LINE variable.

❷   "Age Group" is specified as a spanning header over the CUSTOMER_AGE_GROUP variable.

❸   The variable label for PRODUCT_LINE is set to blank. Because variable labels are still present for QUANTITY and TOTAL_RETAIL_PRICE, the bottom row of labels will not be removed completely. Instead, just the *report-item* label will be removed.

❹   The variable label for CUSTOMER_AGE_GROUP is set to blank. Because variable labels are still present for QUANTITY and TOTAL_RETAIL_PRICE, the bottom row of labels will not be removed completely. Instead, just the text will be removed. Also, since the label is removed for two consecutive columns a merged cell is created.

❺   The ACROSS usage is specified along with a label.

Output 4.12: Spanning Headers Appear Next to ACROSS Values

Product	Age Group	Gender			
		F		M	
		Quantity Ordered	Total Retail Price for This Product	Quantity Ordered	Total Retail Price for This Product
Children	15-30 years	17	$544.00	6	$198.60
	31-45 years	7	$140.50	11	$473.00
	46-60 years	3	$37.80	4	$172.10
	61-75 years	0	0	1	$50.40
Clothes & Shoes	15-30 years	52	$2,496.90	4	$425.40
	31-45 years	43	$2,256.80	69	$3,484.19
	46-60 years	22	$2,046.00	35	$2,299.20
	61-75 years	15	$1,003.20	35	$2,733.00
Outdoors	15-30 years	37	$4,200.70	16	$2,022.00
	31-45 years	31	$5,602.50	66	$6,115.20
	46-60 years	10	$671.80	15	$1,359.60
	61-75 years	4	$456.60	61	$9,433.60
Sports	15-30 years	129	$17,763.91	43	$2,834.99
	31-45 years	76	$8,360.20	94	$7,765.11
	46-60 years	26	$2,610.20	60	$5,723.85
	61-75 years	26	$1,556.32	60	$5,239.80

4.3.3 Place Spanning Headers beside ACROSS Label

As you can see from Output 4.12 there is room for the "Product" and "Age Group" labels to be moved up one more level in the header section. The technique from Section 4.3.2 is used to move them up again. In this section, the key is adding another spanning header at the appropriate place on the COLUMN statement. Example 4.17 demonstrates the technique of adding blank spanning headers in order to move other text up a level in the header section. Output 4.13 shows the final result.

Example 4.17: Place Spanning Headers Beside ACROSS Label

```
options missing='0';
proc report data=orders;
    column ("Product" "" product_line) ❶
           ("Age Group" "" customer_age_group) ❷
           customer_gender,(quantity total_retail_price);
    define product_line / group ""; ❸
    define customer_age_group / group ""; ❹
    define customer_gender / across "Gender";
run;
```

❶ "Product" is specified as a spanning header over the PRODUCT_LINE variable. A second, blank spanning header is placed to its right, positioned right next to the variable name.

❷ "Age Group" is specified as a spanning header over the CUSTOMER_AGE_GROUP variable. A second, blank spanning header is placed to its right, positioned right next to the variable name.

❸ The DEFINE statement for PRODUCT_LINE removes the label.

❹ The DEFINE statement for CUSTOMER_AGE_GROUP does not change. Since label is removed for two consecutive columns, another merged cell is created.

Output 4.13: Spanning Header Appear Next to ACROSS Label

Product	Age Group	Gender			
		F		M	
		Quantity Ordered	Total Retail Price for This Product	Quantity Ordered	Total Retail Price for This Product
Children	15-30 years	17	$544.00	6	$198.60
	31-45 years	7	$140.50	11	$473.00
	46-60 years	3	$37.80	4	$172.10
	61-75 years	0	0	1	$50.40
Clothes & Shoes	15-30 years	52	$2,496.90	4	$425.40
	31-45 years	43	$2,256.80	69	$3,484.19
	46-60 years	22	$2,046.00	35	$2,299.20
	61-75 years	15	$1,003.20	35	$2,733.00
Outdoors	15-30 years	37	$4,200.70	16	$2,022.00
	31-45 years	31	$5,602.50	66	$6,115.20
	46-60 years	10	$671.80	15	$1,359.60
	61-75 years	4	$456.60	61	$9,433.60
Sports	15-30 years	129	$17,763.91	43	$2,834.99
	31-45 years	76	$8,360.20	94	$7,765.11
	46-60 years	26	$2,610.20	60	$5,723.85
	61-75 years	26	$1,556.32	60	$5,239.80

4.3.4 Place Multiple Spanning Headers beside ACROSS Header Rows

You do not always have to have a merged blank cell beside the labels of the variables under the ACROSS or beside the values of the ACROSS. As seen in Example 4.17, those cells are actually spanning headers, so you can place text in them. Example 4.18 inserts text into the second spanning header over the PRODUCT_LINE variable, shown in Output 4.14.

Example 4.18: Place Multiple Spanning Headers in Header Section

```
options missing='0';
proc report data=orders;
   column ("Product" "Category" product_line) ❶
          ("Age Group" "" customer_age_group) ❷
          customer_gender,(quantity total_retail_price);
```

```
        define product_line / group "";
        define customer_age_group / group "";
        define customer_gender / across "Gender";
   run;
```

❶   "Product" is specified as a spanning header over the PRODUCT_LINE variable. A second spanning header, "Category," is also placed over PRODUCT_LINE.

❷   "Age Group" is specified as a spanning header over the CUSTOMER_AGE_GROUP variable. A second, blank spanning header is placed to its right, positioned right next to the variable name.

Output 4.14: Spanning Headers Appear Next to ACROSS Values and Label

Product	Age Group	Gender			
Category		F		M	
		Quantity Ordered	Total Retail Price for This Product	Quantity Ordered	Total Retail Price for This Product
Children	15-30 years	17	$544.00	6	$198.60
	31-45 years	7	$140.50	11	$473.00
	46-60 years	3	$37.80	4	$172.10
	61-75 years	0	0	1	$50.40
Clothes & Shoes	15-30 years	52	$2,496.90	4	$425.40
	31-45 years	43	$2,256.80	69	$3,484.19
	46-60 years	22	$2,046.00	35	$2,299.20
	61-75 years	15	$1,003.20	35	$2,733.00
Outdoors	15-30 years	37	$4,200.70	16	$2,022.00
	31-45 years	31	$5,602.50	66	$6,115.20
	46-60 years	10	$671.80	15	$1,359.60
	61-75 years	4	$456.60	61	$9,433.60
Sports	15-30 years	129	$17,763.91	43	$2,834.99
	31-45 years	76	$8,360.20	94	$7,765.11
	46-60 years	26	$2,610.20	60	$5,723.85
	61-75 years	26	$1,556.32	60	$5,239.80

In Output 4.13, the second level down in the header section had a merged cell two columns wide. In Output 4.14, that cell is divided into two cells. The first cell contains the new spanning header, "Category," for the PRODUCT_LINE variable. The second cell is blank because the text immediately beside CUSTOMER_AGE_GROUP in the COLUMN statement is blank.

4.3.5 Remove ACROSS Label Row

You might be unhappy with the number of rows in the header section created by default. You might want just two rows, which means you have to change "F" and "M" to be more informative, so you can remove the "Gender" label. Example 4.19 removes the ACROSS variable label via the DEFINE statement. Output 4.15 has only two header rows.

Example 4.19: Remove the ACROSS Label Row

```
proc format; ❶
   value $gen
   'F' = 'Female'
   'M' = 'Male';
run;

options missing='0';
proc report data=orders;
   column ("Product" product_line) ❷
         ("Age Group" customer_age_group) ❸
         customer_gender,(quantity total_retail_price);
   define product_line / group ""; ❹
   define customer_age_group / group ""; ❺
   define customer_gender / across '' format=$gen.; ❻
run;
```

❶ Create a format for the CUSTOMER_GENDER values.

❷ "Product" is placed immediately beside PRODUCT_LINE as a spanning header.

❸ "Age Group" is placed immediately beside CUSTOMER_AGE_GROUP as a spanning header.

❹ The variable label for PRODUCT_LINE is set to blank. Because variable labels are still present for QUANTITY and TOTAL_RETAIL_PRICE, the bottom row of labels will not be removed completely. Instead, just the label will be removed.

❺ The variable label for CUSTOMER_AGE_GROUP is set to blank. Because variable labels are still present for QUANTITY and TOTAL_RETAIL_PRICE, the bottom row of labels will not be removed completely. Instead, just the label will be removed. Also, since the text is removed for two consecutive columns a merged cell is created.

❻ The variable label for CUSTOMER_GENDER is set to blank. No labels exist at the top row of the header section, so the row is removed, resulting in just two header rows. The newly created format is applied to the values of CUSTOMER_GENDER, so they are more informative.

Output 4.15: Header Row Containing ACROSS Label Is Removed

Product	Age Group	Female		Male	
		Quantity Ordered	Total Retail Price for This Product	Quantity Ordered	Total Retail Price for This Product
Children	15-30 years	17	$544.00	6	$198.60
	31-45 years	7	$140.50	11	$473.00
	46-60 years	3	$37.80	4	$172.10
	61-75 years	0	0	1	$50.40
Clothes & Shoes	15-30 years	52	$2,496.90	4	$425.40
	31-45 years	43	$2,256.80	69	$3,484.19
	46-60 years	22	$2,046.00	35	$2,299.20
	61-75 years	15	$1,003.20	35	$2,733.00
Outdoors	15-30 years	37	$4,200.70	16	$2,022.00
	31-45 years	31	$5,602.50	66	$6,115.20
	46-60 years	10	$671.80	15	$1,359.60
	61-75 years	4	$456.60	61	$9,433.60
Sports	15-30 years	129	$17,763.91	43	$2,834.99
	31-45 years	76	$8,360.20	94	$7,765.11
	46-60 years	26	$2,610.20	60	$5,723.85
	61-75 years	26	$1,556.32	60	$5,239.80

4.3.6 Counts As Part of ACROSS Values

PROC REPORT creates the header text based on the values of the ACROSS variable. The text of those headers cannot be changed inside of PROC REPORT. For some reports, you might want the header text to be more dynamic, like including the overall count for that category as part of the text of the value.

The header text can be changed in one of three ways:

1. Change the value of the ACROSS variable in the data set.
2. Create a format for the ACROSS variable with the label containing the (n=xx) text.
3. Change the structure of your data so that each value of the current ACROSS variable is its own variable, in other words transpose the data. Then, in the DEFINE statements, assign a label that includes (n=XX).

Of these choices, the second one, creating a format, is probably the easiest and most dynamic. Each time the program is executed, the counts can be determined and the format re-created.

PROC MEANS/SUMMARY or PROC SQL are capable of creating a data set with the values and counts and prevent the need for hardcoding. Example 4.20 uses PROC MEANS to create the counts for the header text. The counts are part of the header in Output 4.16.

Example 4.20: Put Category Totals in Header Text

```
proc means data=orders nway noprint; ❶
   class customer_gender;
   output out=cnts n=count;
run;

data fmt; ❷
   set cnts;
   length label $50;
   start = customer_gender;
   label = catt(customer_gender," (n=", count,")");
   type = "C";
   fmtname = 'gencnt';
   keep start label type fmtname;
run;

proc format cntlin=fmt; ❸
run;

proc report data=orders;
   column customer_age_group customer_gender,quantity;
   define customer_age_group / group;
   define customer_gender / across format=$gencnt.; ❹
run;
```

❶ Create a data set containing unique values of CUSTOMER_GENDER and the count of each of those values. CUSTOMER_GENDER will be the ACROSS variable in the subsequent PROC REPORT step.

❷ Create a data set that contains the necessary variables for a format. Concatenate the CUSTOMER_GENDER and COUNT values into the LABEL variable.

❸ Use the CNTLIN= option on the PROC FORMAT statement to reference the data set with the format information.

❹ Specify the format name on the DEFINE statement for the ACROSS variable CUSTOMER_GENDER.

Output 4.16: Gender Total Counts Are Part of the ACROSS Values

	Customer Gender	
	F (n=277)	M (n=340)
Customer Age Group	Quantity Ordered	Quantity Ordered
15-30 years	235	69
31-45 years	157	240
46-60 years	61	114
61-75 years	45	157

4.4 Nonstandard Reports

The examples in this section are for commonly required reports, but ones that are not as easily created by PROC REPORT as the ones previously discussed in this chapter. ACROSS variable values often must appear in a custom order, and sometimes additional values must be added. This section discusses those circumstances as well as nesting ACROSS variables and hiding columns.

4.4.1 Customized Sort Order

Creating a custom sort order with an ACROSS variable works just like it did in the previous chapter for GROUP variables. You have to create a format with PROC FORMAT and specify the NOTSORTED option. The values in the PROC FORMAT step need to be placed in the order in which you want them to appear from left to right in the final report.

Example 4.21 demonstrates customizing the ACROSS variable sort order. After the format is created, add the ORDER=DATA, FORMAT=, and PRELOADFMT options to the DEFINE statement in PROC REPORT for the ACROSS variable. ORDER_TYPE appears in the customized order in Output 4.17.

Example 4.21: Customize the Order of the ORDER_TYPE Values
```
proc format;
value typefOrd (notsorted) ❶
   3='Internet Sale'❷
   1='Retail Sale'
   2='Catalog Sale';
run;

proc report data=orders;
   column order_type,(quantity total_retail_price);
   define order_type / across format=typefOrd. order=data
          preloadfmt; ❸
   define total_retail_price / 'Retail Price';
run;
```

❶ A format is created with the NOTSORTED option.

❷ The values of ORDER_TYPE are listed in the order in which they should appear in the report from left to right.

❸ The format is specified for ORDER_TYPE. The DEFINE statement must also have the options ORDER=DATA and PRELOADFMT.

Output 4.17: ORDER_TYPE Values Appear in Customized Order

Order Type					
Internet Sale		Retail Sale		Catalog Sale	
Quantity Ordered	Retail Price	Quantity Ordered	Retail Price	Quantity Ordered	Retail Price
226	$21,491.55	559	$44,654.56	293	$33,931.35

4.4.2 Creating Subtotal Columns

Variables with all manner of values can be used as ACROSS, with the values dictating the columns. In some circumstances, subtotals are needed. Think of a report that uses a date variable as ACROSS; you might want to see a subtotal for given date ranges. You have seen that you can create new *report-item*s under an ACROSS, but this is different. This isn't putting another value *under* the ACROSS; it is putting another column *within* the ACROSS.

The ORDERS data set has a delivery date variable, which can be used in a report to show the quantity delivered each day. You would like to see totals for the first half of the week and ones for the second half. In order to have a subtotal column, you need another value of the ACROSS variable. In other words, you need another date, but how do you assign "half week 1" and "half week 2"? You use PROC FORMAT.

PROC FORMAT will let you add categories to your ACROSS variable. Example 4.22 is very similar to Example 4.21 because it creates a format with PROC FORMAT and uses the PRELOADFMT and ORDER=DATA options in PROC REPORT. The format created in Example 4.22 adds the additional categories needed for the subtotal columns, shown in Output 4.18.

Example 4.22: Use a Format to Include Subtotal Columns under ACROSS

```
data orders2;
   set orders;
   ddate = weekday(delivery_date); ❶
run;

proc format; ❷
   value wkdy
   1='Sunday'
   2='Monday'
   3='Tuesday'
   4='Wednesday'
   4.5='Subtotal 1'
   5='Thursday'
   6='Friday'
```

```
        7='Saturday'
        8='Subtotal 2';
run;

options missing='0';
proc report data=orders2 nowd;
    column customer_country ddate,quantity;
    define customer_country / group;
    define ddate /across format=wkdy. preloadfmt order=data '';  ❸

    compute quantity;  ❹
        _c6_  = sum( _c2_, _c3_, _c4_, _c5_ );  ❺
        _c10_ = sum( _c7_, _c8_, _c9_ );
    endcomp;
run;
```

❶ A new variable is created in a DATA step. The DDATE variable is a numeric and contains the weekday value.

❷ A format is created containing the weekday values plus two additional values. These values, 4.5 and 8, will create two new columns in the output.

❸ The DEFINE statement for the ACROSS variable contains the FORMAT=, PRELOADFMT, and ORDER=DATA options.

❹ The compute block for QUANTITY is executed on every row of the report.

❺ An assignment statement is needed for the new columns. The value of the column is the sum of the previous columns. Notice assignment statements are not needed for the other weekdays because the values already exist in the data.

Output 4.18: Columns with Subtotals Are Included

	Sunday	Monday	Tuesday	Wednesday	Subtotal 1	Thursday	Friday	Saturday	Subtotal 2
Customer Country	Quantity Ordered	Quantity Ordered	Quantity Ordered	Quantity Ordered	Quantity Ordered	Quantity Ordered	Quantity Ordered	Quantity Ordered	Quantity Ordered
AU	37	31	30	37	135	27	26	22	75
CA	17	11	18	20	66	19	13	7	39
DE	6	10	17	18	51	27	18	10	55
IL	8	1	0	10	19	5	2	2	9
TR	3	6	5	4	18	15	6	4	25
US	61	66	65	105	297	82	85	75	242
ZA	6	7	9	4	26	6	15	0	21

Instead of creating a half day, 4.5, and a day that doesn't exist, 8, and having to do the calculations, you can take advantage of the multilabel formats because the MLF option is valid for ACROSS variables. Example 4.23 creates and uses a multilabel format to create additional categories for the subtotal columns.

Example 4.23: Use a Multilabel Format to Include Subtotal Columns

```
proc format;
    value wkdy (multilabel notsorted)  ❶
    1='Sunday'
    2='Monday'
```

```
            3='Tuesday'
            4='Wednesday'
            1-4='Subtotal 1'
            5='Thursday'
            6='Friday'
            7='Saturday'
            5-7='Subtotal 2';
    run;

    options missing='0';
    proc report data=orders2;
       column customer_country ddate,quantity;
       define customer_country / group;
       define ddate /across format=wkdy. mlf preloadfmt order=data '';  ❷
    run;
```

❶ When creating the format include the MULTILABEL and NOTSORTED options.

❷ Include the MLF option on the DEFINE statement for the ACROSS to take full advantage of the format.

The output is the same as Output 4.18.

4.4.3 Nesting ACROSS Variables

PROC REPORT does not have a limitation on the number of variables that can be used as an ACROSS or the number of categories of that variable. Nor does it restrict the number of *report-items* stacked underneath the ACROSS. The restricting factor is usually the data or the point at which the report becomes unreadable.

The previous examples used variables that had two to four distinct categories. This made the code easier to understand and the output fit on a page. However, reports that are sent to HTML or Excel do not have page restrictions and ODS attributes can be used to freeze column to make scrolling easier. For these destinations, it is easier to rationalize using a variable that has more categories, using more *report-items* underneath, or nesting ACROSS variables.

Example 4.24 explores using more than one ACROSS variable. The syntax for using multiple variables as ACROSS is straightforward. The two important steps are adding a comma to the COLUMN statement and specifying ACROSS on the DEFINE statement. Output 4.19 displays the results of using two ACROSS variables.

Example 4.24: Nest One ACROSS Variable under Another ACROSS Variable

```
    proc report data=orders;
       column product_line, order_type,(quantity total_retail_price);  ❶
       define product_line / across;  ❷
       define order_type / across format=ordfmt. order=internal;  ❸
       define total_retail_price / 'Retail Price';
    run;
```

❶ The COLUMN statement contains two commas. PRODUCT_LINE is listed first, so it will create the first layer. ORDER_TYPE is also followed by a comma; it will become the second layer.

❷ PRODUCT_LINE is defined as ACROSS.

❸ ORDER_TYPE is defined as ACROSS. The ORDER= option is set to INTERNAL, so the output is in numeric order and not formatted order.

Output 4.19: ORDER_TYPE is Nested Under PRODUCT_LINE

Product Line																							
Children						Clothes & Shoes						Outdoors						Sports					
Order Type						Order Type						Order Type						Order Type					
Retail Sale		Catalog Sale		Internet Sale		Retail Sale		Catalog Sale		Internet Sale		Retail Sale		Catalog Sale		Internet Sale		Retail Sale		Catalog Sale		Internet Sale	
Quantity Ordered	Retail Price	Quantity Ordered	Retail Price	Quantity Ordered	Retail Price	Quantity Ordered	Retail Price	Quantity Ordered	Retail Price	Quantity Ordered	Retail Price	Quantity Ordered	Retail Price	Quantity Ordered	Retail Price	Quantity Ordered	Retail Price	Quantity Ordered	Retail Price	Quantity Ordered	Retail Price	Quantity Ordered	Retail Price
41	$1,400.60	2	$120.20	6	$95.60	180	$10,238.29	64	$4,582.70	31	$1,925.70	99	$8,715.10	100	$14,203.70	38	$5,913.20	306	$23,300.58	124	$14,994.75	151	$13,556.05

Note: This picture is noticeably small. One of the purposes of this picture is to demonstrate that multiple ACROSS variables make tables really wide, which is difficult to legibly fit onto a print page.

Output 4.19 contains a lot of header rows. As mentioned earlier, the report does not have to contain all of those rows. You can remove the labels for PRODUCT_LINE and ORDER_TYPE, which will remove two layers of header rows, as shown in Example 4.25 and Output 4.20.

Example 4.25: Remove Header Rows

```
proc report data=orders;
    column product_line, order_type,(quantity total_retail_price); ❶
    define product_line / across ' '; ❷
    define order_type / across format=ordfmt. order=internal ' '; ❸
    define total_retail_price / 'Retail Price';
run;
```

❶ The COLUMN statement is exactly the same as in the previous example.

❷ The label for PRODUCT_LINE is set to blank. Setting the label to blank removes the header row with that label.

❸ The label for ORDER_TYPE is set to blank. Setting the label to blank removes the header row with that label.

Output 4.20: Header Rows Contain Only the Values of Both ACROSS Variables

Children						Clothes & Shoes					
Retail Sale		Catalog Sale		Internet Sale		Retail Sale		Catalog Sale		Internet Sale	
Quantity Ordered	Retail Price	Quantity Ordered	Retail Price	Quantity Ordered	Retail Price	Quantity Ordered	Retail Price	Quantity Ordered	Retail Price	Quantity Ordered	Retail Price
41	$1,400.60	2	$120.20	6	$95.60	180	$10,238.29	64	$4,582.70	31	$1,923.70

Outdoors						Sports					
Retail Sale		Catalog Sale		Internet Sale		Retail Sale		Catalog Sale		Internet Sale	
Quantity Ordered	Retail Price	Quantity Ordered	Retail Price	Quantity Ordered	Retail Price	Quantity Ordered	Retail Price	Quantity Ordered	Retail Price	Quantity Ordered	Retail Price
99	$9,715.10	103	$14,233.70	38	$5,913.20	239	$23,300.58	124	$14,994.75	151	$13,559.05

Note: Output 4.20 was split into two sections in order to make the font large enough to read. In a browser or a document with orientation set to landscape this would be one continuous wide table.

You know PROC REPORT will let you use a variable twice by creating an alias. The only restriction is that both versions of the variable have to have the same kind of usage. This means that one variable can be nested under itself.

Obviously, using an exact duplicate does not make any sense, as it will just add an unneeded header layer. Instead, you need to make a small tweak, such as changing the format. The first occurrence of the variable can have one format, and the second occurrence can have another format.

The ORDERS data set has a date variable called ORDER_DATE. This variable is perfect for demonstrating how a variable can be nested under itself. A date variable can be formatted to display year, month, day, quarter, week, or weekday. In the following example, ORDER_DATE will be formatted to display year. The second occurrence, the alias ORDDATE, will be formatted as quarter. The report will allow the reader to see whether the quantity purchased fluctuates over time. Example 4.26 uses the ORDER_DATE variable as an ACROSS twice. The results are shown in Output 4.21.

Example 4.26: Use One Variable as ACROSS Twice

```
proc report data=orders;
   column order_date, order_date=orddate,quantity; ❶
   define order_date / across format=year4. order=internal ''; ❷
   define orddate / across format=qtr. order=internal 'Quarter'; ❸
   define quantity / '';
run;
```

❶ ORDER_DATE is listed first with a comma beside it, it will be the first layer. ORDDATE is an alias for ORDER_DATE. It is also followed by a comma and will become the second layer.

❷ ORDER_DATE is defined as ACROSS. The format of YEAR4. creates a row with just the year values. ORDER=INTERNAL ensures that the columns are in chronological order. The label is set to missing, so the top row of the header section is removed.

❸ ORDDATE is defined as ACROSS. The format is QTR. which creates a row with just quarter values. ORDER=INTERNAL ensures that the columns are in chronological order.

Output 4.21: ORDER_DATE Creates All Header Rows

2003				2004				2005				2006				2007			
Quarter				Quarter				Quarter				Quarter				Quarter			
1	2	3	4	1	2	3	4	1	2	3	4	1	2	3	4	1	2	3	4
25	68	75	65	34	53	40	55	25	44	32	52	50	65	60	50	51	100	69	65

4.4.4 Hide a Column under an ACROSS

PROC REPORT will create a column for every variable under an ACROSS. It is not common, but it is possible to prevent one or more of the columns from being included in the final report. These circumstances are ones in which a WHERE statement is too broad. You do not want all of a category removed; just one of the instances of it.

Take as an example the previous code that used ORDER_DATE twice. Maybe a large storm occurred, or a critical system was under repair, or a part of the business was not up and running for part of the year. Therefore, you do not want a specific quarter to appear in the output because the numbers are too different from the norm and you do not want them used for comparison.

The NOZERO option will suppress the display of a column if all of its values are missing or zero. This option can be placed on a DEFINE statement. In a compute block, the problematic column is set to missing. When the report is rendered, the column will be removed. Example 4.27 removes one of the ORDER_DATE columns, shown in Output 4.22.

Example 4.27: Use the NOZERO Option to Hide a Column

```
proc report data=orders;
   column order_date, order_date=orddate,quantity;
   define order_date / across format=year4. order=internal ''
         nozero; ❶
   define orddate / across format=qtr. order=internal 'Quarter';
   define quantity / ' ';

   compute quantity;
      _c12_ = .; ❷
   endcomp;
run;
```

❶ Add the NOZERO option to a DEFINE statement. The option can be placed on either the DEFINE statement for the ACROSS variable or the ANALYSIS variable.

❷ Change the value of the problematic column to missing for all rows.

Output 4.22: One Column is Removed From the Table

2003				2004				2005			2006				2007			
Quarter				Quarter				Quarter			Quarter				Quarter			
1	2	3	4	1	2	3	4	1	2	3	1	2	3	4	1	2	3	4
25	68	75	65	34	53	40	55	25	44	32	50	65	60	50	51	100	69	65

In this output, column 12, the 4th quarter in 2005, was removed.

4.4.5 Vertical Page Breaks

ODS destinations attempt to keep columns together when they share a spanning header. The destination will break the table prior to two columns with a shared header instead of breaking between the columns. However, wide output created with an ACROSS variable might not break at a column that is most logical to you.

Chapter 3 demonstrated one method for handling vertical page breaks for really wide reports by placing the PAGE option on a DEFINE statement for a specific column. That example contains a very large number of individually named and created columns, but what do you do if the table is wide due to the number of values of the ACROSS variable? Placing the PAGE option on the DEFINE statement for the ACROSS variable or the *report-item* underneath it will not generate the desired output.

PROC REPORT does not have an option or straightforward mechanism for inserting a break between values of an ACROSS variable. The only recourse a programmer has is to control the width of the columns. A physical page has a finite width; you can control the width of your columns to match that width and force the ODS destination to trigger a new page at the column that you want it to.

Example 4.28 produces 19 columns and demonstrates the default behavior in a paging destination. In PDF, the first three columns are on page 1 and the other 16 columns (the ones created by the ACROSS variable) are on page 2. Output 4.23a contains page 1 of the PDF file. Output 4.23b contains page 2 of the PDF file.

Example 4.28: Output Very Wide Report to ODS PDF

```
proc format;
   value $cntryAll
        'AU' = 'Australia'
        'CA' = 'Canada'
        'DE' = 'Germany'
        'IL' = 'Israel'
        'MX' = 'Mexico'
        'TR' = 'Turkey'
        'US' = 'United States'
        'ZA' = 'South Africa'
        ;
   run;
```

```
options orientation=landscape leftmargin=.25in rightmargin=.25in
missing='0';
proc report data=orders;
    column product_line customer_age_group order_type customer_country,
        customer_gender,quantity;
    define product_line / group;
    define order_Type / group format=typef.;
    define customer_age_group / group;
    define customer_gender/ across;
    define customer_country / across format=$cntryALL. preloadfmt;
run;
```

Output 4.23a: Top of Page 1 in PDF File

Product Line	Customer Age Group	Order Type
Children	15-30 years	Internet Sale
		Retail Sale
	31-45 years	Catalog Sale
		Internet Sale
		Retail Sale
	46-60 years	Internet Sale
		Retail Sale
	61-75 years	Retail Sale

Output 4.23b: Top of Page 2 in PDF File

Customer Country															
Australia		Canada		Germany		Israel		Mexico		South Africa		Turkey		United States	
Customer Gender		Customer Gender		Customer Gender		Customer Gender		Customer Gender		Customer Gender		Customer Gender		Customer Gender	
F	M	F	M	F	M	F	M	F	M	F	M	F	M	F	M
Quantity Ordered	Quantity Ordered	Quantity Ordered	Quantity Ordered	Quantity Ordered	Quantity Ordered	Quantity Ordered	Quantity Ordered	Quantity Ordered	Quantity Ordered	Quantity Ordered	Quantity Ordered	Quantity Ordered	Quantity Ordered	Quantity Ordered	Quantity Ordered
0	0	0	0	0	0	0	0	0	0	0	0	0	0	2	0
0	0	0	0	0	0	0	0	0	0	0	0	0	0	15	6
0	2	0	0	0	0	0	0	0	0	0	0	0	0	0	0
0	1	0	0	0	0	0	0	0	0	0	0	0	0	0	0
0	4	0	0	0	0	0	0	0	0	0	0	0	0	7	4
3	0	0	0	0	0	0	0	0	0	0	0	0	0	0	0
0	3	0	0	0	0	0	0	0	0	0	0	0	0	0	1
0	0	0	0	0	0	0	0	0	0	0	0	0	0	0	1

The output is not appealing at all. At the very least, you would like to see some of the country columns on the first page. The ugly output is created when the destination chooses the column width and tries to be smart about keeping certain columns together. You can apply a width value to the QUANTITY column to force it to be one inch wide. This overwrites the default behavior and allows more columns to fit on the first page. Example 4.29 demonstrates this technique. Output 4.24a contains page 1 of the PDF file. Output 4.24b contains page 2 of the PDF file.

Example 4.29: Use CELLWIDTH to Control Vertical Page Break

```
options orientation=landscape leftmargin=.25in rightmargin=.25in
missing='0';
proc report data=orders;
   column product_line customer_age_group order_type customer_country,
          customer_gender,quantity;
   define product_line / group;
   define order_Type / group format=typef. id;
   define customer_age_group / group;
   define customer_gender/ across;
   define customer_country / across format=$cntryALL. preloadfmt;
   define quantity / style(column)=[width=1in];
run;
```

Output 4.24a: Top of Page 1 of PDF File Created Using CELLWIDTH

			Customer Country								
			Australia		Canada		Germany		Israel	
			Customer Gender		Customer Gender		Customer Gender		Customer Gender	
			F	M	F	M	F	M	F	M
Product Line	Customer Age Group	Order Type	Quantity Ordered	Quantity Ordered	Quantity Ordered	Quantity Ordered	Quantity Ordered	Quantity Ordered	Quantity Ordered	Quantity Ordered
Children	15-30 years	Internet Sale	0	0	0	0	0	0	0	0
		Retail Sale	0	0	0	0	0	0	0	0
	31-45 years	Catalog Sale	0	2	0	0	0	0	0	0
		Internet Sale	0	1	0	0	0	0	0	0
		Retail Sale	0	4	0	0	0	0	0	0
	46-60 years	Internet Sale	3	0	0	0	0	0	0	0
		Retail Sale	0	3	0	0	0	0	0	0
	61-75 years	Retail Sale	0	0	0	0	0	0	0	0

Output 4.24b: Top of Page 2 of PDF File Created Using CELLWIDTH

			Customer Country								
			Mexico		South Africa		Turkey		United States	
			Customer Gender		Customer Gender		Customer Gender		Customer Gender	
			F	M	F	M	F	M	F	M
Product Line	Customer Age Group	Order Type	Quantity Ordered	Quantity Ordered	Quantity Ordered	Quantity Ordered	Quantity Ordered	Quantity Ordered	Quantity Ordered	Quantity Ordered
Children	15-30 years	Internet Sale	0	0	0	0	0	0	2	0
		Retail Sale	0	0	0	0	0	0	15	6
	31-45 years	Catalog Sale	0	0	0	0	0	0	0	0
		Internet Sale	0	0	0	0	0	0	0	0
		Retail Sale	0	0	0	0	0	0	7	4
	46-60 years	Internet Sale	0	0	0	0	0	0	0	0
		Retail Sale	0	0	0	0	0	0	0	1
	61-75 years	Retail Sale	0	0	0	0	0	0	0	1

The table is now much wider than would fit on a single page. Therefore, ODS PDF no longer divides the output between the first three columns and the rest. The destination will fit as many columns on page 1 as possible and then put the rest of the columns on page 2, 3, and so on. The ID option on the DEFINE statement for ORDER_TYPE ensures the columns containing the GROUP variables will appear on every page.

Depending on your data, you might need to use the PAGE option on the BREAK statement as well in order to insert horizontal page breaks.

Note: If you have a very wide but very short table, the ODS destination might wrap the second half of the table onto the same physical page. There is not an option to force the ODS destination to place the second half of the table onto a new physical page. To force this behavior you must create a second *table,* which the destination will place on a new page. You can do this by running one PROC REPORT step with a WHERE statement that subsets the values of the ACROSS variable. Then run a second PROC REPORT step with a WHERE statement that subsets to the rest of the values of the ACROSS variable.

4.4.6 Use Macro to Create Column References

The previous examples in this chapter were purposefully short in order to simplify the explanations and fit on a page. But in real life, you might have many more categories of an ACROSS or many more variables under the ACROSS. In these situations, entering all of the column references is both cumbersome and error prone. You do not have to enter all of the code; you can let macro program code do it for you.

Let's revisit Example 4.9, the code for creating a new *report-item.*

Example 4.9: Create a New *Report-item* Called ESTPRICE_PER_ITEM

```
proc report data=orders;
   column customer_age_group, (quantity total_retail_price
          estprice_per_item);
   define customer_age_group / across;
   define estprice_per_item / computed 'Est. Item Price'
      format=dollar8.2;

   compute estprice_per_item;
      _c3_  = _c2_  / _c1_;
      _c6_  = _c5_  / _c4_;
      _c9_  = _c8_  / _c7_;
      _c12_ = _c11_ / _c10_;
   endcomp;
run;
```

The number of ACROSS variable values (categories) dictates how many assignment statements are needed. In the above code, CUSTOMER_AGE_GROUP has four values, so four assignment statements are needed.

The absolute column numbers, representing ESTPRICE_PER_ITEM on the left side of the assignment statements, increment by three. This is because three columns appear under each value of the ACROSS.

This code does not contain any *report-item*s on the COLUMN statement before the ACROSS, so the first column number referenced is 1.

The statements follow a pattern. PROC REPORT allows the use of DO loops inside of a compute block, which you can use if you know the number of columns. A normal DATA step DO loop requires you to hardcode the column reference. It is not capable of building the variable name _cn_. However, a %DO loop is capable of building the correct variable names. Macro program code is perfect for situations that require the same code to be repeated multiple times and that have a pattern.

To create the correct macro variable references, you need to know three things.

1. The number of unique values of the ACROSS variable.
2. The number of *report-item*s under the ACROSS variable.
3. The number of *report-item*s to the left of the ACROSS variable.

If you were to write out the logic of the %DO loop, it would be: Start at the left-most column under the ACROSS, which is the number of columns to the left of the ACROSS plus one. Go to the last column under the ACROSS, which is determined by multiplying the number of unique values of the ACROSS by the number of *report-item*s under the ACROSS and adding the number of columns to the left of the ACROSS.

```
%do i=%eval(&numleft+1) %to %eval(&numcat*&numunder+&numleft) %by
&numunder;
    ...assignment statements...
%end;
```

Example 4.30 contains the entire example code converted into a macro program, and Output 4.25 shows the results.

Example 4.30: Use a Macro Program to Create a New *Report-item* Called ESTPRICE_PER_ITEM

```
%let numcat = 4;
%let numleft = 0;
%let numunder = 3;
%macro rep;
%local i;
proc report data=orders;
   column customer_age_group, (quantity total_retail_price
          estprice_per_item);
   define customer_age_group / across;
   define estprice_per_item / computed 'Est. Item Price'
          format=dollar8.2;
```

```
      compute estprice_per_item;
        %do i=%eval(&numleft+1) %to %eval(&numcat*&numunder+&numleft) %by
          &numunder;
          _c%eval(&i+2)_ = _c%eval(&i+1)_ / _c%eval(&i)_;
        %end;
      endcomp;
   run;
   %mend rep;
   %rep
```

Output 4.25: Est. Item Price is a New *Report-item* under the ACROSS Created with a Macro Program

| Customer Age Group | | | | | | | | | | | |
| 15-30 years | | | 31-45 years | | | 46-60 years | | | 61-75 years | | |
Quantity Ordered	Total Retail Price for This Product	Est. Item Price	Quantity Ordered	Total Retail Price for This Product	Est. Item Price	Quantity Ordered	Total Retail Price for This Product	Est. Item Price	Quantity Ordered	Total Retail Price for This Product	Est. Item Price
304	$30,486.50	$100.28	397	$34,197.50	$86.14	175	$14,920.55	$85.26	202	$20,472.92	$101.35

The macro variable references can be used in CALL DEFINE statements as well; you just need to make sure you use double quotation marks around the macro variable.

Chapter 5: Examples – How to Determine When to Pre-Process the Data

5.1 Introduction

Chapters 3 and 4 demonstrated a number of techniques for generating the desired report. For example, you can add dummy variables to your data set to leverage the grouping power of PROC REPORT or include categories in a PROC FORMAT step to ensure that they appear in the report. However, there are just some things it cannot do without the data being pre-processed or restructured. The goal of this chapter is to provide a sampling of the types of reports that require extra work prior to PROC REPORT. For each of these reports, the chapter demonstrates a method that you could use to pre-process your data.

PROC REPORT will not sort a report by an ANALYSIS or COMPUTED *report-item*. You must have the final statistics in a data set used by PROC REPORT for your report to be sorted. This chapter shows how to generate such a report.

The COMPLETEROWS option is covered in Chapter 3. It is a very useful option, but for some reports, it might not create the desired report structure. Multiple sections in this chapter provide methods for generating the desired report in circumstances where COMPLETEROWS cannot or should not be used.

Variables and their labels hold large amounts of information, but PROC REPORT will only allow one usage type. This chapter explains how you can restructure your data to use all pieces of information stored with a variable. Data restructuring is the only way to use a variable's information in both the header and data sections of a report.

ODS destinations and PROC REPORT will wrap or split variable text as best as they can. However, only you know what works best for your data and the reader of a report. You must alter your data values to take full control of when and how a variable's value wraps.

Finally, this chapter discusses report structures that are the most difficult to produce with PROC REPORT. The best thing to do is calculate the values for these types of reports with other procedures. Then use PROC REPORT to output the values in the structure of the data set.

PROC MEANS is used extensively throughout this chapter, but you do not have to use PROC MEANS. You can use any procedure or DATA step technique that you are most comfortable with and gets the job done.

5.2 Sort by Statistic

PROC REPORT cannot sort by an ANALYSIS variable or COMPUTED *report-item*. If you want to sort by a statistic, you have to calculate the statistic first. The statistic(s) can be calculated with the procedure of your choice. For example, PROC SQL, PROC TABULATE, PROC MEANS, and PROC REPORT can all create output data sets that contain summary statistics. Statistical procedures, like PROC LOGISTIC or PROC GLM, might also be used to generate output data sets with more a particular statistic like an odds ratio or a p-value.

You can then define the pre-calculated statistic variable as GROUP or ORDER, which PROC REPORT can sort by. Alternatively, you can create a variable to indicate the desired sort order and use that in the PROC REPORT step.

5.2.1 Grouped Report, No ACROSS Variable

This section demonstrates the steps needed to sort a grouped report by a statistic. These types of reports do not have an ACROSS variable. We have a report with CUSTOMER_COUNTRY, CUSTOMER_AGE_GROUP, and QUANTITY. Both CUSTOMER_COUNTRY have been defined as GROUP. The final report has the values of CALC_QUANTITY sorted in descending order within each country. Example 5.1a demonstrates calculating the needed statistics with PROC MEANS. Example 5.1b shows the PROC REPORT step that sorts the report by the descending value of CALC_QUANTITY. The results are shown in Output 5.1.

Example 5.1a: Pre-Calculate the Sum of QUANTITY within CUSTOMER_COUNTRY

```
proc means data=orders nway noprint; ❶
   class customer_country customer_age_group; ❷
   var quantity; ❸
   output out=order_sum sum=calc_quantity; ❹
run;
```

❶ This example uses PROC MEANS to pre-process the data. The NWAY option instructs PROC MEANS to keep only the most detailed level of the CLASS variable combinations. The NOPRINT option suppresses the printing of a table.

❷ Place the variables that you would define as GROUP in PROC REPORT on the CLASS statement.

❸ QUANTITY is the ANALYSIS variable for which the procedure will calculate a statistic.

❹ The OUTPUT statement sends the final statistics to a data set, ORDER_SUM. The keyword for the desired statistic, SUM=, is used. The summed value is placed in the variable called CALC_QUANTITY.

Example 5.1b: Sort Report by CALC_QUANTITY within CUSTOMER_COUNTRY

```
proc sort data=order_sum;
   by customer_country descending calc_quantity customer_age_group; ❶
run;

proc report data=order_sum; ❷
   column customer_country customer_age_group calc_quantity; ❸
   define customer_country / order format=$cntry.; ❹
run;
```

❶ Use PROC SORT to sort the ORDER_SUM data set by CUSTOMER_COUNTRY and the descending value of CALC_QUANTITY.

❷ Specify the new data set, ORDER_SUM, on the PROC REPORT statement.

❸ The COLUMN statement contains the original GROUP/CLASS variables, CUSTOMER_COUNTRY and CUSTOMER_AGE_GROUP. CALC_QUANTITY is the summed variable from PROC MEANS.

❹ CUSTOMER_COUNTRY is defined as ORDER, so its value does not repeat in the report. The usage of GROUP is an alternative but will result in a note in the log that groups cannot be created because CUSTOMER_AGE_GROUP is a DISPLAY variable.

Output 5.1: Report Sorted by Descending Quantity Ordered within Country

Customer Country	Customer Age Group	Quantity Ordered
Australia	31-45 years	104
	61-75 years	62
	46-60 years	44
Canada	15-30 years	44
	31-45 years	31
	46-60 years	18
	61-75 years	12
Germany	61-75 years	66
	31-45 years	32
	15-30 years	8
Israel	31-45 years	13
	46-60 years	13
	15-30 years	2
South Africa	15-30 years	36
	31-45 years	8
	46-60 years	3
Turkey	31-45 years	29
	15-30 years	11
	61-75 years	3
United States	15-30 years	203
	31-45 years	180
	46-60 years	97
	61-75 years	59

You might find that your report is more complicated than Example 5.1 and simply sorting the data set does not result in the desired PROC REPORT table. In that instance, you should take advantage of PROC REPORT's sorting ability by defining variables as GROUP or ORDER. For example, the CALC_QUANTITY variable can be defined as ORDER with the DESCENDING option to ensure the highest value is output first.

It is possible for the pre-calculated statistic variable to have the same value more than once. If the variable is defined as ORDER, it might result in the second value not being printed in the final report. Recall from Chapter 2 that when a numeric GROUP or ORDER variable is missing, there is not a way to insert a value, so you will need to create a COMPUTED *report-item* to ensure that the pre-calculated statistic is displayed on every row.

5.2.2 Grouped Reports with an ACROSS Variable

As seen in Chapter 4, using an ACROSS variable adds a layer of complexity to the report and to calculating values. Trying to sort by a statistic that is under an ACROSS is a very difficult task.

Before you begin, you must decide whether you want the report sorted by the overall total of the statistic, or you want each column under the ACROSS sorted independently.

Sort by the Statistic for All Values of ACROSS

In the previous example, CUSTOMER_COUNTRY and CUSTOMER_AGE_GROUP were specified as CLASS variables in the PROC MEANS step, so QUANTITY was summed for the combinations of the two variables. The report was sorted so that the value of CALC_QUANTITY dictated the order of the age group within the country. For Australia, the 31-45 year olds purchased the most, but for Canada, the 15-30 year olds purchased the most. If you include an ACROSS variable, like CUSTOMER_GENDER, do you still want the 31-45 year old row to be the first row for Australia?

First, we will look at how to sort the report like the one above, adding only the feature of gender as an ACROSS variable.

The process is very similar to the last section. However, two additional steps are needed. The first new step creates a variable indicating the highest value of CALC_QUANTITY within each country-age group pairing. The IND variable forces PROC REPORT to maintain the sorted order of CALC_QUANTITY within country. Without it, the rows would be sorted by the value of CUSTOMER_AGE_GROUP within country. The second step is to merge the indicator variable onto the original data set. These steps are demonstrated in Example 5.2a. Output 5.2 shows the resulting data set.

Example 5.2a: Pre-Calculate Sum and Create IND Variable to Maintain Order

```
proc means data=orders nway noprint;
   class customer_country customer_age_group; ❶
   var quantity;
   output out=order_sum sum=calc_quantity;
run;

proc sort data=order_sum;
   by customer_country descending calc_quantity; ❷
run;

data order_sum2;
   set order_sum;
   by customer_country; ❸

   retain ind 0; ❹
   if first.customer_country then ind=1; ❺
   else ind+1; ❻
   keep customer_country customer_age_group ind;
run;
```

❶   This step is exactly the same as it was in Example 5.1a. The value of QUANTITY is summed for each combination of country and age group. The variable that will be defined as ACROSS, gender, is not taken into account.

❷ ORDER_SUM is sorted by CUSTOMER_COUNTRY and the descending value of CALC_QUANTITY. CUSTOMER_AGE_GROUP is present but not used. Because the value of CALC_QUANTITY is of the most interest, it will dictate the order of the age group categories. You can add CUSTOMER_AGE_GROUP to the end of the BY statement if you are worried about ties so that age group is sorted alphabetically.

❸ The new DATA step includes a BY statement with just CUSTOMER_COUNTRY.

❹ Create a new variable called IND on the RETAIN statement so that its value is maintained. Specifying an initial value of zero ensures no missing values.

❺ If the observation in the data set is the first occurrence of CUSTOMER_COUNTRY, then set the IND variable to a value of one. The first observation for a country contains the highest value of QUANTITY.

The data set contains more than one instance of CUSTOMER_COUNTRY. It has up to four observations for each value of a given country. Remember that CUSTOMER_AGE_GROUP was also used in PROC MEANS and it has four unique values, which is why there are up to four observations per country. This DATA step ignores CUSTOMER_AGE_GROUP because its value is not needed to determine the sort order of the statistic. However, it is kept on the data set for merging purposes.

❻ For all other observations for a given country, increment the value of IND.

Output 5.2: ORDER_SUM2 Data Set

	Customer_Country	Customer_Age_Group	ind
1	AU	31-45 years	1
2	AU	61-75 years	2
3	AU	46-60 years	3
4	CA	15-30 years	1
5	CA	31-45 years	2
6	CA	46-60 years	3
7	CA	61-75 years	4
8	DE	61-75 years	1
9	DE	31-45 years	2
10	DE	15-30 years	3
11	IL	31-45 years	1
12	IL	46-60 years	2
13	IL	15-30 years	3
14	TR	31-45 years	1
15	TR	15-30 years	2
16	TR	61-75 years	3
17	US	15-30 years	1
18	US	31-45 years	2
19	US	46-60 years	3
20	US	61-75 years	4
21	ZA	15-30 years	1
22	ZA	31-45 years	2
23	ZA	46-60 years	3

After the IND variable is created, it needs to be merged onto the ORDERS data set, which contains all observations and most importantly the CUSTOMER_GENDER variable, which will become the ACROSS variable. Example 5.2b contains the merge step. Then, Example 5.2c uses the merged data set to generate the report. The report is grouped by the country value and then ordered by the IND variable for all of the values of the ACROSS variable (Output 5.3). PROC REPORT is calculating the sum of QUANTITY.

Example 5.2b: Merge IND Variable onto ORDERS Data Set

```
proc sort data=orders;
   by customer_country customer_age_group;
proc sort data=order_sum2;
   by customer_country customer_age_group;

data orders2;
   merge orders order_sum2;
   by customer_country customer_age_group;❶
run;
```

❶ CUSTOMER_AGE_GROUP is used in the PROC SORT step and on the BY statement with the MERGE statement in the DATA step. The value of IND is tied to CUSTOMER_AGE_GROUP. It has a value of one for the age group that should appear first within each country. To get IND on the correct observations in the data set, you must use CUSTOMER_AGE_GROUP on the BY statement.

Example 5.2c: Maintain Sort of QUANTITY within CUSTOMER_COUNTRY with ACROSS Variable

```
options missing='0';
proc report data=orders2; ❶
   column customer_country ind customer_age_group
          customer_gender,quantity; ❷
   define customer_country / group format=$cntry.;
   define ind / group order=internal noprint; ❸
   define customer_age_group / group;
   define customer_gender / across;
run;
```

❶ Use the data set ORDERS2, which contains the IND variable.

❷ The COLUMN statement starts with the outermost grouping variable CUSTOMER_COUNTRY. Then IND is listed because it dictates the order within each country. CUSTOMER_AGE_GROUP is then listed. The grouping variables are followed by the ACROSS, CUSTOMER_GENDER, and QUANTITY.

❸ IND is defined as GROUP with ORDER=INTERNAL, which forces the numeric value to be sorted in ascending sequence. The highest value of QUANTITY corresponds to IND=1, so it will appear on the first row for each country. NOPRINT prevents the column from appearing in the report.

Output 5.3: Report Sorted by Overall Descending Quantity within Country

		Customer Gender	
		F	M
Customer Country	Customer Age Group	Quantity Ordered	Quantity Ordered
Australia	31-45 years	35	69
	61-75 years	13	49
	46-60 years	20	24
Canada	15-30 years	27	17
	31-45 years	26	5
	46-60 years	11	7
	61-75 years	0	12
Germany	61-75 years	0	66
	31-45 years	21	11
	15-30 years	0	8
Israel	31-45 years	0	13
	46-60 years	0	13
	15-30 years	0	2
South Africa	15-30 years	36	0
	31-45 years	8	0
	46-60 years	0	3
Turkey	31-45 years	0	29
	15-30 years	0	11
	61-75 years	0	3
United States	15-30 years	172	31
	31-45 years	67	113
	46-60 years	30	67
	61-75 years	32	27

Sort by the Statistic within Each Value of ACROSS

As mentioned above, there is more than one way to sort a report that has grouping variables and an ACROSS variable. Instead of CUSTOMER_AGE_GROUP being in its own column, it could be placed under each gender value. The sum for QUANTITY for each value of age group can be sorted independently within each value of gender. The final report could have a different age group as the first row for each column of gender.

The desired statistic for the ANALYSIS variable is again calculated before the PROC REPORT step. It is calculated within each combination of the GROUP and ACROSS variables. Then, as in the previous example, an indicator variable is created. The indicator variable designates the first row for each value of the ACROSS within the outside grouping variable.

For this example, the indicator variable designates the highest value of CALC_QUANTITY and its corresponding age group value for each gender within each country. Example 5.3a creates the indicator variable, displayed in Output 5.4.

Example 5.3a: Pre-Calculate Sum and Create IND Variable to Maintain Order under Each ACROSS Value

```
proc means data=orders nway noprint completetypes; ❶
   class customer_country customer_gender customer_age_group; ❷
   var quantity; ❸
   output out=order_sum_under_across sum=calc_quantity; ❹
run;

proc sort data=order_sum_under_across;
   by customer_country customer_gender descending calc_quantity; ❺
run;

data order_sum_under_across2;
   set order_sum_under_across;
   by customer_country customer_gender; ❻

   retain ind 0; ❼
   if first.customer_gender then ind=1; ❽
   else ind+1; ❾
   drop _type_ _freq_;
run;
```

❶   Not all CUSTOMER_AGE_GROUP values occur for each gender within each country. The COMPLETETYPES option ensures that if the age group value is present for a given country, then the output data set contains a record for that age group for both genders.

❷   CUSTOMER_COUNTRY will be a GROUP variable in the PROC REPORT step. CUSTOMER_GENDER will be the ACROSS variable in the PROC REPORT step. CUSTOMER_AGE_GROUP will also be a GROUP variable. Because it will be under gender, it is listed after gender on this CLASS statement.

❸   The analysis variable QUANTITY is placed on the VAR statement.

❹   The OUTPUT statement creates a data set containing the variables from the CLASS statement and the summary values of the analysis variable QUANTITY, stored in the CALC_QUANTITY variable.

❺   The data set created by PROC MEANS is sorted by the outside grouping variable (CUSTOMER_COUNTRY), the ACROSS variable (CUSTOMER_GENDER), and the statistic (QUANTITY).

❻   The outside grouping variable and the ACROSS variable are listed on the BY statement within the DATA step that will create the indicator variable.

❼   Create a new variable called IND on the RETAIN statement, so its value is maintained. Specifying an initial value of zero ensures no missing values.

❽   If the observation in the data set is the first occurrence of CUSTOMER_GENDER (which is nested within CUSTOMER_COUNTRY), then set the IND variable to a value of one. The first observation for a country contains the highest value of CALC_QUANTITY.

❾   For all other observations for a given gender within a country, increment the value of IND.

Output 5.4: ORDER_SUM_UNDER_ACROSS2 Data Set (Partial Listing)

	Customer_Country	Customer_Gender	Customer_Age_Group	calc_quantity	ind
1	AU	F	31-45 years	35	1
2	AU	F	46-60 years	20	2
3	AU	F	61-75 years	13	3
4	AU	F	15-30 years	0	4
5	AU	M	31-45 years	69	1
6	AU	M	61-75 years	49	2
7	AU	M	46-60 years	24	3
8	AU	M	15-30 years	0	4
9	CA	F	15-30 years	27	1
10	CA	F	31-45 years	26	2
11	CA	F	46-60 years	11	3
12	CA	F	61-75 years	0	4
13	CA	M	15-30 years	17	1
14	CA	M	61-75 years	12	2
15	CA	M	46-60 years	7	3
16	CA	M	31-45 years	5	4

Example 5.3b uses the indicator variable in a PROC REPORT step to create a report that is sorted by CALC_QUANTITY within each value of the ACROSS variable (Output 5.5).

Example 5.3b: Maintain Sort of QUANTITY within CUSTOMER_COUNTRY under ACROSS Variable Values

```
options missing='0';
proc report data=order_sum_under_across2; ❶
   column customer_country ind customer_gender,
          (customer_age_group calc_quantity); ❷
   define customer_country / group format=$cntry.;
   define ind / group order=internal noprint; ❸
   define customer_gender / across; ❹
run;
```

❶ Specify the ORDER_SUM_UNDER_ACROSS2 data set to be used by PROC REPORT.

❷ CUSTOMER_COUNTRY is the outside grouping variable and therefore listed first on the COLUMN statement. The IND variable is next. It will force all of the records with the same value to be on the same row of the final report. CUSTOMER_AGE_GROUP is now listed under the ACROSS variable CUSTOMER_GENDER. CALC_QUANTITY in this data set is already summed but is still considered an ANALYSIS variable.

❸ IND is defined as GROUP, with the NOPRINT option, so it is not in the final report. IND is a numeric variable. ORDER=INTERAL ensures that the values are sorted in numeric order.

❹ CUSTOMER_GENDER is defined as ACROSS.

Output 5.5: Report Sorted by Descending Quantity within Each Value of Gender (Partial Listing)

Customer Country	Customer Age Group	Quantity Ordered	Customer Age Group	Quantity Ordered
		Customer Gender		
	F		M	
Australia	31-45 years	35	31-45 years	69
	46-60 years	20	61-75 years	49
	61-75 years	13	46-60 years	24
	15-30 years	0	15-30 years	0
Canada	15-30 years	27	15-30 years	17
	31-45 years	26	61-75 years	12
	46-60 years	11	46-60 years	7
	61-75 years	0	31-45 years	5
Germany	31-45 years	21	61-75 years	66
	15-30 years	0	31-45 years	11
	46-60 years	0	15-30 years	8
	61-75 years	0	46-60 years	0
Israel	15-30 years	0	31-45 years	13
	31-45 years	0	46-60 years	13
	46-60 years	0	15-30 years	2
	61-75 years	0	61-75 years	0

Notice that the CUSTOMER_AGE_GROUP values are in a different order for each value of CUSTOMER_GENDER.

5.3 Use COMPLETEROWS with ACROSS

Chapter 4 includes a brief example of using a DISPLAY or GROUP variable under an ACROSS variable; recall, the examples used a "concise" data set. The chapter does not include any examples of using the COMPLETEROWS option with a report that also uses an ACROSS variable. The reason Chapter 4 does not delve too deeply into using COMPLETEROWS is that, more often than not, those types of reports require pre-processing.

COMPLETEROWS can be used to get all possible values of a GROUP variable under each ACROSS value. However, COMPLETEROWS might cause undesired output in two ways. It might create output with values populated only in a stair-step manner. It might also create output with many additional blank rows. This section explores why you might encounter either type of output and how to pre-process your data to get the desired output.

5.3.1 COMPLETEROWS and a GROUP Variable under an ACROSS Variable

The COMPLETEROWS option creates all possible combinations for the values of the ACROSS variables, even if one or more of the combinations do not occur within the input data set. When COMPLETEROWS is specified and a GROUP variable is placed under an ACROSS, the resulting report is often extremely longer than expected, presents values in a stair-step pattern, or shows values only on the diagonal.

PROC REPORT builds each column separately. Even when you specify an ACROSS variable, each of its columns is created entirely independent of the other columns. The reason you might see values only on the diagonal is that PROC REPORT first creates the column for the first value of the ACROSS. The COMPLETEROWS option tells PROC REPORT to fill in the column with all possible combinations of the ACROSS and the GROUP variables. Then PROC REPORT begins the creation of the second value of the ACROSS. However, the values for the second ACROSS value start at the row where the first column stopped. In other words, PROC REPORT does not move the start position back up to the first row of the report. As it builds the column for the second value of the ACROSS, it again fills the column with all possible combinations of the ACROSS and GROUP variables.

Default Behavior of COMPLETEROWS

Example 5.4 demonstrates this behavior using the same four variables from Section 5.2: CUSTOMER_COUNTRY, CUSTOMER_GENDER, CUSTOMER_AGE_GROUP, and QUANTITY. CUSTOMER_COUNTRY will be a GROUP variable but it will be its own column. CUSTOMER_GENDER will be defined as ACROSS. CUSTOMER_AGE_GROUP will be defined as GROUP and placed under CUSTOMER_GENDER. The results are shown in Output 5.6.

Example 5.4: Demonstrate Undesired Output Generated by COMPLETEROWS

```
proc report data=orders completerows;
   column customer_country customer_gender,
          (customer_age_group quantity);
   define customer_country / group format=$cntry.;
   define customer_gender / across;
   define customer_age_group / group;
run;
```

The resulting table has the stair-step pattern. The entire report is almost two pages long; only part of the first page is shown here.

Output 5.6: Undesired Stair-Step Pattern Generated by COMPLETEROWS

Customer Country	Customer Gender			
	F		M	
	Customer Age Group	Quantity Ordered	Customer Age Group	Quantity Ordered
Australia	15-30 years	68		142
	31-45 years	0		0
	46-60 years	0		0
	61-75 years	0	15-30 years	0
		0	31-45 years	0
		0	46-60 years	0
		0	61-75 years	0
Canada	15-30 years	64		41
	31-45 years	0		0
	46-60 years	0		0
	61-75 years	0	15-30 years	0
		0	31-45 years	0
		0	46-60 years	0
		0	61-75 years	0
Germany	15-30 years	21		85
	31-45 years	0		0
	46-60 years	0		0
	61-75 years	0	15-30 years	0
		0	31-45 years	0
		0	46-60 years	0
		0	61-75 years	0
Israel	15-30 years	0		28
	31-45 years	0		0
	46-60 years	0		0
	61-75 years	0	15-30 years	0
		0	31-45 years	0
		0	46-60 years	0

In Output 5.6, PROC REPORT first created the stand-alone column for country. Then, it built the column for CUSTOMER_GENDER=F and CUSTOMER_AGE_GROUP. The column contains all four possible values of CUSTOMER_AGE_GROUP. The QUANTITY value is the sum for all observations from the input data set where the country was Australia and the gender was female. PROC REPORT starts building the first column for males. The values of CUSTOMER_AGE_GROUP start at the row where the females stopped, the fourth row. All four possible values of CUSTOMER_AGE_GROUP are filled in. The same process is repeated for the next country.

Interestingly, the value of the ANALYSIS variable is always on the first row for each country. The reason is that the ANALYSIS variable value is coming from the summary engine and it associated with a specific value of the GROUP variable. The value is filled in on the row where the GROUP value is present.

Fix COMPLETEROWS Default Behavior

You must pre-process the data to "fix" the above report and get the desired report. Prior to the PROC REPORT step, a data set must be created that already contains all possible combinations of the ACROSS (CUSTOMER_GENDER) and GROUP (CUSTOMER_COUNTRY, CUSTOMER_AGE_GROUP) variables.

PROC MEANS is a very useful tool for the pre-processing step, because it can create categories already in the data set, but it can also add categories that are not present. Previously, in Example 5.3a you saw the use of the COMPLETETYPES option. When used with the PRELOADFMT option, it will insert combinations not present in the input data set.

Example 5.5a demonstrates the steps needed to pre-process the data.

1. Create a format for any GROUP variable that might not have all values present in the data.
2. Use PROC MEANS with COMPLETE TYPES and PRELOADFMT options to create a data set with all desired combinations.
3. Merge the new data set onto the original data set.

The data set created from steps 1 and 2 are shown in Output 5.7.

Example 5.5a: Pre-Process the Data to Get All Combinations of the GROUP and ACROSS Variables

```
proc format;
   value $cagf ❶
   '15-30 years' = '15-30 years'
   '31-45 years' = '31-45 years'
   '46-60 years' = '46-60 years'
   '61-75 years' = '61-75 years'
   ;
run;

proc means data=orders noprint nway completetypes; ❷
   class customer_country customer_gender;
   class customer_age_group / preloadfmt; ❸
   format customer_age_group $cagf.; ❹
   output out=all_combo n=dummy; ❺
run;
```

❶   Create a format for the GROUP variable that might not have all possible values in the data set.

❷   Add the COMPLETETYPES option to the PROC MEANS statement, so all possible combinations are created.

❸   On a CLASS statement for the variable of interest, use the PRELOADFMT option. PRELOADFMT works the same way in PROC MEANS as it does in PROC REPORT. It loads and uses all of the categories present in the format.

❹ The FORMAT statement specifies the format that contains all possible values.

❺ The OUTPUT statement will create a data set with all combinations of the CLASS variables, including the ones inserted via the format. A statistic of some kind is needed so that the N statistic is specified, but it will not be used. Be sure to give the statistic a name that is not currently in your data set.

Output 5.7: ALL_COMBO Data Set (Partial Listing)

	Customer_Country	Customer_Gender	Customer_Age_Group	_TYPE_	_FREQ_	dummy
1	AU	F	15-30 years	7	0	0
2	AU	F	31-45 years	7	19	19
3	AU	F	46-60 years	7	11	11
4	AU	F	61-75 years	7	10	10
5	AU	M	15-30 years	7	0	0
6	AU	M	31-45 years	7	45	45
7	AU	M	46-60 years	7	17	17
8	AU	M	61-75 years	7	27	27
9	CA	F	15-30 years	7	14	14
10	CA	F	31-45 years	7	12	12
11	CA	F	46-60 years	7	5	5
12	CA	F	61-75 years	7	0	0
13	CA	M	15-30 years	7	10	10
14	CA	M	31-45 years	7	4	4
15	CA	M	46-60 years	7	5	5
16	CA	M	61-75 years	7	5	5
17	DE	F	15-30 years	7	0	0
18	DE	F	31-45 years	7	11	11
19	DE	F	46-60 years	7	0	0
20	DE	F	61-75 years	7	0	0
21	DE	M	15-30 years	7	6	6
22	DE	M	31-45 years	7	7	7
23	DE	M	46-60 years	7	0	0
24	DE	M	61-75 years	7	34	34

```
proc sort data=orders;
   by customer_country customer_gender customer_age_group;
run;

data orders2; ❻
   merge orders all_combo;
   by customer_country customer_gender customer_age_group;
run;
```

❻ The data set created by PROC MEANS is merged onto the original data set. The new data set, ORDERS2, now contains at least one record for every CUSTOMER_COUNTRY-CUSTOMER_GENDER-CUSTOMER_AGE_GROUP combination.

Example 5.5b demonstrates the PROC REPORT step, which changed in three ways from Example 5.4. The results are shown in Output 5.8.

1. The merged data set will be used because it contains all combinations.
2. The COMPLETEROWS option is removed because it is no longer necessary.
3. The CUSTOMER_AGE_GROUP variable will be used twice. The first instance will ensure that the groups are on the same row, no matter what gender they are under. The second instance will be the one to display the value under each gender.

Example 5.5b: Use Pre-Processed Data to Display All Values of CUSTOMER_AGE_GROUP under CUSTOMER_GENDER

```
options missing='0';
proc report data=orders2;  ❶
    column customer_country customer_age_group=cag customer_gender,
           (customer_age_group quantity);  ❷
    define customer_country / group format=$cntry.;
    define customer_gender / across;
    define cag / group noprint;  ❸
    define customer_age_group / group;
run;
```

❶ Specify the new, merged data set that contains at least one record for all combinations. The COMPLETEROWS option is no longer needed because the data set already contains all combinations.

❷ The CUSTOMER_AGE_GROUP variable is listed twice on the COLUMN statement. An alias is created from the first instance. The second instance is placed under the ACROSS variable. The second instance is the one you will see in the final report.

❸ Define the alias, CAG, as GROUP and NOPRINT. This instance of CUSTOMER_AGE_GROUP will ensure that the values under gender will start on the desired rows.

Output 5.8: Display All Possible Values of CUSTOMER_AGE_GROUP for Each CUSTOMER_GENDER (Partial Listing)

	Customer Gender			
	F		M	
Customer Country	Customer Age Group	Quantity Ordered	Customer Age Group	Quantity Ordered
Australia	15-30 years	0	15-30 years	0
	31-45 years	35	31-45 years	69
	46-60 years	20	46-60 years	24
	61-75 years	13	61-75 years	49
Canada	15-30 years	27	15-30 years	17
	31-45 years	26	31-45 years	5
	46-60 years	11	46-60 years	7
	61-75 years	0	61-75 years	12
Germany	15-30 years	0	15-30 years	8
	31-45 years	21	31-45 years	11
	46-60 years	0	46-60 years	0
	61-75 years	0	61-75 years	66

Another Method to Avoid the Stair-Step Pattern

Some reports might have the stair-step pattern even if you do not use the COMPLETEROWS option. The report might just be the result of using a GROUP variable under an ACROSS. For those reports, you do not need the pre-processing steps from Example 5.5. (The purpose of the example above is to get all possible values of CUSTOMER_AGE_GROUP under each CUSTOMER_GENDER column.) However, the technique of using the GROUP variable twice is needed. The first instance will prevent PROC REPORT from starting the male column on the row the female column stopped. Instead, the values in the male column will start at the first row of each country. Example 5.6 demonstrates the technique of using a variable twice.

Note: Example 5.6 uses the main ORDERS data set.

Example 5.6: Use Variable Twice to Avoid Stair-Step Pattern

```
proc report data=orders;
   column customer_country customer_age_group=cag customer_gender,
          (customer_age_group quantity);
   define customer_country / group format=$cntry.;
   define customer_gender / across;
   define customer_age_group / group;
   define cag / group noprint;
run;
```

5.3.2 COMPLETEROWS and a DISPLAY Variable under an ACROSS

As mentioned previously, the COMPLETEROWS option might also create output that has many blank rows. This situation is most likely to occur when you have a DIPSLAY variable under an ACROSS variable and a grouping variable that is not under the ACROSS.

In order to understand exactly what happens when COMPLETEROWS and DISPLAY are used together, consider the following code and output, Example 5.7 and Output 5.9. The output is created from the ORDERS_3OBS data set, containing three observations of data. These three records account for two values of a grouping variable (ORDER_TYPE) and three crossing values (CUSTOMER_COUNTRY). The PROC REPORT statement includes the COMPLETEROWS option. CUSTOMER_AGE_GROUP is defined as DISPLAY. The final report has 21 rows!

Example 5.7: Place a DISPLAY Variable under an ACROSS Variable

```
options missing='.';
proc report data=orders_3obs completerows;
   column order_type customer_country, (customer_age_group quantity);
   define order_type / group preloadfmt format=typef. order=internal;
   define customer_country / across format=$cntry.;
   define customer_age_group / display;
run;
```

Output 5.9: A DISPLAY Variable under the ACROSS Might Generate Many Blank Rows

| | Customer Country | | | | | |
| | Australia | | Israel | | United States | |
Order Type	Customer Age Group	Quantity Ordered	Customer Age Group	Quantity Ordered	Customer Age Group	Quantity Ordered
Retail Sale	31-45 years	2		.		.
		.		.		.
		.		.		.
		.	46-60 years	3		.
		.		.		.
		.		.		.
		.		.		.
Catalog Sale		.		.		.
		.		.		.
		.		.		.
		.		.		.
		.		.		.
		.		.	46-60 years	1
Internet Sale		.		.		.
		.		.		.
		.		.		.
		.		.		.
		.		.		.
		.		.		.

The table is created in this order.

1. The first observation is written out (ORDER_TYPE=1, CUSTOMER_COUNTRY=AU, CUSTOMER_AGE_GROUP=31-45 years, QUANTITY=2).

2. A row is written for each of the other observations in the data set regardless of what grouping they might fall in, resulting in 2 blank rows.

3. The second observation is written out (ORDER_TYPE=1, CUSTOMER_COUNTRY=IL, CUSTOMER_AGE_GROUP=46-60 years, QUANTITY=3).

4. A row is written for each of the other observations in the data set regardless of what grouping they might fall in, resulting in 2 blank rows.

5. Then, a row is written out for each observation in the data set that does not belong in the group (ORDER_TYPE=1) that we are currently looking at. In this case, one blank row is written for the ORDER_TYPE=2 observation.

6. The same number of rows will then be written for the remaining groups (ORDER_TYPE=2 and ORDER_TYPE=3).

As you can see, this code demonstrates that using COMPLETEROWS and a DISPLAY variable under an ACROSS, results in many blank rows. If the entire ORDERS data set had been used instead of a subset, the entire table would be almost 250 pages long! It would look much like the picture above with a lot of rows filled with blanks and missing values.

If your report contains many pages of rows with no data, you first need to consider why you are using a DISPLAY variable under an ACROSS variable. Do you really need it? What purpose does it serve? Should its usage be changed to GROUP? Should it be moved from underneath the ACROSS?

You might be able to produce the desired report, but it might take a number of steps prior to PROC REPORT to produce it. The "fix" for this type of report is to use a procedure like PROC MEANS to produce all of the desired combinations prior to PROC REPORT. This method has been demonstrated throughout the previous sections. Another method, which is hinted at in Chapter 4, is to create a concise, pre-summarized data set with all desired combinations and statistics. Finally, consider transposing the data set prior to PROC REPORT.

Depending on your data, you can try using a variable twice on the COLUMN statement as seen in Example 5.6. Otherwise, you might have to both summarize and transpose the data set so that PROC REPORT does not create all of the blank rows or insert values in the stair-step pattern.

Example 5.8 summarizes the data and uses CUSTOMER_AGE_GROUP twice.

Example 5.8: Summarize the Data so That a DISPLAY Variable Is Not Needed under an ACROSS

```
proc sort data=orders out=orders1;
   by customer_country customer_gender customer_age_group;

proc means data=orders1 noprint;
   by customer_country customer_gender customer_age_group;
```

```
      var quantity;
      output out=orders2 sum=;
   run;

   proc report data=orders2;
      column customer_country customer_age_group=cag customer_gender,
             (customer_age_group quantity);
      define customer_country / group format=$cntry.;
      define customer_gender / across;
      define cag / group noprint;
      define customer_age_group / group;
   run;
```

5.4 Use COMPLETEROWS with Multiple GROUP Variables

Chapter 3 explores using the COMPLETEROWS option to produce a row with all categories of a GROUP variable. The chapter does mention that, in some circumstances, using COMPLETEROWS might produce undesired results because it might generate rows that do not make sense for your data.

The example in Chapter 3 uses CUSTOMER_COUNTRY, PRODUCT_LINE, and ORDER_TYPE. The goal of using COMPLETEROWS is to generate rows for all possible values of ORDER_TYPE within each PRODUCT_LINE and CUSTOMER_COUNTRY combination. However, the report contains rows for products that were not actually sold in a given country.

COMPLETEROWS is designed to generate all possible combinations. PROC REPORT does not have a method for indicating that all possible combinations should be generated for only certain values of one GROUP variable. You might want a report that contains all ORDER_TYPE values, but only for country and product combinations that exist in the data. To generate the desired report, you have to pre-process the data. As in previous examples, the most straightforward way of getting the desired report is to insert rows into the data set for combinations that do not exist. Again, PROC MEANS is very useful in creating the desired combinations.

Example 5.9 places the two outside grouping variables, CUSTOMER_COUNTRY and PRODUCT_LINE, on a BY statement instead of a CLASS statement. Placing the variables on the BY statement ensures that only country and product combinations that already exist will be present in the output data set. The BY statement does require you to sort the data first.

Example 5.9a: Insert ORDER_TYPE Values for Existing CUSTOMER_COUNTRY-PRODUCT_LINE Combinations

```
   proc sort data=orders; ❶
      by customer_country product_line order_type;
   run;

   proc format; 
   value typef ❷
      1='Retail Sale'
      2='Catalog Sale'
```

```
      3='Internet Sale';
   run;

   proc means data=orders nway noprint completetypes;  ❸
      by customer_country product_line;  ❹
      class order_type /preloadfmt;  ❺
      format order_type typef.;  ❻
      output out=test n=dummy;  ❼
   run;

   data orders2;  ❽
      merge orders test;
      by customer_country product_line order_type;
   run;
```

❶ The data set must be sorted prior to the PROC MEANS step. All of the GROUP variables should be listed on the BY statement, in the order in which they will be used on the COLUMN statement in PROC REPORT.

❷ Create a format for the GROUP variable that might not have all possible values in the data set.

❸ Add the COMPLETETYPES option to the PROC MEANS statement so that all possible combinations are created.

❹ Place the outermost grouping variables on the BY statement. These variables are the ones for which you want to display only the combinations that already exist in the data.

❺ On a CLASS statement for the variable of interest, use the PRELOADFMT option. PRELOADFMT works the same way in PROC MEANS as it does in PROC REPORT. It loads and uses all of the categories present in the format.

❻ The FORMAT statement specifies the format that contains all possible values.

❼ The OUTPUT statement will create a data set with all combinations of the CLASS variables, including the ones inserted via the format. A statistic of some kind is needed, so the N statistic is specified, but it will not be used. Be sure to give the statistic a name that is not currently in your data set.

❽ Merge the data set created from PROC MEANS with the original data set. The resulting data set will contain rows for all order type values for the country-product combinations that were already present.

After the pre-processing steps have been completed, the PROC REPORT step in Example 5.9b does not require any special steps or options. The COMPLETEROWS option is no longer needed because the data set already contains all of the desired combinations of CUSTOMER_COUNTRY, PRODUCT_LINE, and ORDER_TYPE.

Example 5.9b: Create Report with All ORDER_TYPE Values

```
   options missing='0';
   proc report data=orders2;  ❶
      column customer_country product_line order_type quantity
             total_retail_price;  ❷
      define customer_country / group format=$cntry.;  ❸
```

```
        define order_type / group format=typef.;  ❹
        define product_line  / group;  ❺
run;
```

❶   Specify the new data set on the PROC REPORT statement.

❷   The COLUMN statement lists all of the desired variables from the input data set.

❸   Define CUSTOMER_COUNTRY as a GROUP variable.

❹   Define ORDER_TYPE as a GROUP variable. PRELOADFMT is not needed here, as all possible levels were added in the PROC MEANS step.

❺   Define PRODUCT_LINE as a GROUP variable.

The final report, Output 5.10, now contains a row for every possible value of ORDER_TYPE, but only within the combinations of CUSTOMER_COUNTY and PRODUCT_LINE that exist. Output 5.10 differs from the output in Chapter 3 in the Canada and Germany sections. This report does not contain the Children product.

Output 5.10: Display All Possible Order Types within Country and Product Line Combinations

Customer Country	Product Line	Order Type	Quantity Ordered	Total Retail Price for This Product
Australia	Children	Catalog Sale	2	$120.20
		Internet Sale	4	$59.60
		Retail Sale	7	$348.00
	Clothes & Shoes	Catalog Sale	17	$1,065.70
		Internet Sale	8	$444.40
		Retail Sale	42	$2,830.69
	Outdoors	Catalog Sale	0	0
		Internet Sale	0	0
		Retail Sale	38	$3,206.70
	Sports	Catalog Sale	7	$493.50
		Internet Sale	1	$109.90
		Retail Sale	84	$8,642.80
Canada	Clothes & Shoes	Catalog Sale	3	$81.80
		Internet Sale	3	$173.70
		Retail Sale	0	0
	Sports	Catalog Sale	29	$5,340.58
		Internet Sale	70	$6,355.00
		Retail Sale	0	0
Germany	Clothes & Shoes	Catalog Sale	17	$1,702.70
		Internet Sale	3	$211.40
		Retail Sale	0	0
	Outdoors	Catalog Sale	45	$7,634.50
		Internet Sale	18	$3,636.00
		Retail Sale	0	0
	Sports	Catalog Sale	14	$697.20
		Internet Sale	9	$1,512.80
		Retail Sale	0	0

A number of examples in this chapter have required adding observations to the data set because the combination did not previously exist. This method works really well for these examples because the ANALYSIS variables are being summed and nothing requires the N statistic. Adding observations to your data set might not be appropriate when using the N statistic because you will get a value of 1 (one) instead of 0 (zero).

When you need to use the N statistic, you will have to choose the most appropriate method of producing the desired output. You can use the COMPLETEROWS option and accept that it might produce more rows than desired. Alternatively, you can do all needed summing and processing steps and create a data set that contains all of the information needed for the report, including the desired combinations and rows. Then, use PROC REPORT to simply print out the information.

5.5 Use Information from a Variable in Header and Data Sections

PROC REPORT is very good at a number of different tasks. It can consolidate multiple observations into one row or into one column. It can order data in a specific manner. It can calculate many types of statistics. PROC REPORT cannot create both rows and columns from the same variable, which means that you cannot assign two different tasks to the same variable.

To create a report that uses information from one variable in the header (columns) and data (rows) sections of the report requires pre-processing or restructuring of the data. If you have a categorical variable that you want to use to create headers and rows in the same report, the strategy is straightforward – create a copy (with a new name) of the variable in a DATA step. If you want to use a variable's name or label to create rows and its values to create columns, you have to restructure your data.

A number of scenarios fall under the second circumstance above. Questionnaire data is one such scenario. The data has one observation per respondent and one variable per question. The label of each variable is the question text. The final report should list the text of the question in a column (each row is a question) and subsequent columns should display counts, percentages, or averages for each response. Another scenario is clinical data with pre- and post-surgery measurements. The data has one variable for each measurement. The final report should list the measurement type in a column (each type has its own row) and subsequent columns should list statistics on that measurement.

Both of these scenarios require restructuring of the data set. The data set must contain one variable indicating the row value (the question text or "pre" and "post") and at least one variable containing the response, which could be character or numeric. For the scenarios above, the second variable is most likely to be numeric.

SAS has numerous ways to restructure data to create a new data set. You can use a DATA step, PROC TRANSPOSE, PROC SQL, or the OUT= option on many procedures. Recommending the best method is difficult. The best method depends on the data, the desired report, and the programmer, and it might require many steps. In the end, the best method might be what is easiest and most familiar to the programmer. No matter which method is used, you, as the programmer, must ensure that you have one variable that contains the grouping, or row designation, and one variable that will be analyzed. However, the new data set can also contain other grouping or analysis variables.

This example will use three numeric variables from the ORDERS data set: QUANTITY, TOTAL_RETAIL_PRICE, and DISCOUNT. The final report will contain one row for each of these variables. The first column will indicate the original variable's label. The subsequent columns will contain the N, MEAN, MIN, and MAX statistics.

For the ORDERS data set, it makes the most sense to use PROC TRANSPOSE to create a new data set, seen in Example 5.10a and Output 5.11. The new data set will have one observation per order (ORDER_ID) and product name (PRODUCT_NAME). The columns created by PROC TRANSPOSE will contain the original variables' names, labels, and values. Prior to the PROC TRANSPOSE step, the data must be sorted.

Example 5.10a: Transpose Data by ORDER_ID and PRODUCT_NAME

```
proc sort data=orders;
   by order_id product_name;
run;

proc transpose data=orders out=tranord ❶ prefix=analy ❷;
   by order_id product_name;
   var quantity total_retail_price discount; ❸
run;
```

❶ The name of the restructured data set will be TRANORD.

❷ The name of the new variable, which contains the value of the original variable, will start with 'analy'.

❸ The VAR statement lists the three analysis variables of interest.

Output 5.11: First Ten Observations of TRANORD

	Order_ID	Product_Name	_NAME_	_LABEL_	analy1
1	1230058123	Toncot Beefy-T Emb T-Shirt	Quantity	Quantity Ordered	1
2	1230058123	Toncot Beefy-T Emb T-Shirt	Total_Retail_Price	Total Retail Price for This Product	16.5
3	1230058123	Toncot Beefy-T Emb T-Shirt	Discount	Discount in percent of Normal Total Retail Price	0
4	1230080101	Trekking Tent	Quantity	Quantity Ordered	1
5	1230080101	Trekking Tent	Total_Retail_Price	Total Retail Price for This Product	247.5
6	1230080101	Trekking Tent	Discount	Discount in percent of Normal Total Retail Price	0
7	1230106883	Sharky Swimming Trunks	Quantity	Quantity Ordered	1
8	1230106883	Sharky Swimming Trunks	Total_Retail_Price	Total Retail Price for This Product	28.3
9	1230106883	Sharky Swimming Trunks	Discount	Discount in percent of Normal Total Retail Price	0
10	1230147441	Goggles, Assorted Colours	Quantity	Quantity Ordered	2

The PROC REPORT step on the new data set is straightforward. The COLUMN statement contains the needed variables. The DEFINE statements specify usage and column labels. Example 5.10b demonstrates the PROC REPORT step. Output 5.12 contains the final report.

Example 5.10b: List the Transposed Variables on the COLUMN Statement

```
proc report data=tranord;
   column _label_ analy1,(n  mean min max);
   define _label_ / group 'Order Information';
   define analy1 / 'Order Statistics';
run;
```

Output 5.12: Original Variables' Labels in Rows, Statistics in Columns

Order Information	Order Statistics			
	n	mean	min	max
Discount in percent of Normal Total Retail Price	3	0.3333333	0.3	0.4
Quantity Ordered	617	1.7471637	1	6
Total Retail Price for This Product	617	162.20011	2.6	1937.2

5.6 Wrap Text at a Specific Place

The Listing destination requires the WRAP or FLOW option to make a long text string wrap, or span multiple rows. The Listing destination will honor the SPLIT character when it is part of a data value.

Other ODS destinations will automatically wrap text. In fact, they ignore the WRAP and FLOW options. They do not honor the SPLIT character in data values. The SPLIT character will be displayed in the data column on the report just like any other character. For long data values, the destination will fit as much text on a row within the cell as possible. The amount of text that can fit on a row is based on the font size and cell width, along with other attributes. When it reaches the end of the row, the destination will force a line break and continue the rest of the text. The destination will attempt to insert the line break at a space if possible.

The destination might not wrap a value where you want, or you might have a data value that you want split at a specific place in the text. To control where a value wraps or splits, you must insert a line break command into the actual value using the inline formatting function NEWLINE, for example, ^{newline 1}.

You must place it inside of the actual data value. The data value can be changed via an assignment statement in a DATA step or a compute block. For most programmers, it is easier to make the change in a DATA step. Be sure the length of the variable is long enough to incorporate the inserted command.

The PRODUCT_GROUP variable supplies a general description of the product. For products that fall in the children's line, PRODUCT_GROUP has a comma and a more detailed group value. Example 5.11 and Output 5.13 demonstrate how to convert the comma to a line break command to force the detail text to be on a new line.

Remember to declare and use an ODS ESCAPECHAR.

Example 5.11: Insert NEWLINE Function in PRODUCT_LINE Value

```
ods escapechar="^";
data orders2;
   set orders;
   length product_group2 $75;
   label product_group2 = 'Product Group';
   if product_line = 'Children' then
      product_group2 = tranwrd(product_group, ',' , '^{newline 1}');
   else product_group2 = product_group;
run;

proc report data=orders2;
   column product_line product_group2;
   define product_line / group;
   define product_group2 / group;
run;
```

Output 5.13: Some Product Values Wrap onto a Second Line

Product Line	Product Group
Children	A-Team Kids
	Bathing Suits Kids
	Eclipse Kid's Clothes
	Eclipse Kid's Shoes
	Lucky Guy Kids
	N.D. Gear Kids
	Olssons Kids
	Osprey Kids
	Tracker Kid's Clothes
	Ypsilon Kids
Clothes & Shoes	Eclipse Clothing
	Eclipse Shoes
	Green Tomato
	Knitwear
	LSF
	Orion
	Orion Clothing
	Osprey
	Shoes
	Shorts
	Street Wear
	T-Shirts
	Tracker Clothes

5.7 Incorporate Various Data Pieces into One Report

Chapters 3 and 4 provide a number of really good examples for producing non-default reports, such as including extra summary rows at the bottom of a report or inserting summary columns into the middle of the report. Many of those techniques required adding dummy variables to the data set or additional categories to the format. These strategies might not be effective for some report structures. The best way to generate the desired report structure is to build a data set that looks just like the report and then use PROC REPORT simply to display the data in a pleasing manner.

Clinical reports of adverse events are one report type that might require you to restructure the data set. Clinical reports often have a row for overall totals, then a row for subtotals, and then rows for individual events. In theory, RBREAK and BREAK statements can produce totals and subtotals. The tricky part is creating a grouping variable to capture that correct observations. For some programmers, it is easier to create the observations, columns, and values with other procedures.

A report that requires an observation to be part of two separate groups might also require data restructuring. For example, demographic information could display ethnicity and education. The report should be the breakdown of each ethnicity level, education level, and the combination of the two. In essence, the final report is actually two reports combined into one.

PROC REPORT documentation discusses detail reports and summary reports. Detail reports show information from individual observations from the input data set. Summary reports consolidate multiple observations from the input data set to report summarized, or grouped, information. PROC REPORT cannot create both types of reports in the same step. For example, PROC REPORT will not create a report that has rows for each customer in the top portion of the report and then rows with summary information for country, gender, order type, product line, and so on, in the bottom portion of the report. For those types of reports, you either have to create a lot of dummy grouping variables in the data set and temporary variables in compute blocks, or restructure your data.

5.7.1 Combine Detail and Summary Information

The example in this section demonstrates creating a report that combines detail and summary information. Instead of 'tricking' PROC REPORT into creating the desired report structure, it will be created within a DATA step, and then displayed via PROC REPORT.

The top section of the report will contain one row for each customer. The columns will represent the total number of separate products ordered, the total quantity ordered, and the amount of money spent. The bottom section of the report will contain rows for various categories each customer might fall into, such as gender, age group, and type. Example 5.12a shows the steps to summarize the data for each section and set them together in one data set.

Example 5.12a: Calculate Detail and Summary Information in Two Separate Steps

```
proc sort data=orders;
   by customer_name;
run;
```

```
proc means data=orders noprint; ❶
   by customer_name;
   var quantity total_retail_price;
   output out=top_tots(rename=(_freq_=totn)) sum= /autoname; ❷
run;

proc means data=orders noprint; ❸
   class customer_type customer_age_group customer_gender;
   ways 1; ❹
   var quantity total_retail_price;
   output out=bot_tots(rename=(_freq_=totn)) sum= /autoname; ❺
run;

data all;
   set top_tots(in=in1)
       bot_tots(in=in2); ❻

   length name $100;
   if in1 then do; ❼
      name = customer_name;
   end;
   else if in2 then do; ❽
      if customer_gender ne '' then name = customer_gender;
      else if customer_age_group ne ' ' then
         name = customer_age_group;
      else if customer_type ne '' then name = customer_type;
   end;
run;
```

❶ The first step generates the information for each customer. A customer might purchase multiple products in a single transaction or could have multiple transactions. This step summarizes all the analysis variables into one row for each customer

❷ _FREQ_ is renamed to TOTN. Its value represents the number of separate products purchased. AUTONAME creates a unique variable name for each analysis variable statistic.

❸ This step summarizes the data for all of the observations in the input data set for each of the CLASS variables listed: CUSTOMER_TYPE, CUSTOMER_AGE_GROUP, and CUSTOMER_GENDER.

❹ The WAYS statement restricts the output to the summaries for each of the CLASS variables. The output data set will not contain any combinations, or crossings, of the CLASS variables.

❺ _FREQ_ is renamed to TOTN. Its value represents the number of separate products purchased. AUTONAME creates a unique variable name for each analysis variable statistic.

❻ The two data sets are SET together. They are not merged. The detail information for each customer will appear first in the ALL data set. The summary information for the grouping variables will be under the customer information.

❼ For observations that were in the TOP_TOTS data set (the data set with the customer information), the value of CUSTOMER_NAME is placed in a generic variable called NAME.

❽ For observations that were in the BOT_TOTS data set (the data set with the summary information), the value of each CLASS variable is assigned to the new variable NAME.

You do not have to use PROC MEANS to calculate all of the information. You might need to use PROC FREQ, PROC GLM, or another procedure. The final goal is to create a data set that has one record for each row that you want to have in the final report. It is best to name the variables from each temporary data set the same name, so that when combined, they have one variable that represents each column of the report. Example 5.12b creates the final report, seen in Output 5.14, containing both detail and summary information.

Example 5.12b: Output the Combined Data in One Report

```
proc report data=all split='~'; ❶
   column name totn quantity_sum total_retail_price_sum;❷
   define name / 'Customer Name~Customer Grouping';
   define totn / 'Num Separate~Products Ordered';
   define total_retail_price_sum / 'Dollar Amount';
run;
```

❶ The new data set ALL, containing the information for all parts of the final report is specified. The SPLIT option will be used to control the column headers.

❷ The *report-item*s are listed in the desired order.

Due to space constraints, only the last page of the output is shown.

Output 5.14: Report Contains Detail Rows and Grouped Summary Rows

Customer Name Customer Grouping	Num Separate Products Ordered	Quantity Ordered	Dollar Amount
Rita Lotz	6	8	$687.70
Robert Bowerman	25	37	$2,564.59
Robyn Klem	7	9	$608.60
Roy Siferd	6	11	$293.50
Sandrina Stephano	19	29	$2,810.98
Sanelisiwe Collier	4	9	$1,007.90
Selim Okay	2	4	$485.60
Serdar Yucel	2	3	$186.70
Soberina Berent	7	13	$2,308.28
Susan Krasowski	5	11	$815.40
Tedi Lanzarone	3	5	$374.10
Theunis Brazier	3	3	$292.60
Tommy Mcdonald	5	7	$343.50
Tonie Asmussen	3	4	$278.10
Tulio Devereaux	11	25	$2,303.00
Ulrich Heyde	25	48	$6,545.90
Viola Folsom	11	18	$2,778.80
Wendell Summersby	20	32	$1,583.30
Wilma Yeargan	2	5	$2,087.30
Wynella Lewis	16	32	$1,954.82
Yan Kozlowski	21	33	$2,202.60
F	277	498	$49,747.43
M	340	580	$50,330.04
15-30 years	172	304	$30,486.50
31-45 years	233	397	$34,197.50
46-60 years	105	175	$14,920.55
61-75 years	107	202	$20,472.92
Internet/Catalog Customers	76	138	$14,180.45
Orion Club members high activity	115	188	$14,461.50
Orion Club members medium activity	154	276	$24,164.63
Orion Club Gold members high activity	65	108	$11,600.29
Orion Club Gold members low activity	42	83	$7,484.85
Orion Club Gold members medium activity	77	117	$12,695.87
Orion Club members low activity	88	168	$15,489.87

5.7.2 The Importance of ORDER Variables

Output 5.14 contains the desired information, but it is very unappealing. The reader does not know why the report skips from customer names to "F". The bottom section does not contain any labeling or spacing to tell the reader what the section is for. It fails to explain that the groupings are not mutually exclusive.

NAME defaults to DISPLAY. No variables are defined as GROUP or ORDER, so PROC REPORT does not sort the observations from the input data set. The rows in the final report just happen to be in the correct order because of how the two temporary data sets were set together.

Most reports require full control over the order of the rows. This is where ORDER variables become very useful. Recall that ORDER variables do not consolidate rows from the input data set; they simply enforce a sort order. That capability is perfect for this type of report. When each observation in the data set is unique, you need to ensure that they are written where you want them to be.

ORDER variables also offer the capability of BREAK statements and COMPUTE BEFORE *target* and COMPUTE AFTER *target* blocks. Table (page) breaks can be inserted via the BREAK statement. The compute blocks allow the use of LINE statements with informative text.

The creation of ORDER variables requires forethought; you have to know how they will be used inside of PROC REPORT. When assigning values, remember how PROC REPORT nests these variables if there is more than one on the COLUMN statement. The first one listed on the COLUMN statement creates the initial sort order. The next variable from the COLUMN statement then gives finer control of the order, but only within the values of the first variable.

In general, an ORDER variable that has a unique value for every observation on the input data will work as expected when it is the only ORDER variable. If you use multiple ORDER variables, it is best for the first variable listed to be the broadest one with the fewest number of unique values. As the variables move farther to the right on the COLUMN statement, the number of unique values should increase.

ORDER variables can make the previous report much more appealing and informative. This example will add two ORDER variables to demonstrate how they can be used to enhance the final report. The pre-processing steps remain the same as in the previous example. Example 5.13a adds variables that will be defined as ORDER in the PROC REPORT step.

Example 5.13a: Create ORDER Variables to Designate Sections of the Report

```
proc means data=orders noprint;
   by customer_name;
   var quantity total_retail_price;
   output out=top_tots(rename=(_type_=ord _freq_=totn))
         sum= /autoname; ❶
run;

proc means data=orders noprint;
   class customer_type customer_age_group customer_gender;
   ways 1;
   var quantity total_retail_price;
   output out=bot_tots(rename=(_type_=ord _freq_=totn))
         sum= /autoname; ❷
run;
```

```
data all;
   set top_tots(in=in1)
       bot_tots(in=in2);

   length name $100;
   if in1 then do;
      sec = 1; ❸
      name = customer_name;
   end;
   else if in2 then do;
      sec = 2; ❹
      if customer_gender ne '' then name = customer_gender;
      else if customer_age_group ne ' ' then
         name = customer_age_group;
      else if customer_type ne '' then name = customer_type;
   end;
run;
```

❶ The automatic variable _TYPE_ is renamed to ORD because it will serve as an ordering variable in the PROC REPORT. All records for this data set have a value of zero. ORD is not as important for the observations in this data set as it will be for the BOT_TOTS data set. However, the ORD variable needs to have a value for all records in the final data set.

❷ _TYPE_ is renamed to ORD. The value of ORD will be unique for each CLASS variable. The first variable listed, CUSTOMER_TYPE, will have the lowest value of ORD. The final report needs to maintain the order of the variables as they are listed on the CLASS statement.

❸ All observations from the first data set, the detail section, are given a value of one (1) for the section variable, SEC.

❹ All observations from the second data set, the summary section, are given a value of two (2) for the section variable, SEC.

The creation of the ORDER variables was relatively straightforward. Only the RENAME= option and an assignment statement was needed. The bulk of the changes to the previous code are made in the PROC REPORT step, Example 5.13b. The results of the changes are seen in Output 5.15.

Example 5.13b: Output LINE Statements Based on ORDER Variables

```
proc report data=all split='~';
   column sec ord name totn quantity_sum total_retail_price_sum; ❶
   define sec / order noprint; ❷
   define ord / order noprint;
   define name / 'Customer Name~Customer Grouping';
   define totn / 'Num Separate~Products Ordered';
   define total_retail_price_sum / 'Dollar Amount';

   compute before sec; ❸
      length txt1 $50;
      if sec = 1 then txt1 = 'Individual Customers';
      else txt1 = 'Customer Categories';
      line txt1 $50.; ❹
   endcomp;
```

```
      compute before ord;  ❺
         length txt2 $50;
         if ord = 0 then do;
            num = 0;
            txt2 = '';
         end;
         else if ord = 1 then do;
            num = 50;
            txt2 = 'Breakdown by Customer Gender';
         end;
         else if ord = 2 then do;
            num = 50;
            txt2 = 'Breakdown by Customer Age Group';
         end;
         else if ord = 4 then do;
            num = 50;
            txt2 = 'Breakdown by Customer Type';
         end;
         line txt2 $varying. num;  ❻
      endcomp;
   run;
```

❶ The new variables are placed at the front of the COLUMN statement. This is the customary placement, but as discussed in Chapter 2 they could have been placed at the end of the COLUMN statement. SEC is the broadest level, so it is listed first.

❷ Both of the new variables are defined as ORDER with the NOPRINT option.

❸ This compute block is executed for each value of SEC. SEC was created in the DATA step; it has two unique values.

❹ Write descriptive text for each section of the report.

❺ This compute block is executed for each value of ORD. ORD was generated in each PROC MEANS step; it has four unique values.

❻ Write descriptive text for each of the CLASS variables. The technique of using the $VARYING. format is discussed in Chapter 3.

Output 5.15 includes just a portion of the final report to show the LINE statements created with the ORDER variables.

Output 5.15: ORDER Variables Are Used to Create Section Headers

Customer Name Customer Grouping	Num Separate Products Ordered	Quantity Ordered	Dollar Amount
Ramesh Trentholme	17	24	$1,545.50
Rita Lotz	6	8	$687.70
Robert Bowerman	25	37	$2,564.59
Robyn Klem	7	9	$608.60
Roy Siferd	6	11	$293.50
Sandrina Stephano	19	29	$2,810.98
Sanelisiwe Collier	4	9	$1,007.90
Selim Okay	2	4	$485.60
Serdar Yucel	2	3	$186.70
Soberina Berent	7	13	$2,308.28
Susan Krasowski	5	11	$815.40
Tedi Lanzarone	3	5	$374.10
Theunis Brazier	3	3	$292.60
Tommy Mcdonald	5	7	$343.50
Tonie Asmussen	3	4	$278.10
Tulio Devereaux	11	25	$2,303.00
Ulrich Heyde	25	48	$6,545.90
Viola Folsom	11	18	$2,778.80
Wendell Summersby	20	32	$1,583.30
Wilma Yeargan	2	5	$2,087.30
Wynella Lewis	16	32	$1,954.82
Yan Kozlowski	21	33	$2,202.60
Customer Categories			
Breakdown by Customer Gender			
F	277	498	$49,747.43
M	340	580	$50,330.04
Breakdown by Customer Age Group			
15-30 years	172	304	$30,486.50
31-45 years	233	397	$34,197.50
46-60 years	105	175	$14,920.55
61-75 years	107	202	$20,472.92
Breakdown by Customer Type			
Internet/Catalog Customers	76	138	$14,180.45
Orion Club members high activity	115	188	$14,461.50
Orion Club members medium activity	154	276	$24,164.63
Orion Club Gold members high activity	65	108	$11,600.29
Orion Club Gold members low activity	42	83	$7,484.85
Orion Club Gold members medium activity	77	117	$12,695.87
Orion Club members low activity	88	168	$15,489.87

As you can see from Output 5.15, the inclusion of just two ORDER variables drastically changes the final report. The report is now much more readable and informative. ORDER variables are a very useful tool when creating reports. The key is to define them properly when creating your input data set or pre-processing your data.

The report can look even better with style changes, which are covered in Chapter 6.

5.8 Create the Look of Merged Cells

PROC REPORT will create merged cells in three ways.

1. The SPANROWS option is specified on the PROC REPORT statement. Multiple rows in one column are merged into one cell containing a GROUP or ORDER value.
2. A spanning header is created, either with text on the COLUMN statement or an ACROSS variable over multiple columns. Multiple columns in one row are merged into one cell containing the header text.
3. A LINE statement is used in a compute block. One cell will be created for the row containing the LINE statement text and it will span all of the columns in the report.

PROC REPORT has no other means of creating a merged cell. There are no attributes to specify a merged cell. However, for some reports, you want the final report to look like it has merged cells. This section demonstrates techniques to achieve the look of merged cells.

5.8.1 Merge Vertically

In some reports, the desire is to have a header cell that is merged vertically; in other words, a top and bottom cell become one cell. This is not possible with PROC REPORT. The only method for getting the merged look is to remove the border between the two cells or change the color of the border to match the background. The text will still belong to just one of the cells. Example 5.14 demonstrates changing the border between two header cells, shown in Output 5.16.

Example 5.14: Change Borders to Get Vertically Merged Cell Look

```
proc report data=orders
    style(report)=[rules=cols] ❶
    style(column)=[bordertopwidth=.75pt bordertopcolor=black]; ❷
    column ('Customer Name' customer_name)
            ('^{style[borderbottomwidth=.75pt
                Borderbottomcolor=black]Customer Demographics}' ❸
            customer_country customer_age customer_gender);
    define customer_name / ' ';
    define customer_country / 'Country' format=$cntry.;
    define customer_age / 'Age';
    define customer_gender / 'Gender';
run;
```

❶   Use the RULES= attribute to insert all of the vertical borders.

❷ In the column (data) section of the report, add all of the horizontal borders.

❸ Add a horizontal border for the second spanning header, which is the only part of the header section that needs a horizontal border.

Output 5.16: Border Removed to Get Vertically Merged Cell Look

Customer Name	Customer Demographics		
	Country	Age	Gender
Kyndal Hooks	United States	43	F
Annmarie Leveille	United States	23	F
Najma Hicks	United States	21	F
Yan Kozlowski	United States	38	M

The Customer Name spanning header can be vertically adjusted to move it closer to the cell underneath it. Be aware that you might also have to specify the CELLHEIGHT attribute to ensure that the vertical adjustment is honored. The method above can also be used inside of the data section of the report.

It is possible to create a merged cell with the Report Writing Interface. If you absolutely must have a vertically merged header cell, you have to use the Report Writing Interface. See *SAS® 9.4 Output Delivery System: Advanced Topics.*

Manipulating borders is discussed in detail in Chapter 6.

5.8.2 Merge Horizontally

Other reports require horizontally merged cells, for displaying confidence intervals or p-values. The vertical border between cells can be removed or changed to white, as was done in the previous example. However, the value cannot be forced to span the width of both cells, so this method often is not adequate.

The alternative method is to use two or more PROC REPORT steps to create the output. Each step will be responsible for creating a certain number of columns. The step that creates the rows with the merged-cell look will create fewer columns than the other step.

For example, a report contains five columns with the last row containing two merged cells – columns 2 and 3 looked merged and columns 4 and 5 look merged. One PROC REPORT step will create the output with all five columns. Another PROC REPORT step will create just three columns.

The CELLWIDTH attribute is extremely important in this method. A width will need to be specified for all columns; the default width created by the ODS destination cannot be used. In the second PROC REPORT step, the width of the column (that will look like a merged cell) is set to the sum of the size of the two columns from the first PROC REPORT step. The NOHEADER option is also extremely important. This option should be used on the second and subsequent

PROC REPORT steps to prevent a header row from being created. The goal is to make the second table look like it is part of the first table so that the final report looks like one seamless report.

Example 5.15 creates a cell for each of the values of CUSTOMER_AGE_GROUP, shown in Output 5.17. Then, at the bottom of the report, we want a merged cell that contains the summed information for two of the age groups. The numbers in this example do not mean as much as the structure.

Example 5.15: Two PROC REPORT Steps Are Needed for Horizontally Merged-Cell Look

```
proc report data=orders style(column)=[width=1in]; ❶
   column product_line customer_age_group, quantity;
   define product_line / group;
   define customer_age_group / across;
run;

proc format;
   value $grpage ❷
   "15-30 years", "31-45 years" = 'Cat 1'
   "46-60 years", "61-75 years" = 'Cat 2';
run;

proc report data=orders noheader; ❸
   column dummy customer_age_group, quantity;
   define dummy / computed style(column)=[width=1in]; ❹
   define customer_age_group / across format=$grpage.;
   define quantity / style(column)=[width=2.01in ]; ❺

   compute dummy / char; ❻
      dummy = '';
   endcomp;
run;
```

❶ Set a specific width for all columns in the first PROC REPORT step.

❷ This format will consolidate the CUSTOMER_AGE_GROUP values into two categories.

❸ Specify the NOHEADER option so only the data from the second PROC REPORT step is displayed.

❹ Set a specific width for the first column in this step. It matches that width from the first step since it will not be a merged cell.

❺ Set the width of the columns created by the CUSTOMER_AGE_GROUP variable to be twice the size of the columns from the first PROC REPORT step. These cells will look merged compared to the cells above it.

❻ A dummy COMPUTED *report-item* is created and assigned a blank value.

Note: You might have to manipulate the borders or tweak the cell width values to ensure that the output looks like it contains just one table. The OUTPUTWIDTH= option might be very useful inside of STYLE(REPORT) to ensure that the tables are the exact same width.

Output 5.17: Two Tables Abutted to Get Horizontally Merged Cell Look

	Customer Age Group			
	15-30 years	31-45 years	46-60 years	61-75 years
Product Line	Quantity Ordered	Quantity Ordered	Quantity Ordered	Quantity Ordered
Children	23	18	7	1
Clothes & Shoes	56	112	57	50
Outdoors	53	97	25	65
Sports	172	170	86	86
		701		377

The ODS destination plays a large role in creating the desired output because the ODS destination has to allow you to remove the white space between tables.

The ODS RTF statement has an option called SECTIONDATA that allows you remove the white space between output tables.

```
ods rtf file='merged_look.rtf' sectiondata="\sbknone";
proc report 1 ...
proc report 2 ...
run;
ods rtf close;
```

The ODS PDF destination does not have an option for removing the space between tables, but you can use ODS LAYOUT with ODS PDF to force the tables to abut. Output 5.17 was created in PDF using ODS LAYOUT.

```
ods pdf file="merged_look.pdf" notoc;
ods layout gridded rows=2 row_gutter=0in;
ods region;
proc report 1 ...
ods region;
proc report 2 ...
run;
ods layout end;
ods pdf close;
```

ODS GRIDDED LAYOUT can also be used for HTML output and the ODS destination for Microsoft PowerPoint.

ODS Tagsets.ExcelXP has an option called SKIP_SPACE, which allows you to remove the space between tables that are sent to the same worksheet. However, the second table will not produce the desired appearance. The first PROC REPORT step dictates the number of columns and the width. The table from the second PROC REPORT step will simply be placed underneath the first, taking up only the number of cells corresponding to the number of variables on the COLUMN statement. You will need to post-process the Microsoft Excel file to merge cells.

The ODS destination for Excel does not have a skip space option. However, as demonstrated in Chapter 3, you can hide a specific row, which will allow you to abut the tables. The MERGEACROSS option placed within the TAGATTR= options works better for the Excel destination than it does for the Tagsets.ExcelXP destination, but it still might not produce the desired results. This is because the table is constructed before the MERGEACROSS command has been sent.

Again, the Report Writing Interface can create a merged cell. If using two PROC REPORT steps does not create the desired output, you should consider using the Report Writing Interface. See *SAS 9.4 Output Delivery System: Advanced Topics*.

Chapter 6: Styles – How to Change a Report's Appearance

6.1 Introduction

You now have a good grasp on how to get the numbers and report structure that you need out of PROC REPORT. PROC REPORT is not only a very powerful tool for creating reports in various structures, but it has the capability to add colors, images, hyperlinks, and more. These features help the reader focus on the most important aspects of the report and click to see more detail. This chapter focuses on the styling aspects of PROC REPORT that make the report easier to read.

The chapter begins by demonstrating the use of the border control attributes. These attributes can be used to change or remove borders so that specific columns and rows are visually grouped together.

Trafficlighting is an important tool for conveying relationship and hierarchies. Unlike some reporting procedures, PROC REPORT has the ability to apply trafficlighting based on the values of any cell in the report.

This chapter also demonstrates changing color attributes in the headers of reports and changing attributes of rows generated by LINE statements.

PROC REPORT is not limited to changing just one attribute or just one cell. Section 6.8 shows how borders can be altered at the same time that colors and formats are. The key is changing the attribute in the correct compute block based on execution order.

Finally, the chapter explores including images and URLs as part of the table to enhance not only the appearance, but the information the report conveys.

6.2 STYLE= Option

Style attributes can be applied from any or all of the PROC REPORT statements, using the STYLE<(location(s))>= option. Specifying the location value is optional, but it is best practice to include it. Attribute name and value pairs are listed in brackets after the equal sign. The valid and default values for location vary by statement. The location value can be:

- column
- header
- summary
- report
- lines
- calldef

To specify more than one value of location in the same STYLE= option, separate each value with a space. For example, STYLE(HEADER COLUMN)= will change the attributes in both the header and column areas of the report.

The following statements use the STYLE<(location(s))>= option. The default location is listed.

- PROC REPORT: report
- DEFINE: column and header
- BREAK: summary and lines
- RBREAK: summary and lines
- COMPUTE: lines

Most of the location values are straightforward. *Base SAS Procedures Guide* has a description of each location and a table showing what attributes can be used for that section of the report. Style attributes are applied in the following order. The last one listed takes precedence.

1. Style template created by PROC TEMPLATE and specified on the ODS statement.
2. PROC REPORT statement
3. DEFINE statement
4. BREAK or RBREAK statement
5. COMPUTE statement
6. CALL DEFINE statement

The precedence order means that when specified on the PROC REPORT statement, the header location controls all header cells. When specified on a DEFINE statement, the header location controls the header cell for that specific *report-item*. The same is true for all of the other locations.

The report location can be tricky. Attributes such as RULES=, FRAME=, and BORDERCOLOR= impact every area of the report. OUTPUTWIDTH= (or WIDTH=) is applied to the entire table. Text related attributes, such as FONTSIZE= and FONT=, impact the text created by PRETEXT and POSTTEXT. When associated with the report location, the BACKGROUND= attribute has a different effect in each ODS destination. The most important thing to remember is that if you specify an attribute in the report location, you need to make sure it changes the output in the way you expect. If it does not, you might need to try assigning the attribute in a different location.

This chapter will not cover all possible style attributes that can be applied to PROC REPORT output. It will focus on the most commonly changed attributes.

6.3 Borders

Border lines help draw the focus of the report reader; they help distinguish different pieces of information and hopefully make the report easier to read. Borders for specific sections of the table can be controlled with style templates using the following style attributes:

- FRAME=
- RULES=
- BORDER<LOCATION>WIDTH=
- BORDER<LOCATION>COLOR= (where location=BOTTOM, TOP, LEFT, or RIGHT).

These options, when used in a style template, can turn the borders on and off for a specific section (location) of the report, but they cannot control individual borders within that location. You will need to use these options inside of PROC REPORT to gain granular control of the borders.

In this section, we will first look at the various appearances the FRAME= and RULES= attributes produce. Then, we will explore ways to manipulate the border lines in order to get custom appearances. Due to the fact that we are changing individual borders, we will make all changes within PROC REPORT and not PROC TEMPLATE.

The report, column, and header locations are the most commonly used locations when controlling the borders. The report location is where you would specify the FRAME= and RULES= attributes. This location is used only on the PROC REPORT statement.

When border style attributes are specified, the lines are drawn for the entire width and height of the cell. These attributes should not be used when trying to underline words.

Note: Each ODS destination behaves differently from every other destination. This is especially true when changing borders. For example, in ODS PDF, changing one border results in all four borders being drawn. Also, you might have to specify color and width for the border to be drawn. The code in this section is geared toward use with ODS PDF, but should be applicable in other destinations. Section 6.7.3 specifically addresses changing borders in HTML output.

Note: The border color is set to black throughout this section. The style template for your report might use a different color. You should check the style template for the appropriate color specification.

6.3.1 FRAME= and RULES= Attributes

The FRAME= option controls the borders on the outside of the table. The option can be assigned one of the values listed in Table 6.1.

Table 6.1: FRAME= Values

Value for frame-type	Frame
ABOVE	A border at the top
BELOW	A border at the bottom
BOX	Borders at the top, bottom, and both sides
HSIDES	Borders at the top and bottom
LHS	A border at the left side
RHS	A border at the right side
VOID	No borders
VSIDES	Borders at the left and right sides

The default value for FRAME= varies for each style template. However, BOX is frequently the default. The FRAME= value is at the table level. In some destinations (like Tagsets.RTF), if the table is long enough to span multiple pages, the bottom border might appear only on the last page. In this circumstance, you will have to create a dummy paging variable in order to generate a bottom border on each page. Paging variables are discussed in Chapters 2 and 3. The page break will create multiple tables, one for each page, and the bottom border will be placed on each table.

The RULES= option controls the borders within the table. It can be assigned one of the values listed in Table 6.2.

Table 6.2: RULES= Values

Value for RULES=	Location of Rules
ALL	Between all rows and columns
COLS	Between all columns

Value for RULES=	Location of Rules
GROUPS	Between the table header and the table and between the table and the table footer if there is one
NONE	No borders
ROWS	Between all Rows

Again, the default value for RULES= varies, but ALL is commonly used.

The code in Example 6.1 creates output that specifies the RULES= attribute, seen in Table 6.2. Changing the value specified for RULES= produces Figure 6.1, which demonstrates the look each value creates. Please note that the value of FRAME=BOX is inherited from the style template.

Example 6.1: Changing the RULES= Attribute

```
proc report data=orders style(report)=[rules=ALL];
   column product_line customer_gender quantity total_retail_price;
   define product_line / group;
   define customer_gender / group;
run;
```

Figure 6.1: Various Border Looks in ODS PDF Created by Changing the RULES= Attribute

Rules=all

Product Line	Customer Gender	Quantity Ordered	Total Retail Price for This Product
Children	F	27	$722.30
	M	22	$894.10
Clothes & Shoes	F	132	$7,802.90
	M	143	$8,941.79
Outdoors	F	82	$10,931.60
	M	158	$18,930.40
Sports	F	257	$30,290.63
	M	257	$21,563.75

Rules=cols

Product Line	Customer Gender	Quantity Ordered	Total Retail Price for This Product
Children	F	27	$722.30
	M	22	$894.10
Clothes & Shoes	F	132	$7,802.90
	M	143	$8,941.79
Outdoors	F	82	$10,931.60
	M	158	$18,930.40
Sports	F	257	$30,290.63
	M	257	$21,563.75

Rules=groups

Product Line	Customer Gender	Quantity Ordered	Total Retail Price for This Product
Children	F	27	$722.30
	M	22	$894.10
Clothes & Shoes	F	132	$7,802.90
	M	143	$8,941.79
Outdoors	F	82	$10,931.60
	M	158	$18,930.40
Sports	F	257	$30,290.63
	M	257	$21,563.75

Rules=none

Product Line	Customer Gender	Quantity Ordered	Total Retail Price for This Product
Children	F	27	$722.30
	M	22	$894.10
Clothes & Shoes	F	132	$7,802.90
	M	143	$8,941.79
Outdoors	F	82	$10,931.60
	M	158	$18,930.40
Sports	F	257	$30,290.63
	M	257	$21,563.75

Rules=rows

Product Line	Customer Gender	Quantity Ordered	Total Retail Price for This Product
Children	F	27	$722.30
	M	22	$894.10
Clothes & Shoes	F	132	$7,802.90
	M	143	$8,941.79
Outdoors	F	82	$10,931.60
	M	158	$18,930.40
Sports	F	257	$30,290.63
	M	257	$21,563.75

6.3.2 Column (Data) Borders

For some reports, borders need to be changed or added to both the header location and the column location. The following examples will concentrate on the column location. Section 6.3.3 will concentrate on the header location.

Example 6.2 places vertical borders between the columns, as seen in Output 6.1. The only horizontal border will be between the headers and the data. Remember, when STYLE(COLUMN) is used on the PROC REPORT statement, it controls all of the columns within the body of the table.

Example 6.2: Insert Borders between Columns

```
proc report data=orders style(report)=[rules=groups] ❶
    style(column)=[borderleftcolor=black borderleftwidth=.1pt
                   borderrightcolor=black borderrightwidth=.1pt]; ❷
    column product_line customer_gender quantity total_retail_price;
    define product_line / group;
    define customer_gender / group;
run;
```

❶ Rules=groups will draw the horizontal border between the headers and the data.

❷ Style(column)= controls the attributes for all of the columns in the output. A left and right border will be drawn for all columns.

Output 6.1: A Border is Placed under the Headers and between the Columns

Product Line	Customer Gender	Quantity Ordered	Total Retail Price for This Product
Children	F	27	$722.30
	M	22	$894.10
Clothes & Shoes	F	132	$7,802.90
	M	143	$8,941.79
Outdoors	F	82	$10,931.60
	M	158	$18,930.40
Sports	F	257	$30,290.63
	M	257	$21,563.75

In Example 6.2, borders were placed between all columns. In Example 6.3, we want to place just one vertical border to distinguish the last column from all of the other columns. Output 6.2 displays the horizontal border between the headers and the data.

Example 6.3: Insert a Border for One Column

```
proc report data=orders style(report)=[rules=groups]; ❶
    column product_line customer_gender quantity total_retail_price;
    define product_line / group;
    define customer_gender / group;
    define quantity / style(column header)=[borderrightcolor=black
           borderrightwidth=.1pt]; ❷
    define total_retail_price / style(column header)=
           [borderleftcolor=black borderleftwidth=.1pt]; ❸
run;
```

❶ Rules=groups will draw the horizontal border between the headers and the data.

❷   Style(column header)= controls the attributes for the QUANTITY column in both the data and header areas of the report. Only the right border will be drawn for this column.

❸   Style(column report)= controls the attributes for the TOTAL_RETAIL_PRICE column in both the data and header areas of the report. Only the left border will be drawn for this column.

Output 6.2: A Border Is Drawn to Distinguish the Last Column

Product Line	Customer Gender	Quantity Ordered	Total Retail Price for This Product
Children	F	27	$722.30
	M	22	$894.10
Clothes & Shoes	F	132	$7,802.90
	M	143	$8,941.79
Outdoors	F	82	$10,931.60
	M	158	$18,930.40
Sports	F	257	$30,290.63
	M	257	$21,563.75

The goal of the final example in this section is to insert border lines between groups of data. Ideally the border would be placed on the first row of each grouping because it is easy to determine which row that is based on a nonmissing GROUP/ORDER variable value. However, the ODS destination controls where a page break occurs, so we cannot use the first row in a grouping to control the border because our override might affect the border between the header and data. To place a border on the last row of a group, an extra grouping variable needs to be created. Then inside of PROC REPORT, border control attributes can be used in a CALL DEFINE statement.

The report created in Example 6.4 is first grouped by PRODUCT_LINE, and then by CUSTOMER_GENDER. The border line needs to be placed at the bottom of each PRODUCT_LINE grouping. The key to this method is determining the last CUSTOMER_GENDER value within a PRODUCT_LINE value. Pre-processing is required, including two PROC SORT steps and two DATA steps.

The data has to be pre-processed to create the new group variable, which is an indicator for the last CUSTOMER_GENDER within PRODUCT_LINE. The indicator variable is then placed in the COLUMN statement and defined as a GROUP (or ORDER) variable.

The result is shown in Output 6.3.

Example 6.4: Insert Border Lines between Groups

```
proc sort data=orders(keep=product_line customer_gender)
     out=unique nodupkey; ❶
   by product_line customer_gender;
run;
```

❷
```
data unique;
   set unique;
   by product_line customer_gender;
   if last.product_line;
   rename customer_gender=last_gender;
run;
```

❸
```
data orders2;
   merge orders unique;
   by product_line;
run;

proc report data=orders2 style(report)=[rules=groups];  ❹
   column product_line last_gender ❺ customer_gender quantity
         total_retail_price;
   define product_line / group;
   define customer_gender / group;
   define last_gender / group noprint;  ❻

   compute last_gender;  ❼
      if not missing(last_gender) then hold=last_gender;
   endcomp;

   compute customer_gender;  ❽
      if hold = customer_gender then do;
         call define(_row_,'style','style=[borderbottomwidth=.1pt
            borderbottomcolor=black]');
      end;
   endcomp;
run;
```

❶ Get a unique list of PRODUCT_LINE and CUSTOMER_GENDER combinations.

❷ From the unique list, keep only the last CUSTOMER_GENDER value within each value of PRODUCT_LINE. Rename CUSTOMER_GENDER to LAST_GENDER.

❸ Merge the LAST_GENDER variable onto the original ORDERS data set.

❹ Rules=groups will draw the horizontal border between the headers and the data.

❺ Place LAST_GENDER on the COLUMN statement prior to the CUSTOMER_GENDER variable.

❻ Define LAST_GENDER as a GROUP variable and use the NOPRINT option so that the column is not included in the final report.

❼ Create a temporary variable called HOLD that will contain the value of LAST_GENDER for all observations.

❽ Determine if the CUSTOMER_GENDER value matches the value in HOLD within each value of PRODUCT_LINE. If it matches, then use a CALL DEFINE statement to insert a border under that row.

Output 6.3: A Border is Inserted between Values of Product Line

Product Line	Customer Gender	Quantity Ordered	Total Retail Price for This Product
Children	F	27	$722.30
	M	22	$894.10
Clothes & Shoes	F	132	$7,802.90
	M	143	$8,941.79
Outdoors	F	82	$10,931.60
	M	158	$18,930.40
Sports	F	257	$30,290.63
	M	257	$21,563.75

The last value of CUSTOMER_GENDER is the same value for each value of PRODUCT_LINE in this example, but that might change if the data was subset or a new version of the data was provided. And, it might not be the case in your data. The purpose is to demonstrate how to determine the last row with the PRODUCT_LINE grouping.

This example placed a border under the last row of PRODUCT_LINE, but this technique can be used to do anything you need to do to the last row, like change values, colors, or formats.

6.3.3 Header Borders

Controlling the borders in the header section of a report can be challenging. The header section has one row of cells that contain the labels for the individual columns, but as you learned in Chapters 3 and 4, spanning headers create additional rows, as do ACROSS variables. An ACROSS variable will create a row containing the values of the variable and another row containing the label of the ACROSS variable. Each of the cells containing a header can be controlled individually. The key is knowing what created the cell – a variable value, variable label, or a spanning header.

Example 6.5 shows how an ACROSS variable affects borders. The values of CUSTOMER_GENDER will become headers with corresponding columns underneath, as shown in Output 6.4. The goal is to draw a border under the values of CUSTOMER_GENDER and above the individual column headers created by the other *report-items*.

Example 6.5: Change Borders for ACROSS Variable Headers

```
proc report data=orders style(report)=[rules=groups]; ❶
   column product_line customer_age_group
customer_gender,(quantity total_retail_price); ❷
   define product_line / group;
   define customer_age_group / group;
   define customer_gender / across ''
         style(header)=[borderbottomwidth=.1pt
         borderbottomcolor=black]; ❸
```

```
        define total_retail_price / 'Total Retail Price';
run;
```

❶ Rules=groups will draw the horizontal border between the headers and the data.

❷ Putting a comma after CUSTOMER_GENDER and putting QUANTITY and TOTAL_RETAIL_PRICE inside of parentheses will place a column for QUANTITY and TOTAL_RETAIL_PRICE under each value of CUSTOMER_GENDER.

❸ Style(header)= controls the attributes for the CUSTOMER_GENDER header cells. CUSTOMER_GENDER does not have a header label, but the attributes also apply to its values because it is defined as an ACROSS variable. A bottom border will be drawn under the M and F values.

Output 6.4: A Border Is Drawn under the ACROSS Variable Values

			F		M
Product Line	**Customer Age Group**	**Quantity Ordered**	**Total Retail Price**	**Quantity Ordered**	**Total Retail Price**
Children	15-30 years	17	$544.00	6	$198.60
	31-45 years	7	$140.50	11	$473.00
	46-60 years	3	$37.80	4	$172.10
	61-75 years	.	.	1	$50.40
Clothes & Shoes	15-30 years	52	$2,496.90	4	$425.40
	31-45 years	43	$2,256.80	69	$3,484.19
	46-60 years	22	$2,046.00	35	$2,299.20
	61-75 years	15	$1,003.20	35	$2,733.00
Outdoors	15-30 years	37	$4,200.70	16	$2,022.00
	31-45 years	31	$5,602.50	66	$6,115.20
	46-60 years	10	$671.80	15	$1,359.60
	61-75 years	4	$456.60	61	$9,433.60
Sports	15-30 years	129	$17,763.91	43	$2,834.99
	31-45 years	76	$8,360.20	94	$7,765.11
	46-60 years	26	$2,610.20	60	$5,723.85
	61-75 years	26	$1,556.32	60	$5,239.80

Borders that surround spanning headers cannot be controlled individually with the STYLE(HEADER)= option. Inline formatting must be used to control individual spanning headers. The syntax for inline formatting is

```
^{style <style-element-name><[style-attribute-specification(s)]>
formatted text}
```

In this case, ^ is the ODS ESCAPECHAR. The *escape-character* should be one of the following rarely used characters: @, ^, or \. The backslash (\) should not be used for RTF output.

Example 6.6 demonstrates how to place a border underneath a spanning header. Output 6.5 will look much like the previous example. The difference is how the text was created.

Example 6.6: Change Borders for a Spanning Header

```
ods escapechar="^"; ❶
proc report data=orders style(report)=[rules=groups]; ❷
   column product_line customer_age_group
          ('^{style [borderbottomwidth=.1pt
          borderbottomcolor=black]Order value}'
          quantity total_retail_price); ❸
   define product_line / group;
   define customer_age_group / group ;
   define total_retail_price / 'Total Retail Price';
run;
```

❶ Declare an ODS ESCAPECHAR so that inline formatting can be used to draw borders in this example.

❷ Rules=groups will draw the horizontal border between the headers and the data.

❸ Inline formatting is used to draw a border under the spanning header "Order value."

Output 6.5: A Border is Drawn Under a Spanning Header

| Product Line | Customer Age Group | Order value | |
		Quantity Ordered	Total Retail Price
Children	15-30 years	23	$742.60
	31-45 years	18	$613.50
	46-60 years	7	$209.90
	61-75 years	1	$50.40
Clothes & Shoes	15-30 years	56	$2,922.30
	31-45 years	112	$5,740.99
	46-60 years	57	$4,345.20
	61-75 years	50	$3,736.20
Outdoors	15-30 years	53	$6,222.70
	31-45 years	97	$11,717.70
	46-60 years	25	$2,031.40
	61-75 years	65	$9,890.20
Sports	15-30 years	172	$20,598.90
	31-45 years	170	$16,125.31
	46-60 years	86	$8,334.05
	61-75 years	86	$6,796.12

Inline formatting can be used to draw multiple borders to create a look not available through STYLE(HEADER)=. Example 6.7 and Output 6.6 demonstrate using inline formatting to draw all of the borders within the header section.

Example 6.7: Draw Vertical and Horizontal Borders with Inline Formatting

```
proc report data=orders style(report)=[rules=groups]; ❶
   column ('Product Line' product_line) ❷
          ('^{style [borderrightwidth=.1pt borderrightcolor=black]}
```

```
                    Customer Age Group' customer_age_group ) ❸
                    ('^{style [borderbottomwidth=.1pt
                    borderbottomcolor=black]Order value}' quantity
                    total_retail_price); ❹
        define product_line / group ''; ❺
        define customer_age_group / group ''
                style(header)=[borderrightwidth=.1pt
                borderrightcolor=black]; ❻
        define total_retail_price / 'Total Retail Price';
    run;
```

❶   Rules=groups will draw the horizontal border between the headers and the data.

❷   "Product Line" is a spanning header, which will align with the other spanning headers.

❸   "Customer Age Group" is a spanning header, which will align with the other spanning headers. Inline formatting is used to add a right border to the cell, which will draw a border line between "Customer Age Group" and "Order value."

❹   Inline formatting is used to draw a border under the spanning header "Order Value."

❺   The column header for PRODUCT_LINE is set to blank. This means a blank cell will be placed immediately above the first data value.

❻   The column header for CUSTOMER_AGE is set to blank. This means a blank cell will be placed immediately above the first data value. Style(header)= inserts a border on the right side of the blank cell, which will draw a border line between "" and "Quantity Ordered."

Output 6.6: Borders Separate the Header into Sections

Product Line	Customer Age Group	Order value	
		Quantity Ordered	Total Retail Price
Children	15-30 years	23	$742.60
	31-45 years	18	$613.50
	46-60 years	7	$209.90
	61-75 years	1	$50.40
Clothes & Shoes	15-30 years	56	$2,922.30
	31-45 years	112	$5,740.99
	46-60 years	57	$4,345.20
	61-75 years	50	$3,736.20
Outdoors	15-30 years	53	$6,222.70
	31-45 years	97	$11,717.70
	46-60 years	25	$2,031.40
	61-75 years	65	$9,890.20
Sports	15-30 years	172	$20,598.90
	31-45 years	170	$16,125.31
	46-60 years	86	$8,334.05
	61-75 years	86	$6,796.12

TIP: For some reports, getting the desired borders might require trial and error. You might want to remove all borders and add specific borders until you get the desired appearance. Also, in some cases, you might need to specify a border in a certain spot, but you can change the color to match the background so that it is not seen.

6.4 Trafficlighting

A very common task for report creators is to apply coloring to the background or foreground of certain cells so that they stand out. This is called trafficlighting. The type of trafficlighting that is needed depends on the report, but you can highlight a cell based on its value or the value of another cell. You can also highlight an entire row or color cells in a diagonal pattern. In this section, we will explore how to trafficlight cells for each of these tasks.

6.4.1 Color Based on Cell's Value

The most common technique is to change the foreground or background of a cell based on its value. This method is used to draw attention to values that are above a certain threshold or have fallen below it. This method can also simply distinguish one group from another.

The color assignment can be made on two different statements, the DEFINE statement and the CALL DEFINE statement. Both statements produce the same result.

Example 6.8 changes the background of the TOTAL_RETAIL_PRICE column, as seen in Output 6.7. The color will be based on a range of possible values, usually the lowest value is assigned the lightest color, and the highest value assigned to the darkest color. The color values are assigned in a PROC FORMAT step.

Example 6.8: Apply a Background Color Via the DEFINE Statement

```
proc format;
    value pricefmt ❶
        . = 'red'
        low - 0 = 'red'
        0 <- 10000 = 'cxe0ecf4'
        10000 <- 30000 ='cxfe9929'
        30000 <- high = 'yellow'
        ;
run;

proc report data=orders;
    column customer_country quantity costprice_per_unit
           total_retail_price;
    define customer_country / group format=$cntry.;
    define total_retail_price / 'Retail Price'
           style(column)=[background=pricefmt.]; ❷
run;
```

❶ Create a format with the desired ranges. The specified color can be a predefined SAS color, RGB value, HLS value, RGBA value, or a CMYK value.

❷ Inside of the style(column)= option on the DEFINE statement put the BACKGROUND= attribute and specify its value as the format name created in the first step. Each time a row is generated for TOTAL_RETAIL_PRICE, the value is evaluated against the format and the appropriate color value is assigned to the background.

Output 6.7: Background Color of Retail Price Varies Based on What Value Range It Falls Into

Customer Country	Quantity Ordered	Cost Price Per Unit	Retail Price
Australia	210	$4,851.35	$17,321.49
Canada	105	$2,293.80	$11,951.08
Germany	106	$4,065.55	$15,394.60
Israel	28	$516.95	$1,559.50
South Africa	47	$1,250.35	$5,149.90
Turkey	43	$1,656.15	$5,175.80
United States	539	$11,171.98	$43,525.10

Output 6.7 can also be achieved by applying the format in a CALL DEFINE statement within a compute block, as shown in Example 6.9. The attribute name and value pair, background=pricefmt., remains the same.

Example 6.9: Apply Background Color Via a CALL DEFINE Statement

```
proc report data=orders;
    column customer_country quantity costprice_per_unit
           total_retail_price;
    define customer_country / group format=$cntry.;
    define total_retail_price / 'Retail Price';
    compute total_retail_price;
        call define(_col_,'style','style=[background=pricefmt.]'); ❶
    endcomp;
run;
```

❶ The attribute name and value pair is placed in the third argument of the CALL DEFINE statement. The value of TOTAL_RETAIL_PRICE is evaluated for each cell of the column.

Applying styles via a CALL DEFINE statement uses more memory and CPU than applying it via a DEFINE statement. Therefore, if memory is a concern, and the style can be applied on the DEFINE statement, the DEFINE statement is the better method.

6.4.2 Color Based on Another *Report-item*

Trafficlighting can also be assigned to one column based on the value of another column. In this situation, the color assignment must be done with a CALL DEFINE statement within a compute block. It is important to pay attention to which variable is placed on the COMPUTE statement and which column is referenced as the first argument of the CALL DEFINE statement. Remember from Chapter 2 that PROC REPORT works left to right based on the order of the *report-items* on the COLUMN statement. You must be sure you are not referencing a *report-item* that is to the right of the one on the COMPUTE statement.

Example 6.10 assigns a background color to the TOTAL_RETAIL_PRICE column based on the value of the CUSTOMER_COUNTRY variable, as shown in Output 6.8.

Example 6.10: Use CALL DEFINE Statement to Change Attributes

```
proc report data=orders;
   column customer_country quantity costprice_per_unit
          total_retail_price;
   define customer_country / group format=$cntry.;
   define total_retail_price / 'Retail Price';
   compute total_retail_price; ❶
      if customer_country in ('US' 'DE' 'CA') then ❷
        call define(_col_,'style','style=[background=cxfe9929]'); ❸
      else if customer_country = 'AU' then
        call define(_col_,'style','style=[background=cxe0ecf4]');
      else
        call define(_col_,'style','style=[background=yellow]');
   endcomp;
run;
```

❶ TOTAL_RETAIL_PRICE is placed on the COMPUTE statement because it is the column that we want to apply the color to, and because it is the last variable on the COLUMN statement. All of the values of the other columns have already been populated.

❷ Write IF/ELSE IF conditions that will divide the CUSTOMER_COUNTRY values into the desired groupings.

❸ In the CALL DEFINE statement the _COL_ reference can be used as the first argument because TOTAL_RETAIL_PRICE is on the COMPUTE statement and that is the column in which the color will change. In the third argument, assign the desired color to each country grouping.

Output 6.8: Background Color Changes for Each Cell Based on Country

Customer Country	Quantity Ordered	Cost Price Per Unit	Retail Price
Australia	210	$4,851.35	$17,321.49
Canada	105	$2,293.80	$11,951.08
Germany	106	$4,065.55	$15,394.60
Israel	28	$516.95	$1,559.50
South Africa	47	$1,250.35	$5,149.90
Turkey	43	$1,656.15	$5,175.80
United States	539	$11,171.98	$43,525.10

CALL DEFINE statements can be used to do more than set the background color in just one column. You can change multiple columns, multiple attributes, or assign an attribute to an entire row. Example 6.11 changes the foreground color to red and the font weight to bold and italicizes the data for the rows that do not meet certain criteria, in this case, the countries that have not achieved the goal of selling 50 units. The results are shown in Output 6.9.

Example 6.11: Highlight Specific Rows

```
proc report data=orders;
    column customer_country quantity costprice_per_unit
           total_retail_price;
    define customer_country / group format=$cntry.;
    define total_retail_price / 'Retail Price';
    compute total_retail_price;
        if quantity.sum < 50 then ❶
            call define(_row_,'style','style=[foreground=red
                      font_weight=bold font_style=italic]'); ❷
    endcomp;
run;
```

❶ The IF condition specifies that QUANTITY.SUM is less than 50. QUANTITY is an ANALYSIS variable, so it must be referred to by *variable-name.statistic* in the compute block. Also, TOTAL_RETAIL_PRICE is listed after QUANTITY on the COLUMN statement, so the value of QUANTITY is available in this compute block.

❷ The first argument in the CALL DEFINE statement is _row_, which means that the style attributes will be applied to every column in the row that satisfies the IF condition. In the third argument, three attribute name and value pairs are listed to change the foreground color, the font weight, and the font style.

Output 6.9: Rows with a Quantity Less Than 50 Are Red and Italic

Customer Country	Quantity Ordered	Cost Price Per Unit	Retail Price
Australia	210	$4,851.35	$17,321.49
Canada	105	$2,293.80	$11,951.08
Germany	106	$4,065.55	$15,394.60
Israel	*28*	*$516.95*	*$1,559.50*
South Africa	*47*	*$1,250.35*	*$5,149.90*
Turkey	*43*	*$1,656.15*	*$5,175.80*
United States	539	$11,171.98	$43,525.10

A color attribute can also pull its value from the value of a variable. You might have a variable in your data set that contains the color assignment that you want to use. Or, the color value might be contained in the text of another *report-item* that is used in the report. When the color variable already exists in the input data set, be sure to place it correctly on the COLUMN statement so that its value is available in the compute block that you are using.

CUSTOMER_GROUP has three values, one of which contains the word "Gold." Example 6.12 applies gold as the foreground color to three of the four columns when CUSTOMER_GROUP is "Orion Club Gold members." The result is shown in Output 6.10.

Example 6.12: Change Foreground Color Based on a Color Variable

```
proc report data=orders;
   column customer_country customer_group quantity costprice_per_unit
          total_retail_price;
   define customer_country / group format=$cntry.;
   define customer_group / group;
   define total_retail_price / mean 'Mean Retail Price';
   compute total_retail_price; ❶
      if index(customer_group,'Gold') then color = 'cxcc4c02'; ❷
         else color = 'black';
   ❸ call define('customer_group','style',
                   'style=[foreground='||color||']');
      call define('quantity.sum','style',
                   'style=[foreground='||color||']');
      call define('costprice_per_unit.sum','style',
                   'style=[foreground='||color||']');
      call define('total_retail_price.mean','style',
                   'style=[foreground='||color||']');
   endcomp;
run;
```

❶   Use TOTAL_RETAIL_PRICE on the COMPUTE statement because it is the last variable on the COLUMN statement, and we need to assign the foreground color to multiple columns.

❷   Create a temporary variable to hold the desired color value. If CUSTOMER_GROUP contains the word "Gold", then assign the color to gold. Otherwise, assign the color to black.

❸   A CALL DEFINE statement is needed for each of the columns that we want to modify. Be sure to use the appropriate variable reference in the first argument depending on the variable type, GROUP or ANALYSIS. The third argument is built using the concatenation (||) operator. Notice the variable name COLOR does not appear directly inside of quotation marks. This is because COLOR is a variable name, and its value needs to be concatenated into the string. If COLOR is inside of quotation marks, no format will be applied because FOREGROUND=COLOR has no meaning to the CALL DEFINE statement.

Output 6.10: Customer Group with Gold in the Name Are Highlighted

Customer Country	Customer Group Name	Quantity Ordered	Cost Price Per Unit	Mean Retail Price
Australia	Internet/Catalog Customers	13	$429.60	$106.13
	Orion Club Gold members	24	$552.05	$90.91
	Orion Club members	173	$3,869.70	$144.26
Canada	Internet/Catalog Customers	5	$132.55	$226.43
	Orion Club Gold members	30	$653.65	$215.99
	Orion Club members	70	$1,507.60	$217.08
Germany	Internet/Catalog Customers	48	$1,695.55	$261.84
	Orion Club Gold members	48	$2,146.70	$281.88
	Orion Club members	10	$223.30	$191.24
Israel	Internet/Catalog Customers	5	$76.55	$125.67
	Orion Club Gold members	2	$77.65	$79.30
	Orion Club members	21	$362.75	$73.14
South Africa	Orion Club Gold members	17	$508.15	$169.56
	Orion Club members	30	$742.20	$230.29
Turkey	Orion Club Gold members	7	$432.25	$234.00
	Orion Club members	36	$1,223.90	$190.75
United States	Internet/Catalog Customers	67	$1,205.90	$157.63
	Orion Club Gold members	180	$4,247.60	$150.27
	Orion Club members	292	$5,718.48	$134.53

6.4.3 Color on the Diagonal

The ORDERS data set does not lend itself to a practical example of highlighting cells on the diagonal. To demonstrate the technique, a small data set is created. The variable value of one column is compared to the header of another column inside of the PROC REPORT step of Example 6.13. When the values match, the corresponding cell is highlighted, as in Output 6.11.

Example 6.13: Color Cell in a Diagonal Pattern

```
data test; ❶
input x $ a b c;
datalines;
a 1 2 3
b 4 5 6
c 7 8 9
;
run;

%macro rep(colvars);
    %local word_cnt ordervar i;
    %let word_cnt=%sysfunc(countw(&colvars)); ❷
    %let ordervar=%scan(&colvars.,1,' '); ❸
```

```
proc report data=test;
    col &colvars dummy;  ❹
    define &ordervar / order;
    define dummy / noprint;

    compute dummy;
        %do i=2 %to &word_cnt;  ❺
            %let chkvar=%scan(&colvars.,&i.,' ');  ❻
            if &ordervar="&chkvar" then call define(
                "&chkvar..sum",'style','style=[background=cxfe9929]');  ❼
        %end;
    endcomp;
    run;
%mend;

%rep (x a b c)  ❽
```

❶   Create a data set with one variable that contains the variable names of the other variables.

❷   Count the number of variables in the macro parameter &COLVARS. In this example &WORD_CNT resolves to 4.

❸   Assign the first variable of &COLVARS to the macro variable &ORDERVAR. &ORDERVAR resolves to x, which is the character variable that contains the names of the other variables.

❹   Put &COLVARS as well as a DUMMY variable on the COLUMN statement. The DUMMY variable will be used on the COMPUTE statement, so all values are in place when adding the color on the diagonal.

❺   The %DO loop will go from column number two (2) to the value of &WORD_CNT (4), that is, the last variable in &COLVARS.

❻   Assign &CHKVAR to the name of the columns. &CHKVAR will change each time through the loop.

❼   Use an IF condition to determine whether the row value for &ORDERVAR (x) is the same as the current column variable. When the IF condition is true, change the background of that cell to an orange color. The first argument of the CALL DEFINE statement is the current value of &CHKVAR followed by .sum because the variables are numeric and therefore default to ANALYSIS.

❽   The macro call lists the variables that are in the final table, starting with the character variable that contains the name of the other variables.

Output 6.11: Color on the Diagonal

x	a	b	c
a	1	2	3
b	4	5	6
c	7	8	9

6.5 Trafficlighting under an ACROSS Variable

In this section, we will use the same examples as before, but we add a new wrinkle by including an ACROSS variable. Trafficlighting can be more challenging when there is an ACROSS variable, because you have to have an assignment statement for each one of the columns that you want to apply color to.

6.5.1 Color Based on Cell's Value

Example 6.14 changes the background of the TOTAL_RETAIL_PRICE column. The color in Output 6.12 will be based on a range of possible values. The code now uses CUSTOMER_AGE_GROUP as an ACROSS variable, so there are four columns of TOTAL_RETAIL_PRICE.

Example 6.14: Traffic Light Using a Format

```
proc format;
   value pricefmt ❶
      . = 'red'
      low - 0 = 'red'
      0 <- 10000 = 'cxe0ecf4'
      10000 <- 30000 ='cxfe9929'
      30000 <- high = 'yellow'
      ;
run;

options missing='';
proc report data=orders;
   column customer_country customer_age_group,
          (quantity costprice_per_unit total_retail_price);
   define customer_country / group format=$cntry.;
   define customer_age_group /across; ❷
   define total_retail_price / 'Retail Price'
          style(column)=[background=pricefmt.]; ❸
run;
```

❶   The format is created as it was in Example 6.8.

❷   CUSTOMER_AGE_GROUP is added as an ACROSS variable. Its values become headers with a column for QUANTITY, COSTPRICE_PER_UNIT, and TOTAL_RETAIL_PRICE under each value.

❸   Inside of the style(column)= option on the DEFINE statement, put the BACKGROUND= attribute and specify its value as the format name created in the first step ❶. Each time a row is output for TOTAL_RETAIL_PRICE, the value is evaluated against the format and the appropriate color value is assigned to the background. This is done for all four columns of TOTAL_RETAIL_PRICE.

Output 6.12: Background Color Is Changed for Columns under an ACROSS

| Customer Country | Customer Age Group | | | | | | | | | | | |
| | 15-30 years | | | 31-45 years | | | 46-60 years | | | 61-75 years | | |
	Quantity Ordered	Cost Price Per Unit	Retail Price	Quantity Ordered	Cost Price Per Unit	Retail Price	Quantity Ordered	Cost Price Per Unit	Retail Price	Quantity Ordered	Cost Price Per Unit	Retail Price
Australia				104	$1,879.80	$6,607.59	44	$1,107.10	$3,450.90	62	$1,864.45	$7,263.00
Canada	44	$911.45	$6,124.58	31	$979.20	$4,146.40	18	$286.15	$1,158.90	12	$117.00	$521.20
Germany	8	$195.85	$496.90	32	$1,530.75	$5,711.60				66	$2,338.95	$9,186.10
Israel	2	$77.65	$158.60	13	$244.15	$645.30	13	$195.15	$755.60			
South Africa	36	$883.60	$4,169.60	8	$224.65	$687.70	3	$142.10	$292.60			
Turkey	11	$554.85	$1,655.60	29	$1,029.55	$3,333.50				3	$71.75	$186.70
United States	203	$4,522.20	$17,881.22	180	$3,500.93	$13,065.41	97	$2,334.00	$9,262.55	59	$814.85	$3,315.92

Notice that now that we have added an ACROSS variable, we see red for the missing values and only two of the other three colors appear. When applying colors, you will have to keep in mind that all colors might not be used in a more detailed table.

6.5.2 Color Based on Another *Report-item*

Example 6.15 assigns a background color to the TOTAL_RETAIL_PRICE column based on the value of the CUSTOMER_COUNTRY variable, as seen in Output 6.13. The earlier example, Example 6.10, had three CALL DEFINE statements, one for each country grouping. Now that CUSTOMER_AGE_GROUP is an ACROSS variable, four CALL DEFINE statements are needed within each of the three country groupings.

Example 6.15: Change TOTAL_RETAIL_PRICE Background Based on Country Value

```
options missing='';
proc report data=orders;
   column customer_country customer_age_group,
          (quantity costprice_per_unit total_retail_price);
   define customer_country / group format=$cntry.;
   define customer_age_group /across; ❶
   define total_retail_price / 'Retail Price';
   compute total_retail_price;
      if customer_country in ('US' 'DE' 'CA') then do;
         call define('_c4_','style','style=[background=cxfe9929]');
         call define('_c7_','style','style=[background=cxfe9929]'); ❷
         call define('_c10_','style','style=[background=cxfe9929]');
         call define('_c13_','style','style=[background=cxfe9929]');
      end;
      else if customer_country = 'AU' then do;
         call define('_c4_','style','style=[background=cxe0ecf4]');
         call define('_c7_','style','style=[background=cxe0ecf4]'); ❸
         call define('_c10_','style','style=[background=cxe0ecf4]');
         call define('_c13_','style','style=[background=cxe0ecf4]');
      end;
      else do;
         call define('_c4_','style','style=[background=yellow]');
         call define('_c7_','style','style=[background=yellow]'); ❹
         call define('_c10_','style','style=[background=yellow]');
         call define('_c13_','style','style=[background=yellow]');
```

```
        end;
    endcomp;
run;
```

❶ CUSTOMER_AGE_GROUP is defined as an ACROSS variable. Its values become headers with a column for QUANTITY, COSTPRICE_PER_UNIT, and TOTAL_RETAIL_PRICE under each value.

❷ When the first IF condition is true, the appropriate color value is assigned as the background in a CALL DEFINE statement for all for TOTAL_RETAIL_PRICE columns.

❸ A different color is assigned to the TOTAL_RETAIL_PRICE columns when the country value is Australia.

❹ All other countries fall in the ELSE condition. The TOTAL_RETAIL_PRICE columns are assigned a third background color.

Output 6.13: Background Color Is Changed Based on Customer Country

Customer Country	Customer Age Group											
	15-30 years			31-45 years			46-60 years			61-75 years		
	Quantity Ordered	Cost Price Per Unit	Retail Price	Quantity Ordered	Cost Price Per Unit	Retail Price	Quantity Ordered	Cost Price Per Unit	Retail Price	Quantity Ordered	Cost Price Per Unit	Retail Price
Australia				104	$1,879.80	$6,607.59	44	$1,107.10	$3,450.90	62	$1,864.45	$7,263.00
Canada	44	$911.45	$6,124.58	31	$979.20	$4,146.40	18	$286.15	$1,158.90	12	$117.00	$521.20
Germany	8	$195.85	$496.90	32	$1,530.75	$5,711.60				66	$2,338.95	$9,186.10
Israel	2	$77.65	$158.60	13	$244.15	$645.30	13	$195.15	$755.60			
South Africa	36	$883.60	$4,169.60	8	$224.65	$687.70	3	$142.10	$292.60			
Turkey	11	$554.85	$1,655.60	29	$1,029.55	$3,333.50				3	$71.75	$186.70
United States	203	$4,522.20	$17,881.22	180	$3,500.93	$13,065.41	97	$2,334.00	$9,262.55	59	$814.85	$3,315.92

The code from Example 6.15 can be cumbersome, especially if the ACROSS variable has more than four values or if you place more than three *report-item*s under the ACROSS. The code can be placed inside of a macro program. Macro variables are created and assigned so that they will provide the number of categories for the ACROSS variable, as well as the number of *report-item*s before the ACROSS, and the number of *report-item*s under the ACROSS. The macro program will then create the needed column references for the CALL DEFINE statements. Example 6.16 demonstrates using macro logic to assign background color to columns under an ACROSS.

Example 6.16: Use a Macro Program to Apply Attribute Changes

```
proc sql noprint;
select count(distinct customer_age_group) into: cntageg ❶
from book.orders;
quit;

%macro rep;
   %local varsleft varsunder i;
   /* the number of variables before the across */
   %let varsleft=1; ❷
   /* number of variables under the across */
   %let varsunder=3; ❸
```

```
proc report data=orders;
    column customer_country customer_age_group,
           (quantity costprice_per_unit total_retail_price);
    define customer_country / group format=$cntry.;
    define customer_age_group /across;
    define total_retail_price / 'Retail Price';
    compute total_retail_price;
        if customer_country in ('US' 'DE' 'CA') then do;  ❹
            %do i=%eval(&varsleft+&varsunder) ❺ %to
            %eval(&cntageg*&varsunder+&varsleft) %by &varsunder;  ❻
              call define(
                 "_c&i._",'style','style=[background=cxfe9929]');  ❼
            %end;
        end;
        ❽
        else if customer_country = 'AU' then do;
            %do i=%eval(&varsleft+&varsunder) %to
            %eval(&cntageg*&varsunder+&varsleft) %by &varsunder;
              call define(
                 "_c&i._",'style','style=[background=cxe0ecf4]');
            %end;
        end;
        else do;
            call define(
               "_c&i._",'style','style=[background=yellow]');
        end;
    endcomp;
run;

%mend rep;

%rep
```

❶ Determine the number of distinct categories for the ACROSS variable CUSTOMER_AGE_GROUP. Put this number in a macro variable that will be used inside of a compute block in PROC REPORT. In this example, &CNTAGEG resolves to four.

❷ Put the number of *report-item*s on the COLUMN statement that are to the left of the ACROSS variable. This should include any *report-item*s defined as NOPRINT.

❸ Put the number of *report-item*s on the COLUMN statement that are under the ACROSS variable. This should include any *report-item*s defined as NOPRINT.

❹ An IF condition checks the value of CUSTOMER_COUNTRY.

❺ In this example we want to change the background color for the TOTAL_RETAIL_PRICE columns. The first column number for TOTAL_RETAIL_PRICE is four. We want to start the loop at column four, so we add &VARSLEFT and &VARSUNDER. If we wanted to start with a different column, the equation inside of %EVAL would need to change. You will need to think through the starting and ending column number when applying this example to your data.

❻ The last column number for TOTAL_RETAIL_PRICE is 13. The number of CUSTOMER_AGE_GROUP categories multiplied by the number of *report-item*s under

CUSTOMER_AGE_GROUP plus the number of *report-item*s to the left of the ACROSS gives us 13 (4*3+1). Since we need to change only TOTAL_RETAIL_PRICE columns, we will loop through the columns by the number of *report-item*s under the ACROSS.

❼ Because the macro program loops through each column of TOTAL_RETAIL_PRICE, we need only one CALL DEFINE statement per pass for each country grouping to assign the appropriate background color. "_c&i._" resolves to _c4_, _c7_, _c10_, and _c13_.

❽ Repeat steps 4-7 for the other values of CUSTOMER_COUNTRY.

The output created is the same as in Output 6.13.

The purpose of Examples 6.15 and 6.16 is to demonstrate that a CALL DEFINE statement is required for each column that requires a style change. Both examples can be simplified by creating a temporary variable that holds the color value needed for each country. Then the technique from Example 6.12 can be applied, which will reduce the number of CALL DEFINE statements required to produce the table in Output 6.13. Use the method that makes the most sense to you and is easiest for you to update.

The goal of Example 6.17 is to change the foreground color to red and bold and italicize the font for the TOTAL_RETAIL_PRICE columns that do not meet certain criteria. In this example the countries that have not achieved the goal of selling 10 units will be changed. The QUANTITY goal changed from 50 in the previous version of this example to 10 because we cannot expect 50 units to be sold within each age group. As with the previous example, this one requires more CALL DEFINE steps than the example without an ACROSS variable. This table structure requires evaluating the QUANTITY column that is under the same age group value as the TOTAL_RETAIL_PRICE column. Output 6.14 displays the style changes to the text.

Example 6.17: Change Attributes Based on Another Variable under the ACROSS

```
options missing='';
proc report data=orders;
   column customer_country customer_age_group,
(quantity costprice_per_unit total_retail_price);
   define customer_country / group format=$cntry.;
   define customer_age_group /across;
   define total_retail_price / 'Retail Price';
   compute total_retail_price;
      if _c2_ < 10 then ❶ call define('_c4_','style',
       'style=[foreground=red font_weight=bold font_style=italic]'); ❷
      if _c5_ < 10 then call define('_c7_','style',
       'style=[foreground=red font_weight=bold font_style=italic]');
      if _c8_ < 10 then call define('_c10_','style',
       'style=[foreground=red font_weight=bold font_style=italic]');
      if _c11_ < 10 then call define('_c13_','style',
       'style=[foreground=red font_weight=bold font_style=italic]');
   endcomp;
run;
```

❶ One IF condition is needed for each of the QUANTITY columns. The QUANTITY column numbers are 2, 5, 8, and 11.

❷ The TOTAL_RETAIL_PRICE column numbers are 4, 7, 10, and 13. Columns 2 and 4 are under CUSTOMER_AGE_GROUP "15-30 years," which is why those are paired together, and so on. You have already seen the foreground=, font_weight=, and font_style= attribute specifications.

Output 6.14: Attributes for Retail Price Based on Quantity Ordered

Customer Country	Customer Age Group											
	15-30 years			31-45 years			46-60 years			61-75 years		
	Quantity Ordered	Cost Price Per Unit	Retail Price	Quantity Ordered	Cost Price Per Unit	Retail Price	Quantity Ordered	Cost Price Per Unit	Retail Price	Quantity Ordered	Cost Price Per Unit	Retail Price
Australia				104	$1,879.80	$6,607.59	44	$1,107.10	$3,450.90	62	$1,864.45	$7,263.00
Canada	44	$911.45	$6,124.58	31	$979.20	$4,146.40	18	$286.15	$1,158.90	12	$117.00	$521.20
Germany	8	$195.85	*$496.90*	32	$1,530.75	$5,711.60				66	$2,338.95	$9,186.10
Israel	2	$77.65	*$158.60*	13	$244.15	$645.30	13	$195.15	$755.60			
South Africa	36	$883.60	$4,169.60	8	$224.65	*$687.70*	3	$142.10	*$292.60*			
Turkey	11	$554.85	$1,655.60	29	$1,029.55	$3,333.50				3	$71.75	*$186.70*
United States	203	$4,522.20	$17,881.22	180	$3,500.93	$13,065.41	97	$2,334.00	$9,262.55	59	$814.85	$3,315.92

TIP: Use the SHOWALL option on the PROC REPORT statement to display all columns, even ones designated as NOPRINT. Then when you count the columns to get the needed column number, you are sure to have the right number.

Again, the main goal of Example 6.17 is to demonstrate that each column under an ACROSS variable must have its own CALL DEFINE statement. Example 6.17 has one statement for each column that needs to change but the code can be simplified. An ARRAY statement and DO loop can be used to generate all four statements. For example:

```
compute total_retail_price;
    array cn{4} _c2_ _c5_ _c8_ _c11_;
    do i=1 to 4;
        if cn{i} < 10 then call define(
            i*3+1,'style','style=[foreground=red font_weight=bold]');
    end;
endcomp;
```

6.5.3 Color on the Diagonal

For some reports, the values on the diagonal are the most important and need to be highlighted to draw the readers' attention. Highlighting on the diagonal makes the most sense when a GROUP variable and an ACROSS variable have an increasing ordered value; for example, CUSTOMER_AGE_GROUP starts with the youngest age group and ends with the oldest age group. When an ACROSS variable is used to create the columns, highlighting the diagonal cells is straightforward because the column number can be compared to the row number.

The ACROSS variable, CUSTOMER_AGE_GROUP, has a logical increasing order in Example 6.18 and Output 6.15. PRODUCT_LINE is used as the GROUP variable. PRODUCT_LINE does not have an obvious logical order, but it does have four groups, which helps demonstrate highlighting the cells on the diagonal. Presumably, your data would have two variables closely linked with a matching number of distinct categories.

Example 6.18: Apply Color in a Diagonal Pattern under an ACROSS

```
proc sql noprint;
select count(distinct customer_age_group) into: cntageg ❶
from orders;
quit;

options missing='';
proc report data=orders;
   column product_line customer_age_group;
   define product_line /group;
   define customer_age_group /across;
   compute before product_line; ❷
      row_num+1;
   endcomp;
   compute customer_age_group;
      do i=1 to &cntageg; ❸
      ❹❺ if row_num=i then call define(i+1,'style',
                            'style=[background=cxfe9929]');
      end;
   endcomp;
run;
```

❶   Determine the number of distinct categories for the ACROSS variable CUSTOMER_AGE_GROUP. Put this number in a macro variable that will be used inside of a compute block in PROC REPORT.

❷   PRODUCT_LINE is the GROUP variable. Before each value of PRODUCT_LINE, increment a temporary counter variable. The ROW_NUM variable contains the row number.

❸   Use a DO loop to scroll through each column created by CUSTOMER_AGE_GROUP. The macro variable created in step 1 tells the DO loop when to stop.

❹   The IF condition row_num=i determines whether the row number and the category number for CUSTOMER_AGE_GROUP match.

❺   A CALL DEFINE statement is used to change the background color to orange. The first argument of the CALL DEFINE statement is the column number for the column that needs to be highlighted. The DO loop scrolls from one to the number of age categories, but column one is actually the PRODUCT_LINE value, so 1 needs to be added to i so that the appropriate column is highlighted.

Output 6.15: Cells Highlighted on the Diagonal under an ACROSS Variable

	Customer Age Group			
Product Line	15-30 years	31-45 years	46-60 years	61-75 years
Children	14	11	3	1
Clothes & Shoes	35	62	35	27
Outdoors	33	61	18	35
Sports	90	99	49	44

6.6 Color in Headers

Sections 6.4 and 6.5 discuss various ways of changing the color for cells within the details section of the report. This section addresses changing the color of the header cells. Header cell attributes can be changed only within a style element in PROC TEMPLATE or by using the STYLE(HEADER)= option on the PROC REPORT or DEFINE statements. Header attributes cannot be changed in a CALL DEFINE statement.

6.6.1 STYLE(HEADER)= on PROC REPORT Statement

As mentioned at the start of this chapter, there is an order of precedence when applying attributes based on which statement the style override is placed. When you use STYLE(HEADER)= on the PROC REPORT statement, those attributes are applied to every header cell, as seen in Example 6.19 and Output 6.16.

Example 6.19: Assign Attributes to All Header Cells

```
proc report data=orders
     style(header)=[background=green foreground=white]; ❶
   column product_category customer_gender quantity
         total_retail_price;
   define product_category / group;
   define customer_gender / group;
   define total_retail_price / 'Retail Price';
run;
```

❶ All headers have the same green background and white foreground. If the report contained spanning headers, those cells would also have the same coloring.

Output 6.16: All Header Cells Have a Background of Green and Foreground of White

Product Category	Customer Gender	Quantity Ordered	Retail Price

6.6.2 STYLE(HEADER)= on DEFINE Statement

Placing the STYLE(HEADER)= option on the DEFINE statement will override the same attributes applied within STYLE(HEADER)= on the PROC REPORT statement. However, when placed on the DEFINE statement, the attributes change only for the header of that specific column. Example 6.20 changes the background color for the CUSTOMER_GENDER column header in Output 6.17.

Example 6.20: Change the Header Attributes for Gender

```
proc report data=orders
     style(header)=[background=green foreground=white]; ❶
   column product_category customer_gender quantity
         total_retail_price;
   define product_category / group;
   define customer_gender / group style(header)=[
         background= cxfe9929]; ❷
```

```
      define total_retail_price / 'Retail Price';
run;
```

❶   All headers are initially assigned the same green background and white foreground.

❷   The background color is changed for the CUSTOMER_GENDER column header. Notice that only the background color is specified, so the foreground color of white is inherited from style(header)= on the PROC REPORT statement.

Output 6.17: The Gender Header Background Color Is Changed

6.6.3 Spanning Header

Spanning headers also take their style attributes from the STYLE(HEADER)= option on the PROC REPORT statement. The only way to change the attributes of the spanning header is through inline formatting, as demonstrated in Example 6.21 and Output 6.18.

Example 6.21: Change Spanning Header Attributes with Inline Formatting

```
ods escapechar="^";
proc report data=orders; ❶
   column product_category customer_gender
          ('^{style [background=green foreground=white]
           Sales Information}' ❷
           quantity total_retail_price);
   define product_category / group;
   define customer_gender / group;
   define total_retail_price / 'Retail Price';
run;
```

❶   For this example, style(header)= is not used on the PROC REPORT statements. The attributes' values come from the header element in the style template.

❷   Inline formatting is used to change the background color to green and foreground color to white for just the spanning header.

Output 6.18: The Spanning Header Has a Green Background and White Foreground

In HTML output, background colors applied to spanning headers will put color only behind the words. The color will not be applied to the entire cell. Inline formatting used to change the background color of a spanning header is ignored in the ODS Excel and ODS Tagsets.ExcelXP destinations.

For these destinations, you will need to create a new variable in the data set; the value will be the spanning header text. The new variable needs to be defined as an ACROSS variable and its background color can be changed in STYLE(HEADER)= on the DEFINE statement. Example 6.22 shows the necessary steps to change the background color of a spanning header in HTML and Excel output.

Example 6.22: Change Spanning Header Attributes for HTML and Excel Output

```
data orders2;
   set orders;
   acrvar = "Sales Information";
run;

proc report data=orders2;
   column product_category customer_gender acrvar,
          (quantity total_retail_price);
   define product_category / group;
   define customer_gender / group;
   define acrvar / across '' style(header)=[background=green
          foreground=white];
   define total_retail_price / 'Retail Price';
run;
```

The output produced by Example 6.22 looks like Output 6.18.

6.6.4 ACROSS Variable Label and Value Headers

Attributes from the STYLE(HEADER)= option on a DEFINE statement for an ACROSS variable apply to both the label and value cells. Example 6.23 applies a yellow background to the ACROSS variable CUSTOMER_GENDER, shown in Output 6.19.

Example 6.23: Apply Attributes to ACROSS Variable Headers

```
proc report data=orders;
   column product_category customer_gender,
          (quantity total_retail_price);
   define product_category / group;
   define customer_gender / across style(header)=[background=yellow];
   define total_retail_price / 'Retail Price';
run;
```

Output 6.19: The Label and Values for Gender Have a Yellow Background

	Customer Gender			
	F		M	
Product Category	Quantity Ordered	Retail Price	Quantity Ordered	Retail Price

6.6.5 ACROSS Value Headers

Example 6.8 demonstrates applying a background color to a cell using a format. The exact same method is applicable to ACROSS variable values. The difference is that the color appears in the header section of the report instead of the data section. Example 6.24 applies a different color to each of the headers containing a value of the ACROSS variable CUSTOMER_GENDER, as shown in Output 6.20.

Example 6.24: Use a Format to Apply Background Color

```
proc format;
   value $gen ❶
      "M" = "cxe0ecf4"
      "F" = "cxc51b8a"
      ;
run;

proc report data=orders;
   column product_category customer_gender,
         (quantity total_retail_price);
   define product_category / group;
   define customer_gender / across style(header)=[background=$gen.]; ❷
   define total_retail_price / 'Retail Price';
run;
```

❶ Create a format specifying the desired color for each value of the ACROSS variable.

❷ Set the background color to the name of the format containing the desired colors. The cell containing the variable label will inherit its attributes from the header element of the style template.

Output 6.20: Each Gender Value Has a Different Background Color

	Customer Gender			
	F		M	
Product Category	Quantity Ordered	Retail Price	Quantity Ordered	Retail Price

6.6.6 ACROSS Label versus ACROSS Values

The results in Output 6.20 show the background color changes for the values of CUSTOMER_GENDER. The background color for the label is taken from STYLE(HEADER)= on the PROC REPORT statement or the corresponding element in the style template. It is possible for the label to have a different color than what is specified in those elements.

Example 6.22 demonstrates one method for getting that type of output by creating a new variable in the data set. Another method is using inline formatting on a spanning header, which can be used to output the label text for the ACROSS variable. Example 6.25 demonstrates using the inline formatting method, with the results shown in Output 6.21.

Example 6.25: Use a Spanning Header to Write ACROSS Label

```
proc format;
   value $gen ❶
      "M" = "cxe0ecf4"
      "F" = "cxc51b8a"
      ;
run;

ods escapechar="^";
proc report data=orders;
   column product_category ('^{style [background=yellow]Customer
         Gender}' ❷ customer_gender, (quantity total_retail_price));
   define product_category / group;
   define customer_gender / across ''
         style(header)=[background=$gen.]; ❸
   define total_retail_price / 'Retail Price';
run;
```

❶ Create a format specifying the desired color for each value of the ACROSS variable.

❷ Use inline formatting to set a color in a spanning header above the ACROSS variable and the *report-items* stacked underneath it.

❸ Change the CUSTOMER_GENDER label to null so that its default value will not appear. The spanning header in step 2 ❷ will now act as its label. Set the background color to the name of the format containing the desired colors.

Output 6.21: A Spanning Header Provides the ACROSS Label and Background Color

	Customer Gender			
	F		M	
Product Category	Quantity Ordered	Retail Price	Quantity Ordered	Retail Price

Remember that inline formatting in a spanning header behaves differently in each ODS destination. Use the technique from Example 6.22 if the color from the inline formatting does not fill the entire cell.

6.7 LINE Statements

By default, the text that is created by a LINE statement is centered. However, you can change the justification and other style attributes with the STYLE(LINES)= option on the PROC REPORT statement or with STYLE= option on the COMPUTE statement. Attributes in STYLE(LINES)= will apply to all LINE statements within the report. Attributes from the COMPUTE statement will be applied to only the LINE statements from that compute block.

In Example 6.26, the text written via the LINE statement (the values for CUSTOMER_COUNTRY) is now left-justified and the background is changed to light blue, as seen in Output 6.22.

Example 6.26: Apply Attributes to a LINE Statement

```
proc report data=orders;
   column customer_country customer_group quantity total_retail_price;
   define customer_country / group noprint;
   define customer_group / group;
   define total_retail_price / 'Retail Price';
   compute before customer_country / style={just=l
         background=lightblue};
      line customer_country $cntry.;
   endcomp;
run;
```

Output 6.22: The Row from the LINE Statement Has a Blue Background

Customer Group Name	Quantity Ordered	Retail Price
Australia		
Internet/Catalog Customers	13	$1,061.30
Orion Club Gold members	24	$1,545.50
Orion Club members	173	$14,714.69
Canada		
Internet/Catalog Customers	5	$679.30
Orion Club Gold members	30	$3,239.80
Orion Club members	70	$8,031.98
Germany		
Internet/Catalog Customers	48	$6,545.90
Orion Club Gold members	48	$7,892.50
Orion Club members	10	$956.20
Israel		
Internet/Catalog Customers	5	$377.00
Orion Club Gold members	2	$158.60
Orion Club members	21	$1,023.90
Turkey		
Orion Club Gold members	7	$1,170.00
Orion Club members	36	$4,005.80
United States		
Internet/Catalog Customers	67	$5,516.95
Orion Club Gold members	180	$16,079.02
Orion Club members	292	$21,929.13
South Africa		
Orion Club Gold members	17	$1,695.60
Orion Club members	30	$3,454.30

Style attributes for multiple LINE statements from the same compute block cannot be controlled separately. However, for some reports it might be necessary to have two LINE statements at the same place in the table but with different attributes. Chapter 3 explains that PROC REPORT cannot have two compute blocks at the same *location* (BEFORE or AFTER). The example in that chapter demonstrates creating a new grouping variable that changes values at the same time the first grouping variable value changes. Examples 6.27a and 6.27b use the same technique to place two LINE statements at the same place with different attributes. Example 6.27b uses the BEFORE location. Therefore, the LINE statements are written in the order the variables appear on the COLUMN statement from left to right. The first grouping variable on the COLUMN statement writes the top LINE statement.

Example 6.27a: Create a Copy of CUSTOMER_COUNTRY

```
data orders2;
   set orders;
   c_country = customer_country;
run;
```

You can now use the copy, C_COUNTRY, as necessary. Example 6.27b writes one LINE statement from two compute blocks, which will appear together in the table. The order of the LINE statements in the output is based on the order of the CUSTOMER_COUNTRY and C_COUNTRY variables in the COLUMN statement. The orange divider rows are written first. Those rows are created with the CUSTOMER_COUNTRY variable, so CUSTOMER_COUNTRY should be the first variable in the COLUMN statement. Then, C_COUNTRY is used to create the blue rows that contain the text value for CUSTOMER_COUNTRY, as seen in Output 6.23.

Example 6.27b: Use the Copy of CUSTOMER_COUNTRY to Write a Second LINE Statement

```
proc report data=orders2;
   column customer_country c_country customer_group quantity
          total_retail_price;
   define customer_country / group noprint;
   define c_country / group noprint;
   define customer_group / group;
   define total_retail_price / 'Retail Price';
   compute before c_country /style={just=l background=lightblue};
      line customer_country $cntry.;
   endcomp;
   compute before customer_country /style={background=cxfe9929};
      line ' ';
   endcomp;
run;
```

Output 6.23: Each LINE Statement Has Its Own Attributes

Customer Group Name	Quantity Ordered	Retail Price
Australia		
Internet/Catalog Customers	13	$1,061.30
Orion Club Gold members	24	$1,545.50
Orion Club members	173	$14,714.69
Canada		
Internet/Catalog Customers	5	$679.30
Orion Club Gold members	30	$3,239.80
Orion Club members	70	$8,031.98
Germany		
Internet/Catalog Customers	48	$6,545.90
Orion Club Gold members	48	$7,892.50
Orion Club members	10	$956.20
Israel		
Internet/Catalog Customers	5	$377.00
Orion Club Gold members	2	$158.60
Orion Club members	21	$1,023.90
Turkey		
Orion Club Gold members	7	$1,170.00
Orion Club members	36	$4,005.80
United States		
Internet/Catalog Customers	67	$5,516.95
Orion Club Gold members	180	$16,079.02
Orion Club members	292	$21,929.13

6.8 Advanced Color and Border Assignments

This section provides an example of changing many parts of the output in one program. It combines many of the previously discussed techniques, such as creating temporary variables, using a multilabel format to add a value to an ACROSS variable, and changing individual borders.

6.8.1 Apply Multiple Styles on One Cell

The purpose of Example 6.28 is to demonstrate how to build on styling attributes already in place and to show how the styling attributes interact. This example is more sophisticated than previous examples, but even this example could be more advanced. Please be aware the report in this example is being sent to the ODS RTF destination. The same code might not produce the same output in other destinations, specifically the borders.

Output 6.24, the final report created by Examples 6.28a and 6.28b, will have four sections, one for each value of PRODUCT_LINE. Each section needs a different background color and thick borders. The final report also contains date columns. The columns representing year totals need to have a left border and a thicker right border.

Example 6.28a: Create a Format and Make Changes to the Style Template

```
data crfmt;  ❶
    fmtname='mydatef';
    hlo='MS';
    begin='01JAN2003'D;
    finish='31DEC2007'D;

    numq=intck('qtr',begin,finish);
    numy=intck('year',begin,finish);

    do i=0 to numq;
        start=intnx('qtr',begin,i);
        end=intnx('qtr',begin,i,'E');
        label=put(start,yyq6.);
        output;
    end;

    do i=0 to numy;
        start=intnx('year',begin,i);
        end=intnx('year',begin,i,'E');
        label=year(start);
        output;
    end;
run;

proc sort data=crfmt;  ❷
    by end descending start;
run;

proc format cntlin=crfmt;
run;

proc template;  ❸
    define style mypearl;
    parent=styles.pearl;
    style Table from Table /
        cellpadding = 4pt
        borderspacing = 0pt
        borderwidth = 1pt
        frame = box
        rules = rows
        bordercolor = black
        bordercollapse = collapse;
```

```
      end;
   run;
```

❶ Create a data set with format information. The format will have one label for each quarter between the BEGIN and FINISH values, as well as a label for each corresponding year.

❷ Sort the data set to ensure that the quarter labels for each year appear before the year label.

❸ Create a custom style template. This changes the RULES=, BORDERCOLOR=, and BORDERSPACING= attributes from their original values.

Example 6.28b: Apply Various Style Changes at Both the Row and Column Level

```
ods escapechar="^";
options missing='' orientation=landscape nocenter;
ods rtf file='test.rtf'  style=mypearl; ❶
proc report data=orders spanrows style(header)=[background=vpap];
   column ('^{style[borderrightcolor=black borderrightwidth=2pt]}'
          ('^{style[borderrightcolor=black
            borderrightwidth=1pt]Product}' product_line)
          ('^{style[borderrightcolor=black
            borderrightwidth=2pt]Customer Groups}' customer_group))
          order_date,total_retail_price; ❷
   define product_line / group ''
        style(column)=[borderrightcolor=black borderrightwidth=1pt
        vjust=c just=c];
   define customer_group / group ''
        style(column)=[borderrightcolor=black borderrightwidth=2pt]; ❸
   define order_date / across format=mydatef. 'Order Date' mlf
        preloadfmt order=data;
   define total_retail_price / '';
   break after product_line / summarize suppress;

   compute before product_line;
      pcnt+1; ❹
   endcomp;

   compute product_line;
      ❺
      if pcnt = 1 then call define(_row_,'style',
                'style={background=vlibg}');
      else if pcnt = 2 then call define(_row_,'style',
                'style={background=khaki}');
      else if pcnt = 3 then call define(_row_,'style',
                'style={background=aliceblue}');
      else if pcnt = 4 then call define(_row_,'style',
                'style={background=ligy}');

      if product_line ne '' and _break_ = '' then do;
         call define(_row_,'style/merge',
                'style={bordertopcolor=black bordertopwidth=2pt}'); ❻
```

```
                     ❼
            if pcnt = 1 then call define(_col_,'style',
                    'style={borderbottomcolor=vlibg}');
            else if pcnt = 2 then call define(_col_,'style',
                    'style={borderbottomcolor=khaki}');
            else if pcnt = 3 then call define(_col_,'style',
                    'style={borderbottomcolor=aliceblue}');
            else if pcnt = 4 then call define(_col_,'style',
                    'style={borderbottomcolor=ligy}');
        end;
    endcomp;

    compute after product_line / style={background=lightgrey
                bordertopcolor=black borderbottomcolor=black
                borderbottomwidth=2pt bordertopwidth=2pt};  ❽
        line ' ';
        customer_group = 'Totals';
        call define('customer_group','style',
                    'style=[font_weight=bold font_style=italic]');
    endcomp;

    compute total_retail_price;
        call define('_c7_','style','style={borderleftcolor=black
                    borderleftwidth=1pt borderrightcolor=black
                    borderrightwidth=2pt}');
        call define('_c8_','style','style={borderleftcolor=black}');

        call define('_c12_','style','style={borderleftcolor=black
                    borderleftwidth=1pt borderrightcolor=black
                    borderrightwidth=2pt}');
        call define('_c13_','style','style={borderleftcolor=black}');

        call define('_c17_','style','style={borderleftcolor=black
                    borderleftwidth=1pt borderrightcolor=black
                    borderrightwidth=2pt}');
        call define('_c18_','style','style={borderleftcolor=black}');

        call define('_c22_','style','style={borderleftcolor=black
                    borderleftwidth=1pt borderrightcolor=black
                    borderrightwidth=2pt}');
        call define('_c23_','style','style={borderleftcolor=black}');  ❾

        if upcase(_break_) = 'PRODUCT_LINE' then do i=3 to 27;  ❿
            call define(i,'format','dollar10.');
        end;
    endcomp;
run;
ods rtf close;
```

❶ Specify the custom style template created in the PROC TEMPLATE step.

❷ Add thick black borders to the right side of the spanning headers for the PRODUCT_LINE and CUSTOMER_GROUP columns. This visually separates the headers for these *report-item*s from the headers for the date columns.

❸ Add a thick right border to the CUSTOMER_GROUP column to visually separate it from the date columns.

❹ Create a counter variable, PCNT, for the PRODUCT_LINE value. Each value will have a unique counter value.

❺ Assign a background color for all rows within each PRODUCT_LINE value.

❻ This statement places a thick border between the header and the first detail row. The 'STYLE/MERGE' option adds this specification to the specifications from the other CALL DEFINE statements. If 'STYLE' option was used, the background colors would be stripped from the top rows.

❼ A border is created between the detail rows and the summary row created by the BREAK statement. The border needs to be removed in the PRODUCT_LINE column. It is removed by changing its color to match the background color.

❽ Change the style attributes for the LINE statement output via this compute block: change the background color of the row to light gray and add thick top and bottom borders.

❾ For each of the year columns, add a black left border and a thicker black right border.

❿ Change the format on the summary row for all of the ANALYSIS columns. These columns are referred to by the column number, 3-27.

Output 6.24: Multiple Attribute Changes Are Applied to Every Cell – Partial Listing

Product	Customer Groups	Order Date							
		2003Q1	2003Q2	2003Q3	2003Q4	2003	2004Q1	2004Q2	2004Q3
Children	Orion Club Gold members							$6.50	
	Orion Club members			$131.00		$131.00		$21.80	$75.20
	Totals			$131		$131		$28	$75
Clothes & Shoes	Internet/Catalog Customers		$210.30	$302.40		$512.70			
	Orion Club Gold members	$16.50	$562.50	$353.00	$415.20	$1,347.20	$421.50	$200.20	
	Orion Club members	$75.00	$767.40	$465.80	$1,080.30	$2,388.50	$307.30	$167.50	$382.70
	Totals	$92	$1,540	$1,121	$1,496	$4,248	$729	$368	$383
Outdoors	Internet/Catalog Customers	$128.40		$146.80		$275.20	$369.80		
	Orion Club Gold members	$247.50	$391.70	$1,602.90	$1,110.90	$3,353.00		$840.80	$6.20
	Orion Club members	$190.40	$744.90	$362.00	$525.30	$1,822.60	$1,100.70	$442.50	
	Totals	$566	$1,137	$2,112	$1,636	$5,451	$1,471	$1,283	$6
Sports	Internet/Catalog Customers	$109.20	$310.20	$434.85		$854.25		$95.70	
	Orion Club Gold members	$178.50	$711.00	$946.50	$2,541.48	$4,377.48	$183.90	$518.10	$3,322.70
	Orion Club members	$446.10	$3,520.90	$3,082.70	$619.30	$7,669.00	$487.00	$1,701.07	$546.90
	Totals	$734	$4,542	$4,464	$3,161	$12,901	$671	$2,315	$3,870

6.8.2 Color Every Other Row

Example 6.4 used _ROW_ as the first argument in the CALL DEFINE statement for inserting a border between groups. Example 6.11 used _ROW_ as the first argument in a CALL DEFINE statement to apply the FOREGROUND= and BOLD= attributes to every cell in a given row. The previous example, Example 6.28, applied a color based on a specific value of product. All of these examples based the decision to change the attributes on a specific value of a specific *report-item*. Setting of attributes does not have to be based on a value already in the data. The decision to change an attribute could be based on the row number itself. For example, the background color attribute could be applied to every other row or every third row in the final report. Example 6.29 demonstrates how to determine a row number, and then, based on that row number, apply a background color to entire row. The result is shown in Output 6.25.

Example 6.29: Use the MOD Function to Determine Even and Odd Rows for Coloring

```
proc report data=orders;
    column customer_country customer_group quantity total_retail_price;
    define customer_country / group format=$cntry.;
    define customer_group / group;

    compute customer_country;  ❶
        row_num + 1;  ❷
            if mod(row_num,2) = 0 then
                call define(_row_,'style','style=[background=lightgrey]');  ❸
    endcomp;
run;
```

❶ Any compute block associated with a *report_item* is executed on every row. Any variable can be used, but general practice is to use either the first or last variable from the COLUMN statement as the *report-item*.

❷ Increment a temporary variable, ROW_NUM, each time the compute block is executed, which is every row.

❸ The MOD function determines the remainder from the division of the first argument by the second argument. Dividing by two gives a zero on even rows. The background color is set to light gray on even rows.

Output 6.25: Every Other Row Has a Light Gray Background

Customer Country	Customer Group Name	Quantity Ordered	Total Retail Price for This Product
Australia	Internet/Catalog Customers	13	$1,061.30
	Orion Club Gold members	24	$1,545.50
	Orion Club members	173	$14,714.69
Canada	Internet/Catalog Customers	5	$679.30
	Orion Club Gold members	30	$3,239.80
	Orion Club members	70	$8,031.98
Germany	Internet/Catalog Customers	48	$6,545.90
	Orion Club Gold members	48	$7,892.50
	Orion Club members	10	$956.20
Israel	Internet/Catalog Customers	5	$377.00
	Orion Club Gold members	2	$158.60
	Orion Club members	21	$1,023.90
South Africa	Orion Club Gold members	17	$1,695.60
	Orion Club members	30	$3,454.30
Turkey	Orion Club Gold members	7	$1,170.00
	Orion Club members	36	$4,005.80
United States	Internet/Catalog Customers	67	$5,516.95
	Orion Club Gold members	180	$16,079.02
	Orion Club members	292	$21,929.13

6.8.3 Change Borders in HTML Output

Borders in HTML do not always act like they do in other destinations. In general, you can change the color or thickness in STYLE<(location(s))>= options. You can also change them with inline formatting commands as long as the cell has text. (If the cell does not have text, add a non-breaking space so that HTML treats the cell like it has text.) The tricky task is removing borders in HTML.

Example 6.4 inserted borders between PRODUCT_LINE groups. If you run the exact same code from that example and send the report to HTML, it looks like Output 6.26.

Output 6.26: HTML Output Inserted Unwanted Borders Between Rows

Product Line	Customer Gender	Quantity Ordered	Total Retail Price for This Product
Children	F	27	$722.30
	M	22	$894.10
Clothes & Shoes	F	132	$7,802.90
	M	143	$8,941.79
Outdoors	F	82	$10,931.60
	M	158	$18,930.40
Sports	F	257	$30,290.63
	M	257	$21,563.75

Depending on the style used to create the HTML file, all of the borders look the same or the border between the groups is thicker and darker but all borders still exist. One method for removing the borders is to change the color to match the background, which is demonstrated by Example 6.30 and Output 6.27. You might have to look up the style template code in order to determine the exact color value for each part of the report.

Example 6.30: Add a Condition to Change Some Border Colors to White

```
proc report data=orders2
     style(report)=[rules=groups]
     style(header)=[bordercolor=cxEDF2F9] ❶
     style(column)=[borderrightwidth=0pt borderleftwidth=0pt]; ❷
  column product_line last_gender customer_gender quantity
         total_retail_price;
  define product_line / group;
  define customer_gender / group;
  define last_gender / group noprint;

  compute last_gender;
     if not missing(last_gender) then hold=last_gender;
  endcomp;

  compute customer_gender;
     if hold = customer_gender then do;
        call define(_row_,'style','style=[borderbottomwidth=.1pt
           borderbottomcolor=cx919191]');
     end;
        else do;
        call define(_row_,'style','style=[borderbottomwidth=1pt
           borderbottomcolor=white]'); ❸
     end;
  endcomp;
run;
```

❶   Change the BORDERCOLOR attribute value to the blue color (cxEDF2F9) that matches the header background color.

❷   Set the width for the vertical borders in the column (data) section of the report to zero so that notches do not appear in the gray horizontal border drawn by the CALL DEFINE statement.

❸   For all of the rows that are not the last one in the group, change the bottom border color to white, which matches the white background of the report.

Output 6.27: Remove Border Lines between Groups in HTML Output

Product Line	Customer Gender	Quantity Ordered	Total Retail Price for This Product
Children	F	27	$722.30
	M	22	$894.10
Clothes & Shoes	F	132	$7,802.90
	M	143	$8,941.79
Outdoors	F	82	$10,931.60
	M	158	$18,930.40
Sports	F	257	$30,290.63
	M	257	$21,563.75

6.8.4 Special Instructions for the ODS Destination

One of the advanced features of the STYLE= option is that it allows PROC REPORT to pass special destination-specific instructions to the ODS destination where the report is being rendered. Chapter 3 touched on this concept briefly with the explanation of the TAGATTR= attribute. This attribute passes Excel-specific instructions. TAGATTR= can be used with both the Tagsets.ExcelXP and the ODS destination for Excel. RTF command codes can be passed to Microsoft Word when creating RTF documents. HTML tags can also be passed to HTML-based output, most often with the HTMLSTYLE= attribute.

To PROC REPORT and SAS, the instructions are simple text strings. The ODS destination is responsible for interrupting the instructions and executing the command. You must be careful when passing special instructions to the ODS destination because SAS does little to no syntax checking on the string. SAS gives the programmer the power to pass the instruction, but assumes that the programmer has entered a valid command. If the command is incorrect, it is unlikely that an error or warning is printed to the log. It is more likely that an incorrect command alters the output in an unexpected way or produces a corrupt file.

It is common to need to send special instructions in output generated for Excel. The special instruction might be to apply an Excel-specific format, for example, changing negative numbers so that they are displayed in red. A special instruction might also be used to hide a row, as demonstrated in Chapter 3. The TAGATTR= attribute is also capable of passing formulas to Excel.

The formula in Example 6.31 simply divides one number by another, but it demonstrates the technique of using the STYLE= option to insert special instructions for Excel. Output 6.28 highlights the formula for one cell. The formula is applied to all rows for a given column, but it could have been applied via a CALL DEFINE statement and limited to one row or one cell.

Example 6.31: Use STYLE= to Send a Formula to Excel

```
ods excel file="Output6-28.xlsx";
proc report data=orders;
   column customer_age_group customer_gender quantity
          total_retail_price new;
   define customer_age_group / group;
   define customer_gender / group;
   define new / computed 'Price per Unit'
      style(column)={tagattr='format:Currency formula:RC[-1]/RC[-2]'};
   compute new;
      new = 0;  ❶
   endcomp;
run;
ods excel close;
```

❶ The COMPUTED variable needs a value before the formula can be applied. Setting NEW to zero ensures that the formula is applied and a value is present in the final table.

Output 6.28: Values For the Last Column Are Generated By a Formula

	A	B	C	D	E
1	Customer Age Group	Customer Gender	Quantity Ordered	Total Retail Price for This Product	Price per Unit
2	15-30 years	F	235	$25,005.51	=D2/C2
3		M	69	$5,480.99	$79.43
4	31-45 years	F	157	$16,360.00	$104.20
5		M	240	$17,837.50	$74.32
6	46-60 years	F	61	$5,365.80	$87.96
7		M	114	$9,554.75	$83.81
8	61-75 years	F	45	$3,016.12	$67.02
9		M	157	$17,456.80	$111.19

The number of special instructions for each destination is too large and the capability too vast to cover in detail in this book. Example 6.31 is designed simply to make you aware of the possibilities that are open to you. The need for special instructions gets smaller with each new release of SAS, because the capabilities are being built into the ODS destinations or into new style attributes. However, as in this example, there are cases when they are the best option.

6.9 Images

Images are vital to many types of reports. Images can be company logos, graphs, and photos. This section explores images and how they can be incorporated into a PROC REPORT table. Images can be placed at the top or bottom of the report, as well as within cells of the table. Both the PREIMAGE= and POSTIMAGE= attributes can be used to insert images. The size and DPI of the image are important factors in the final appearance of the report. Image files should be high quality and relatively small. Images that are six inches tall and six inches wide are unlikely to fit in a table cell without dramatically affecting the rest of the table.

Note: Images cannot be used with reports sent to the Tagsets.ExcelXP destination. Also, the ODS destination for PowerPoint cannot place images inside of cells; this is a restriction in Microsoft PowerPoint. PowerPoint does allow images to be placed at the top or bottom of the report.

6.9.1 Place an Image above or below a Report Table

Recall from earlier in the chapter that STYLE(REPORT)= applies to the report as a whole. STYLE(REPORT)= is the option needed to insert images above or below the report table. Borders or lines might not surround the image, but the image is part of the table. If the image should be its own output object, it should be placed in a TITLE, FOOTNOTE, or ODS TEXT= statement or output via PROC ODSTEXT.

Place Image above the Table

Example 6.32 demonstrates using the PREIMAGE= attribute to place a logo above the table, as seen in Output 6.29.

Example 6.32: Use PREIMAGE=

```
proc report data=orders style(report)=[preimage="cologo.tif"]; ❶
    column customer_type n;
    define customer_type / group;
run;
```

❶ PREIMAGE= places the image above the table. Because it is part of the table, the image will not be repeated if the table spans multiple pages.

Output 6.29: PREIMAGE= Places the Logo Above the Table

ABC

Customer Type Name	n
Internet/Catalog Customers	76
Orion Club members high activity	115
Orion Club members medium activity	154
Orion Club Gold members high activity	65
Orion Club Gold members low activity	42
Orion Club Gold members medium activity	77
Orion Club members low activity	88

Place Image below the Table

Example 6.33 demonstrates using the POSTIMAGE= attribute to place a logo below the table, as seen in Output 6.30.

Example 6.33: Use POSTIMAGE=

```
proc report data=orders style(report)=[postimage="saslogo.jpg"]; ❶
   column customer_type n;
   define customer_type / group;
run;
```

❶ STYLE(REPORT)= applies to the report as a whole. POSTIMAGE= puts the image below the report but the image is still considered part of the table. Because it is placed at the bottom of the table, the image will not be repeated if the table spans multiple pages.

Output 6.30: POSTIMAGE= Places the Logo Below the Table

Customer Type Name	n
Internet/Catalog Customers	76
Orion Club members high activity	115
Orion Club members medium activity	154
Orion Club Gold members high activity	65
Orion Club Gold members low activity	42
Orion Club Gold members medium activity	77
Orion Club members low activity	88

ABC

6.9.2 Place an Image inside of the Table

Insert an Image in a Cell with a Value

An image can be placed in a cell by using a CALL DEFINE statement or STYLE(COLUMN)= on the DEFINE statement to specify the PREIMAGE= and POSTIMAGE= attributes. Example 6.34 uses a CALL DEFINE statement to place an image in a cell that also contains another value, as seen in Output 6.31. Inside of a cell, the POSTIMAGE= attribute will place the image after the value.

Example 6.34: Insert an Image via a CALL DEFINE Statement

```
proc report data=orders;
   column customer_type n;
   define customer_type / group;
   compute n;
      if index(customer_type,'Gold') then
         call define(_col_,'style','style=[postimage="check.gif"]');
   endcomp;
run;
```

Output 6.31: The N Column Contains a Value and an Image

Customer Type Name	n
Internet/Catalog Customers	76
Orion Club members high activity	115
Orion Club members medium activity	154
Orion Club Gold members high activity	65 ✓
Orion Club Gold members low activity	42 ✓
Orion Club Gold members medium activity	77 ✓
Orion Club members low activity	88

Insert an Image in a COMPUTED Column

Example 6.35 is very similar to Example 6.34, but this time, the check mark will be placed in its own column in Output 6.32. The COMPUTED variable CHECK does not have an actual value; the value is technically missing. This example defines CHECK as character on the COMPUTE statement so that a period (for missing) is not placed in the cell if the MISSING system option is not set.

Example 6.35: Insert an Image into a New Column via a CALL DEFINE Statement

```
proc report data=orders;
   column customer_type n check;
   define customer_type / group;
   define check /computed ' ';

   compute check /char length=20;
      if index(customer_type,'Gold') then
         call define(_col_,'style','style=[postimage="check.gif"]');
   endcomp;
run;
```

Output 6.32: A COMPUTED Columns Contains an Image

Customer Type Name	n	
Internet/Catalog Customers	76	
Orion Club members high activity	115	
Orion Club members medium activity	154	
Orion Club Gold members high activity	65	✓
Orion Club Gold members low activity	42	✓
Orion Club Gold members medium activity	77	✓
Orion Club members low activity	88	

Insert a Different Image for Each Value

The POSTIMAGE= style attribute enables images to be embedded in a PROC REPORT column based on the value of a variable. POSTIMAGE requires a quoted string or a fileref. A fileref cannot be created in a COMPUTE block. However, POSTIMAGE does enable you to specify a format. The format resolves to a quoted string. The same logic applies to the PREIMAGE= style attribute.

Example 6.36 demonstrates how to place a different image in each cell, shown in Output 6.33. The image used is dependent upon the value of ORDER_TYPE. Be sure to include the full pathname as part of the LABEL value when creating the format that points to the image file.

Example 6.36: Create a Format Containing the Image Paths for Each Value

```
proc format;
    value mypic ❶
        1 = "goldmedal.png"
        2 = "silvermedal.png"
        3 = "bronzemedal.png";

    value blank ❷ other=" ";
run;

proc report data=orders;
    column order_type image;
    define order_type / group format=typef.;
    define image / computed ' ' style(column)=[preimage=mypic.] ❸
            format=blank.; ❹
    compute image;
        image = order_type; ❺
    endcomp;
run;
```

❶ Create format information that links the desired image file to a specific value of the variable of interest. The starting values match the values of ORDER_TYPE. The labels values should contain the appropriate file path.

   The image files can have any name. For some programmers, it makes sense to name the images the same as the variable value.

❷ Create a format that will change the displayed value to a blank.

❸ PREIMAGE= inside of STYLE(COLUMN)= is assigned the name of the format that contains the image names.

❹ The FORMAT= option is assigned the BLANK. format created in step 2 ❷. The IMAGE variable will contain values. This format prevents those values from appearing in the final output.

❺ Set IMAGE to the value of ORDER_TYPE. The formats applied on the DEFINE statement place the image in the cell.

Output 6.33: A Separate Image Is Displayed for Each ORDER_TYPE Value

Insert a BACKGROUND Image

An image can also be set as the background image of a cell using the BACKGROUNDIMAGE= attribute. The BACKGROUNDIMAGE= attribute is valid only in a select number of ODS destinations, which limits its usefulness. The size of the image versus the width and height of the cell also plays an important role in the final appearance of the report. Images that are bigger than the cell will look truncated. Images that are smaller than the cell might repeat in order to fill the entire cell. For images that you intend to use as background images, it is best to create them with a specific height and width, and then apply that same height and width to the cell in the PROC REPORT step.

HTML is one of the valid destinations for using the BACKGROUNDIMAGE= attribute, so it will be used to demonstrate the technique. Example 6.37 uses the same images as Example 6.36 and inserts the appropriate image as the background image to the ORDER_TYPE column in Output 6.34.

Example 6.37: Use BACKGROUNDIMAGE=

```
proc report data=orders;
   column order_type;
   define order_type / group format=typef.
         style(column)=[just=c cellwidth=1in cellheight=1in]; ❶
   compute order_type;
      ❷
      if order_type = 1 then call define(_col_,'style',
         'style=[backgroundimage="goldmedal.tiff"]');
      else if order_type = 2 then call define(_col_,'style',
         'style=[backgroundimage="silvermedal.tiff"]');
```

```
        else if order_type = 3 then call define(_col_,'style',
          'style=[backgroundimage="bronzemedal.tiff"]');
    endcomp;
run;
```

❶ The image size is 1in by 1in. Therefore, both the CELLWDITH= and CELLHEIGHT= attributes are set to 1in to ensure that the background image fits well.

❷ Apply the BACKGROUNDIMAGE= attribute in a CALL DEFINE statement.

Output 6.34: Each ORDER_TYPE Value Has a Unique Background Image

6.10 URLs

Reports often require hyperlinks. The hyperlinks could be to a single website or to files that contain information related to your report (known as drill-down reports). In this section, we will look at how to create both types of hyperlinks. The URL= attribute creates the hyperlinks and can be associated with a header or a cell value.

Each destination designates a hyperlinked cell differently. Adobe software will place a blue border around a cell when there is a hyperlink unless you turn it off via the style template. Adobe will place a note icon in the corner of the cell when the FLYOVER= attribute is applied. Microsoft Word will have a flyover with instructions to press Ctrl+Click when you hover over a hyperlinked cell in RTF files. Both applications will change the cursor to a hand when you hover over the cell. Hyperlinks are easily distinguishable in HTML as they tend to be underlined and in a different font color. HMTL allows you to place a hyperlink on individual words within a cell. Most other ODS destinations place the hyperlink on the cell as a whole. Therefore, you cannot place multiple hyperlinks within one cell.

Example 6.38 creates a custom style template that will be used throughout this section of the chapter. The output being created is sent to PDF; by default, PDF will surround hyperlinks with blue boxes. The custom style template removes the blue boxes.

Example 6.38: Create Style Template That Removes the Blue Hyperlink Box

```
ods path(prepend) work.templat(update);  ❶
proc template;
   define style styles.pearl2;
       parent=styles.pearl;
       style body from document /
               linkcolor=_undef_;  ❷
   end;
run;

ods pdf file='url.pdf' notoc style=pearl2;
```

❶ Set the ODS PATH to start with WORK.TEMPLAT because this custom style does not need to be stored. It is just temporary.

❷ Set the LINKCOLOR= attribute to undefined in order to remove the blue boxes around hyperlinks.

6.10.1 Hyperlink to a Static Location

The URL= attribute can be set to a hardcoded value. In Example 6.39, STYLE(HEADER)= for CUSTOMER_TYPE contains URL= and it specifies a link to www.sas.com, as seen in Output 6.35.

Example 6.39: Place Hyperlink to a Static Location in Header Cell

```
proc report data=orders;
   column customer_type n;
   define customer_type / group
style(header)=[url="http://www.sas.com" flyover="SAS"];
run;
```

Output 6.35: PDF Designates the Flyover for the Hyperlinked Cell with a Note Icon

≡ Customer Type Name	n
Internet/Catalog Customers	76
Orion Club members high activity	115
Orion Club members medium activity	154
Orion Club Gold members high activity	65
Orion Club Gold members low activity	42
Orion Club Gold members medium activity	77
Orion Club members low activity	88

The URL= attribute can also be used in a CALL DEFINE statement. Notice in Example 6.40 the second argument is STYLE. This allows use of the URL= and the FLYOVER= attributes in the same CALL DEFINE statement. The result is shown in Output 6.36.

Example 6.40: Use CALL DEFINE to Add a URL Hyperlink and a Flyover

```
proc report data=orders;
   column customer_type n;
   define customer_type / group;
   compute n;
      call define(_col_,'style','style=[url=http://www.sas.com
                   flyover="SAS"]');
   endcomp;
run;
```

Output 6.36: Each N Cell Has a Hyperlink and a Flyover Note Icon

Customer Type Name	n
Internet/Catalog Customers	≡ 76
Orion Club members high activity	≡115
Orion Club members medium activity	≡154
Orion Club Gold members high activity	≡ 65
Orion Club Gold members low activity	≡ 42
Orion Club Gold members medium activity	≡ 77
Orion Club members low activity	≡ 88

6.10.2 Link to Numerous Files

The second argument in CALL DEFINE can also be URL. It requires only the name URL; you do not include the equal sign (=). Using URL as the second argument is the same as using the URL= attribute, in that it makes the entire cell a link. However, the third argument must contain only the URL value. The third argument can be a variable. Example 6.41 creates a variable called LINK, which allows for multiple locations or files. LINK is created within the compute block to point to a file with a name that matches the current value of the CUSTOMER_TYPE variable. The result is shown in Output 6.37. Be sure to include the first part of the full path to the location of the file when creating the LINK variable.

Example 6.41: Assign a Different Hyperlink Value to Each CUSTOMER_TYPE Value

```
proc report data=orders;
   column customer_type n;
   define customer_type / group;
   compute customer_type;
      length link $100;
      link = cats(customer_type,".pdf");
      call define(_col_,'url',link);
   endcomp;
run;
```

Output 6.37: Each Customer Type Value Links to a Different File

Customer Type Name	n
Internet/Catalog Customers	76
Orion Club members high activity	115
Orion Club members medium activity	154
Orion Club Gold members high activity	65
Orion Club Gold members low activity	42
Orion Club Gold members medium activity	77
Orion Club members low activity	88

Because the FLYOVER= attribute is not used in this example, and the link color is changed to undefined, it is not always easy to tell in PDF output that a link is associated with a particular cell. Output 6.38 is what the same output looks like in HTML.

Output 6.38: HTML Indicates Each Cell Is a Hyperlink

Customer Type Name	n
Internet/Catalog Customers	76
Orion Club members high activity	115
Orion Club members medium activity	154
Orion Club Gold members high activity	65
Orion Club Gold members low activity	42
Orion Club Gold members medium activity	77
Orion Club members low activity	88

Since the FLYOVER= attribute is not used in Example 6.41, and the link color is changed to undefined, it is not always easy to determine that a link is associated with a particular cell in PDF output. The TEXTDECORATION= attribute can be used to underline the text, so it appears more like a traditional link. Example 6.42 demonstrates the additional CALL DEFINE statement needed in the compute block to apply the TEXTDECORATION= attribute.

Example 6.42: Apply TEXTDECORATION= Attribute to Link Text

```
compute customer_type;
   length link $100;
   link = cats(customer_type,".pdf");
   call define(_col_,'url',link);
   call define(_col_,'style','style=[textdecoration=underline]');
endcomp;
```

Output 6.39: TEXTDECORATION= Helps Distinguish Links in PDF Cells

Customer Type Name	n
Internet/Catalog Customers	76
Orion Club members high activity	115
Orion Club members medium activity	154
Orion Club Gold members high activity	65
Orion Club Gold members low activity	42
Orion Club Gold members medium activity	77
Orion Club members low activity	88

Chapter 7: Table of Contents – How to Manipulate with CONTENTS= and PROC DOCUMENT

7.1 Introduction

The final step to mastering PROC REPORT is learning how to control the Table of Contents nodes and labels. A table of contents is a very useful and necessary tool for navigating through a long, multipage report. PROC REPORT has the ability to control the entries in the table of contents. PROC REPORT has the CONTENTS= option on many statements that allows you to change the node labels. This chapter will examine the various uses of the CONTENTS= option. Then the chapter will explore how you can use ODS Document destination and PROC DOCUMENT to change the content nodes created by PROC REPORT and replay the report with a new table of contents.

7.2 Default Nodes

The default table of contents that PROC REPORT creates has three node levels. The first node is the procedure label. The second node is the report label. The third node is the table label. The first two node levels are straightforward and easily manipulated. The third node level is the hardest to understand and control. Example 7.1 produces the default table of contents nodes.

Example 7.1: Default TOC Nodes

```
proc report data=orders;
    column product_line quantity total_retail_price;
    define product_line / group;
run;
```

Output 7.1: Default TOC Nodes and Labels

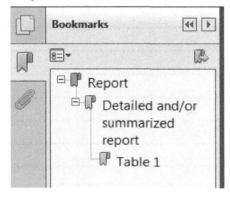

1. **The procedure label:** The first node, the procedure label, is controlled by the ODS PROCLABEL statement. The label can be assigned to any string value. The label can be set to blank, but the node cannot be eliminated completely unless you use PROC DOCUMENT, which is discussed later in this chapter.

2. **The report label:** The second node is controlled by the CONTENTS= option on the PROC REPORT statement. The text value is static. It can hold only one value. It can be eliminated completely by assigning a null value, CONTENTS=' '.

3. **The table label:** The third node always defaults to "Table 1". This node is controlled by the CONTENTS= option on the BREAK statement. The BREAK statement must also have the PAGE option specified to change the node label. This means you must have a paging variable. If you do not need table breaks but need to control the node label, you can assign the paging variable to have the same value for every observation in the input data set. The text value is static. It can hold only one value. The node can be eliminated completely by assigning a null value, CONTENTS=' '.

Example 7.2 changes the default labels. The changes are displayed in Output 7.2. The *location* value on the BREAK statement must be BEFORE.

Example 7.2: Change Default Node Labels

```
data orders;
    set orders;
    dummy = 1;
run;
```

```
ods proclabel = 'Sales Data';
proc report data=orders contents='Product Line';
   column dummy product_line quantity total_retail_price;
   define dummy / group noprint;
   define product_line / group;
   break before dummy / contents='Full Report' page;
run;
```

Output 7.2: Default Nodes Labels Changed to Informative Text

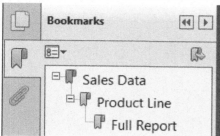

7.3 BY-Variable Nodes

Using a BY variable adds a node level to the table of contents. Example 7.3 demonstrates the table of contents generated by a BY variable, shown in Output 7.3.

Example 7.3: BY-Variable Nodes

```
proc sort data=orders;
   by customer_age_group;
run;

proc report data=orders;
   by customer_age_group;
   column product_line quantity total_retail_price;
   define product_line / group;
run;
```

Output 7.3: Default BY-Variable Node Labels

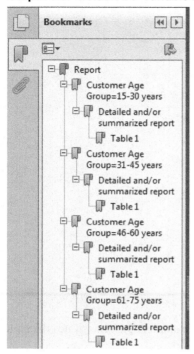

As you can see, the BY-variable node is in the form *BY-variable name = BY-variable value.* The BY-group value becomes the second node level. The report label moves down to the third level. The table label becomes the fourth level. PROC REPORT does not have the ability to change this structure. The CONTENTS= option does not resolve #BYVAR or #BYVAL.

To change the node label for each BY group, the PROC REPORT step needs to be placed inside of a macro program. The macro program has to run once for each BY group. Moving the PROC REPORT step inside of a macro program eliminates the need for a BY statement. Therefore, the code reverts to the default structure of creating three node levels and those node labels can be modified, as demonstrated in Example 7.4 and Output 7.4.

Example 7.4: Change BY-Variable Node Labels

```
proc sort data=orders;
   by customer_age_group;
run;

%macro bynode(byvar);
   %local i;
   ods proclabel = "&byvar"; ❶
   proc report data=orders contents=""; ❷
      where customer_age_group="&byvar";
      column product_line quantity total_retail_price;
```

```
        define product_line / group;
    run;
%mend bynode;

data _null_;
    set orders;
    by customer_age_group;
    if first.customer_age_group then
        call execute('%bynode('||customer_age_group||')');   ❸
run;
```

❶   The PROCLABEL is set to the value of the BY variable. Recall that PROCLABEL controls the first node. This statement changes the text from the default of "The Report Procedure" to the more informative text of the BY value.

❷   The report label node is eliminated completely.

❸   The macro containing the PROC REPORT code is executed once for each value of the BY variable CUSTOMER_AGE_GROUP.

Output 7.4: Change Procedure Label to BY-Variable Value

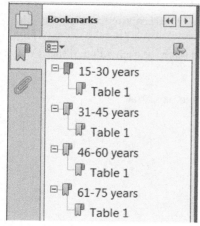

The table label, the second node in Output 7.4, can be removed using a BREAK BEFORE statement. Using the BY variable as paging variable is the easiest solution because you already know that each time PROC REPORT runs, the BY variable will have only one value for the report. Example 7.5 removes the second node in Output 7.5.

Example 7.5: Eliminate Another BY-Variable Node Level

```
proc sort data=orders;
    by customer_age_group;
run;

%macro bynode(byvar);
ods proclabel = "&byvar";❶
proc report data=orders contents="";   ❷
```

```
      where customer_age_group="&byvar";
      column customer_age_group product_line quantity total_retail_price;
      define customer_age_group / group noprint; ❸
      define product_line / group;
      break before customer_age_group / contents='' page; ❹
   run;
   %mend bynode;

   data _null_;
      set orders;
      by customer_age_group;
      if first.customer_age_group then
         call execute('%bynode('||customer_age_group||')'); ❺
   run;
```

❶ The PROCLABEL is set to the value of the BY variable.

❷ The report label node is eliminated completely.

❸ CUSTOMER_AGE_GROUP is added to the COLUMN statement and defined as GROUP with the NOPRINT option. GROUP is needed, so the BREAK statement can be used. NOPRINT prevents the column from appearing in the report.

❹ The BREAK BEFORE statement with the CONTENTS= and PAGE options control the value of the table label node. This code eliminates the node completely by setting the value of null.

❺ The macro containing the PROC REPORT code is executed once for each value of the BY variable CUSTOMER_AGE_GROUP.

Output 7.5: TOC Contains Only One Node Level with BY-Value as Label

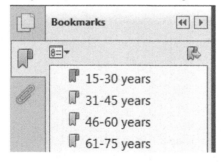

7.4 DEFINE Statement CONTENTS=

The DEFINE statement has a CONTENTS= option, but it is ignored unless the PAGE option is also specified. For basic PROC REPORT output, this option can be used to change the third node, the table label. This method is an alternative to needing to add a paging variable. However, the CONTENTS= option on the DEFINE statement does not allow you to completely eliminate the node like it does on the BREAK statement. Example 7.6 modifies the label of the third node using the DEFINE statement, shown in Output 7.5.

Example 7.6: Change Third Node Level Label Using the DEFINE Statement

```
proc report data=orders;
   column product_line quantity total_retail_price;
   define product_line / group contents='Product Line' page;
run;
```

Output 7.6: Third Node Label Changed to More Informative Text

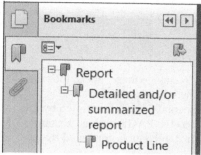

As mentioned above, the CONTENTS= option is valid only with the PAGE option used. The PAGE option on a DEFINE statement is used to create a horizontal page break when the table is very wide. Remember that for non-Listing ODS destinations, the PAGE option actually creates a table break. When a second table is generated, the table of contents has two entries in the third node level, one label for each of the tables. The entry values are in the form *Col1-ColN*, where Col1 is the first column name on that page and ColN is the last column name on that page. Example 7.7 uses the PAGE option and creates multiple table entries in Output 7.7.

Example 7.7: Use the PAGE Option on a DEFINE Statement

```
proc report data=orders;
   column customer_id customer_name customer_age customer_gender
          customer_birthdate customer_country customer_group
          customer_type product_name quantity total_retail_price;

   define customer_id / group;
   define customer_name / group;
   define customer_age / group;
   define customer_gender / group;
   define customer_birthdate / group;
   define customer_country / group format=$cntry.;
   define customer_group / group;
   define customer_type / group;
   define product_name / group page;
run;
```

Output 7.7: Node Label Created By PAGE Option on DEFINE Statement

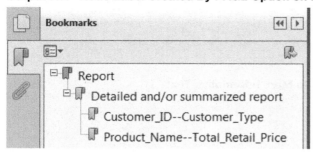

Output 7.7 contained the *report-item* names as the table label. To change these labels, the CONTENTS= option is needed on two DEFINE statements. The label for the first table is controlled by the first variable for that table. The label for the second table is controlled by the variable that triggers the second table, that is, the variable that has the PAGE option. Example 7.8 uses the CONTENTS= on two DEFINE statements to control the table labels generated by the PAGE option in Output 7.8.

Example 7.8: Use the PAGE and CONTENTS= Options on a DEFINE Statement

```
proc report data=orders;
    column customer_id customer_name customer_age customer_gender
           customer_birthdate customer_country customer_group
           customer_type product_name quantity total_retail_price;

    define customer_id / group contents='Customer Info, Entry 1';
    define customer_name / group;
    define customer_age / group;
    define customer_gender / group;
    define customer_birthdate / group;
    define customer_country / group format=$cntry.;
    define customer_group / group;
    define customer_type / group;
    define product_name / page contents='Customer Info, Entry 2';
run;
```

Output 7.8: Node Label Created By CONTENTS= Option on DEFINE Statement

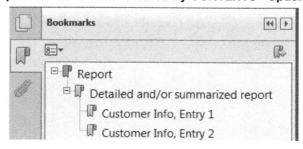

7.5 BREAK Statement CONTENTS=

In general, the BREAK statement is used to create a new table by using the PAGE option. For each new table, the table of contents contains an entry. The entry will have the label "Table N", where N is the table number. CUSTOMER_COUNTRY has seven unique values. When it is placed on a BREAK statement with the PAGE option, the table of contents has seven table entries, as shown by Example 7.9 and Output 7.9.

Example 7.9: Place PAGE Option on the BREAK AFTER Statement

```
proc report data=orders;
   column customer_country product_line quantity total_retail_price;
   define customer_country / group;
   define product_line / group;
   break after customer_country / page;
run;
```

Output 7.9: Node Label Created by PAGE Option on BREAK AFTER Statement

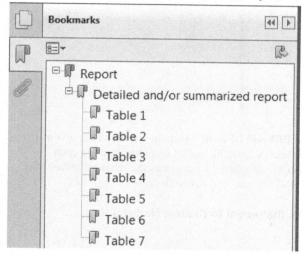

As we have seen in previous examples, the CONTENTS= option on the BREAK statement can be used to change the text for the table label, to change the text on the third node level, or to eliminate the node completely. The text for the table label is static, so it cannot take on the values of the GROUP variable CUSTOMER_COUNTRY. Example 7.10 demonstrates specifying static text in the CONTENTS= option on a BREAK AFTER statement. The result is shown in Output 7.10.

Example 7.10: Use the PAGE and CONTENTS= Options on a BREAK AFTER Statement

```
proc report data=orders;
   column customer_country product_line quantity total_retail_price;
   define customer_country / group;
   define product_line / group;
   break after ❶customer_country / page contents='Customer Country';❷
run;
```

❶ The *location* on the BREAK statement is AFTER. This is **not** best practice when trying to control the table labels via the CONTENTS= option. The entry for the first table will differ from the entry for the other tables.

❷ CONTENTS= assigns the same text for Tables 2-7.

Output 7.10: Node Label Created by PAGE and CONTENTS= Option on BREAK AFTER Statement

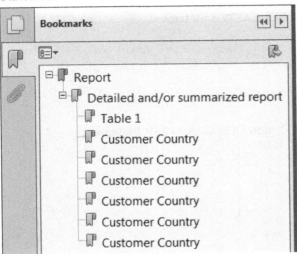

Best practice is to control the table label on a BREAK BEFORE statement. However, even when placed on a BREAK BEFORE statement, the text is static. It cannot be controlled for each individual table with the CONTENTS= option. Example 7.11 generates the table of contents in Output 7.11, which has the text from CONTENTS= repeated seven times.

Example 7.11: Change Location on BREAK Statement to Change Node Label

```
proc report data=orders;
    column customer_country product_line quantity total_retail_price;
    define customer_country / group;
    define product_line / group;
    break before customer_country / page contents='Customer Country';
run;
```

Output 7.11: BEFORE Location on BREAK Statement Changes a Third Level Node Label

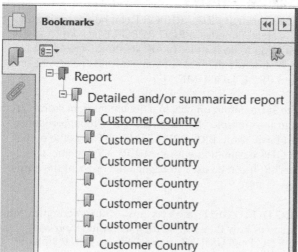

7.6 RBREAK Statement CONTENTS=

The RBREAK statement also has a CONTENTS= option. The option is valid only when also used with the BEFORE *location*, the PAGE option, and the SUMMARIZE option. Another entry will be added to the third node level. Due to the restrictive nature of this option on the RBREAK statement, it might not be practical to use in most business situations. Example 7.12 demonstrates the additional entry generated by the RBREAK statement. The result is shown in Output 7.12.

Example 7.12: Use the PAGE and CONTENTS= Options on an RBREAK Statement

```
proc report data=orders;
   column customer_country product_line quantity total_retail_price;
   define customer_country / group;
   define product_line / group;
   rbreak before  / contents="Summary" page summarize;
run;
```

Output 7.12: RBREAK Statement Adds a Node Labeled Summary

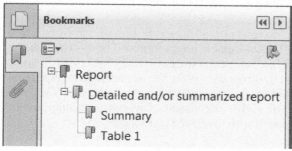

7.7 ODS DOCUMENT and PROC DOCUMENT

Controlling the number of nodes and their labels through PROC REPORT can be frustrating and difficult. In some cases, as with the BREAK statement nodes, PROC REPORT has only a small amount of control. For some reports, the best thing to do is to let PROC REPORT create the bare minimum number of necessary nodes. Then, restructure the table of contents and change the entry labels with the ODS Document destination and PROC DOCUMENT.

The ODS Document destination is designed to store output objects in a document item store. From the stored information, you can produce output for multiple ODS destinations without rerunning the original PROC or DATA step. In its most basic form, PROC DOCUMENT sends the output objects in a document item store to any open ODS destination with the REPLAY statement. However, PROC DOCUMENT is more powerful; it can be used to change the order of the output objects as well as to restructure the table of contents.

The ODS DOCUMENT destination and PROC DOCUMENT are very powerful and complex tools in Base SAS. This book just touches the surface of how they can be used in conjunction with PROC REPORT. For more information on PROC DOCUMENT, please refer to *SAS 9.4 Output Delivery System: User's Guide* and the *SAS 9.4 Output Delivery System: Procedures Guide* Another great reference is the book *PROC DOCUMENT by Example Using SAS* by Michael Tuchman.

7.7.1 ODS DOCUMENT Convention

The syntax for the ODS DOCUMENT destination is the same as for other destinations. You must first open the destination, and then, after data and procedure steps, close the destination.

```
ods document name=temp;
proc report …
run;
ods document close;
```

The default behavior of the ODS DOCUMENT statement is Update access mode. Update mode appends any new procedure information to an already existing document item store. The code in this section will specify the Write access mode. This mode deletes anything existing in the item store and starts from scratch each time. The purpose is to avoid any confusion regarding the contents of the item store. The document store will be called TEMP. By default, this will be stored in WORK. The name can be changed to something more meaningful and prefaced with a libref so that the document store is permanently stored.

Also, please be aware the CUSTOMER_COUNTRY variable uses a format. For this code, the format and ODS DOCUMENT were created in the same SAS session. ODS DOCUMENT stores temporary formats as part of the document and those are used when the document is replayed. Permanent formats are not saved into the document. In your code, you must make sure SAS knows where user-defined formats are located when you replay a document. This can be accomplished with a PROC FORMAT or an OPTIONS statement with the FMTSEARCH option.

7.7.2 PROC DOCUMENT Statements and Options

In the next two sections, PROC DOCUMENT is used to display the contents of the document item store created by ODS DOCUMENT. The sections will use only the LIST statement. The LIST statement does exactly what the name implies – it writes a list of the contents of each entry in the document. On the LIST statement, two options are needed: LEVELS= and DETAILS. The LEVELS= option will be set to ALL so that the output contains every entry and path in the item store. The DETAILS option is used, so that you can see the TYPE and LABEL variable values for each path.

In the final two sections of this chapter, the MAKE, SETLABEL, and COPY statements will be used. The MAKE statement is used to create a new directory. All changes made within the item store will be placed in a new directory to avoid confusion and inadvertent changes to the items created by PROC REPORT. SETLABEL is used to assign node labels. The COPY statement is used to copy items created by PROC REPORT to the new directory. Again, this is to avoid inadvertent changes. PROC DOCUMENT has other methods besides COPY that use less space, but for the sake of simplicity, the examples use only the COPY statement.

PROC DOCUMENT allows RUN-Group processing. Interactively, you can submit multiple statements and execute them without terminating the procedure. Therefore, the RUN statement is very important; it must be used to ensure that all statements are executed. The procedure must end with a QUIT statement to be properly terminated.

7.7.3 Default Items

It is important to understand the entries PROC REPORT places into the document item store. The first step is to view the default behavior. Example 7.13 below creates an item store from a simple PROC REPORT step, shown in Output 7.13.

Example 7.13: Store PROC REPORT Output Object in a Document Item Store

```
ods document name=temp(write);❶
proc report data=orders; ❷
   column product_line quantity total_retail_price;
   define product_line / group;
run;
ods document close; ❸

proc document name=temp; ❹
   list / levels=all details; ❺
run;
quit;
```

❶ Open the ODS DOCUMENT destination specifying the item store name and the access mode.

❷ This is a basic PROC REPORT step that does not change any of the node labels.

❸ Close the ODS DOCUMENT destination.

❹   The ODS DOCUMENT destination does not create printed output. To view the contents of the document store, you need a PROC DOCUMENT step. The newly created document store, TEMP, is specified.

❺   The LIST statement will list the contents of the document store. The LEVELS= and DETAILS options ensure that all the related information is printed.

Output 7.13: Default Item Store Generated by PROC REPORT

			Size							
Obs	Path	Type	in Bytes	Created	Modified	Symbolic Link	Template	Label		Page Break
1	\Report#1	Dir		07NOV2015:16:29:10	07NOV2015:16:29:10			The Report Procedure		
2	\Report#1\Report#1	Dir		07NOV2015:16:29:10	07NOV2015:16:29:10			Detailed and/or summarized report		
3	\Report#1\Report#1\Report#1	Table	1616	07NOV2015:16:29:10	07NOV2015:16:29:10					Before

Listing of: \Work.Temp
Order by: Insertion
Number of levels: All

Recall that PROC REPORT creates three node levels by default. The document store has three items.

1. The first item, Observation 1, corresponds to the procedure label created by the ODS PROCLABEL statement. The item type is "Dir", which is not an output object. This item is the top of the directory structure that contains the output objects. The label column in the output shows the default value of "The Report Procedure".

2. The second item, Observation 2, is also type "Dir", so it creates a subdirectory. This item corresponds to the report label controlled by the CONTENTS= option on the PROC REPORT statement. The label column contains the text "Detailed and/or summarized report", which you have seen.

3. The final item, Observation 3, is the actual output object – the table created by PROC REPORT. The label value is missing due to the timing sequence of ODS DOCUMENT creating the observation and PROC REPORT supplying the correct label.

Previously in this chapter, the PAGE option was added to a BREAK statement and the resulting table of contents has seven Table N nodes. Though the table of contents was changed by the inclusion of the PAGE option, the item store contains only one table entry, as demonstrated by Example 7.14 and seen in Output 7.14. Again, this is because of a timing issue; PROC REPORT had yet to create all seven tables when the entry in the item store was created.

Example 7.14: Use PAGE option on BREAK Statement and Generate Item Store

```
ods document name=temp(write);
proc report data=orders;
   column customer_country product_line quantity total_retail_price;
   define customer_country / group;
   define product_line / group;
   break after customer_country / page;
run;
ods document close;

proc document name=temp;
   list / levels=all details;
```

```
run;
quit;
```

Output 7.14: Document Item Store Generated with PAGE Option on BREAK Statement

			Size						
Listing of: \Work.Temp\
Order by: Insertion
Number of levels: All

Obs	Path	Type	Size in Bytes	Created	Modified	Symbolic Link	Template	Label	Page Break
1	\Report#1	Dir		07NOV2015:16:33:54	07NOV2015:16:33:54			The Report Procedure	
2	\Report#1\Report#1	Dir		07NOV2015:16:33:54	07NOV2015:16:33:54			Detailed and/or summarized report	
3	\Report#1\Report#1\Report#1	Table	2024	07NOV2015:16:33:54	07NOV2015:16:33:54				Before

The document store will always have at least two items. One item will be a directory. The second item will be the table output object. Removing the second- and third-level nodes in the table of contents through PROC REPORT still produces two entries in the document store, which is demonstrated by Example 7.15 and Output 7.15.

Example 7.15: Remove Two Node Levels from TOC
```
data orders;
   set orders;
   dummy = 1;
run;

proc report data=orders contents='';
   column dummy product_line quantity total_retail_price;
   define dummy / group noprint;
   define product_line / group;
   break before dummy / contents='Full Report' page;
run;
```

Output 7.15: Document Item Store When Two Node Levels Are Removed From TOC

Listing of: \Work.Temp\
Order by: Insertion
Number of levels: All

Obs	Path	Type	Size in Bytes	Created	Modified	Symbolic Link	Template	Label	Page Break
1	\Report#1	Dir		07NOV2015:16:37:06	07NOV2015:16:37:06			The Report Procedure	
2	\Report#1\Report#1	Table	1648	07NOV2015:16:37:06	07NOV2015:16:37:06				Before

7.7.4 BY-Variable Item List

When a BY statement is used, a subdirectory is added to the document store under the main directory for each value of the BY variable. Each subdirectory has a sequence number. The sequence number is an integer that is unique for each subdirectory or entry. Multiple BY variables do not change the subdirectory structure. They do increase the number of subdirectories the item store contains because there will be one for each combination of the BY-variable values.

For example 7.16, the variable CUSTOMER_AGE_GROUP has five unique values. Therefore, five subdirectories are added. The first subdirectory is called ByGroup1#1, the next is called ByGroup2#1, and so on. Under each BY value directory is another subdirectory, and in that subdirectory is the table output object. The results are shown in Output 7.16.

Example 7.16: Include a BY Statement in the PROC REPORT Step

```
proc sort data=orders;
   by customer_age_group;
run;

ods document name=temp(write);
proc report data=orders;
   by customer_age_group;
   column product_line quantity total_retail_price;
   define product_line / group;
run;
ods document close;

proc document name=temp;
   list / levels=all details;
run;
quit;
```

Output 7.16: Document Item Store Generated with BY Statement

Listing of: \Work.Temp\
Order by: Insertion
Number of levels: All

Obs	Path	Type	Size in Bytes	Created	Modified	Symbolic Link	Template	Label	Page Break
1	\Report#1	Dir		07NOV2015:16:39:31	07NOV2015:16:39:31			The Report Procedure	
2	\Report#1\ByGroup1#1	Dir		07NOV2015:16:39:31	07NOV2015:16:39:31			Customer Age Group=15-30 years	
3	\Report#1\ByGroup1#1\Report#1	Dir		07NOV2015:16:39:31	07NOV2015:16:39:31			Detailed and/or summarized report	
4	\Report#1\ByGroup1#1\Report#1\Report#1	Table	1616	07NOV2015:16:39:31	07NOV2015:16:39:31				Before
5	\Report#1\ByGroup2#1	Dir		07NOV2015:16:39:31	07NOV2015:16:39:31			Customer Age Group=31-45 years	
6	\Report#1\ByGroup2#1\Report#1	Dir		07NOV2015:16:39:31	07NOV2015:16:39:31			Detailed and/or summarized report	
7	\Report#1\ByGroup2#1\Report#1\Report#1	Table	1616	07NOV2015:16:39:31	07NOV2015:16:39:31				Before
8	\Report#1\ByGroup3#1	Dir		07NOV2015:16:39:31	07NOV2015:16:39:31			Customer Age Group=46-60 years	
9	\Report#1\ByGroup3#1\Report#1	Dir		07NOV2015:16:39:31	07NOV2015:16:39:31			Detailed and/or summarized report	
10	\Report#1\ByGroup3#1\Report#1\Report#1	Table	1616	07NOV2015:16:39:31	07NOV2015:16:39:31				Before
11	\Report#1\ByGroup4#1	Dir		07NOV2015:16:39:31	07NOV2015:16:39:31			Customer Age Group=61-75 years	
12	\Report#1\ByGroup4#1\Report#1	Dir		07NOV2015:16:39:31	07NOV2015:16:39:31			Detailed and/or summarized report	
13	\Report#1\ByGroup4#1\Report#1\Report#1	Table	1616	07NOV2015:16:39:31	07NOV2015:16:39:31				Before

7.7.5 Parent Node with Multiple Child Nodes

The nodes and item lists can all be overwhelming and confusing, but you have to know the structure of the item store before you can manipulate it. That is the good news – you can change the structure! This section contains examples of using PROC DOCUMENT to change the structure of the item list, which ultimately changes the nodes in the table of contents in the output.

One common desire for the table of contents is to have one parent node with multiple child nodes. The PAGE and CONTENTS= options on the BREAK statement do not create multiple items in the item store, so there is nothing to manipulate to create child nodes. The section on BY-variable nodes demonstrated making each BY value a node, but those nodes did not have a parent node. This is where PROC DOCUMENT comes in. PROC DOCUMENT can create a parent node with a meaningful label and then move multiple child nodes underneath it, again with meaningful labels.

Creating one parent node with multiple child nodes is a two-step process.

1. The first step, seen in Example 7.17a, is to create a document item store containing the PROC REPORT output, a BY statement is required to create the required number of items.
2. The second step, seen in Example 7.17b, is to create a new directory in the item store and move the output objects to that directory with the desired label.

The table of contents generated by the result of these two steps can be seen in Output 7.17.

Example 7.17a: Create Document Item Store Containing PROC REPORT Output

```
proc sort data=orders;
   by customer_country;
run;

ods document name=temp(write); ❶
proc report data=orders contents=''; ❷
   by customer_country;
   format customer_country $cntry.;
   column customer_country product_line quantity total_retail_price;
   define customer_country / group;
   define product_line / group;
   break before ❸ customer_country / page contents=''; ❹
run;
ods document close;
```

❶ Open the ODS DOCUMENT destination. No other destination is being used. The final report will be created in the final step using PROC DOCUMENT and sent to the ODS PDF destination.

❷ The report label node is eliminated completely.

❸ BEFORE must be specified as the location.

❹ The PAGE option is required in order to use the CONTENTS= option. CONTENTS= is set to a null value so that PROC REPORT does not generate a Table 1 node.

Example 7.17b: Move Item Store Entries to a New Directory Structure

```
proc document name=temp; ❶
   make \parentchild; ❷
   setlabel \parentchild "Country Sales"; ❸

   ❹
   setlabel \Report#1\ByGroup1#1\Report#1 "Australia";
   copy \Report#1\ByGroup1#1\Report#1 to \parentchild#1;

   setlabel \Report#1\ByGroup2#1\Report#1 "Canada";
   copy \Report#1\ByGroup2#1\Report#1 to \parentchild#1;

   setlabel \Report#1\ByGroup3#1\Report#1 "Germany";
   copy \Report#1\ByGroup3#1\Report#1 to \parentchild#1;
```

```
        setlabel \Report#1\ByGroup4#1\Report#1 "Israel";
        copy \Report#1\ByGroup4#1\Report#1 to \parentchild#1;

        setlabel \Report#1\ByGroup5#1\Report#1 "Turkey";
        copy \Report#1\ByGroup5#1\Report#1 to \parentchild#1;

        setlabel \Report#1\ByGroup6#1\Report#1 "United States";
        copy \Report#1\ByGroup6#1\Report#1 to \parentchild#1;

        setlabel \Report#1\ByGroup7#1\Report#1 "South Africa";
        copy \Report#1\ByGroup7#1\Report#1 to \parentchild#1;
    run;

    ods pdf file="CountrySales.pdf"; ❺
        replay \parentchild; ❻
    run;
    ods pdf close;
    quit;
```

❶ Specify the document item store TEMP created in Example 7.17a.

❷ The MAKE statement creates a new directory called PARENTCHILD. The new directory will be the parent node in the final output.

❸ Set the label for the parent node. The label text will be "Country Sales".

❹ Create a label for each one of the child nodes. The label text should correspond to the specified path. Copy the output object and place it under the new parent node. A SETLABEL and COPY statement is needed for each one of the BY values.

❺ Open the final destination that you want the output created in, in this case, ODS PDF.

❻ Use the REPLAY statement, specifying the newly created folder PARENTCHILD that contains the desired structure and node labels.

Output 7.17: One Parent and Multiple Child Node TOC Generated by PROC DOCUMENT

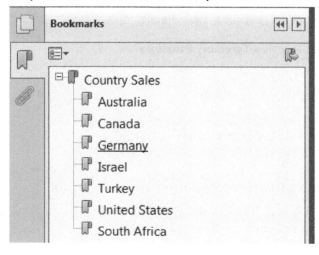

The above code hardcoded all of the SETLABEL and COPY statements. This can be a tedious process and it opens the door for typographical errors. This step can be placed inside of a macro program instead, so that the macro does all of the heavy lifting. Using a macro program to update the item store requires more steps to the process of creating one parent node with multiple child nodes.

1. The first step is to create a document item store containing the PROC REPORT output.
2. The next step is creating a data set that contains the item list from the store.
3. The third step is to create macro variables for each path and label that needs to be manipulated.
4. The final step is creating a new item structure, with the desired node levels, and replaying the new structure to the desired ODS destination.

The code in Example 7.18a starts after the PROC REPORT step and the close of the ODS DOCUMENT destination from Example 7.17a. Example 7.18a creates a data set from the items stored in the document. Output 7.18 shows the data set. Example 7.18b creates macro variables. The values are seen in Output 7.19. Example 7.18c contains the macro code that creates SETLABEL and COPY statements for each country.

Example 7.18a: Create Data Set Containing Document Item Store Values

```
ods output properties=itemlist; ❶
proc document name=temp;
   list / levels=all details; ❷
run;
quit;
```

❶ Create a data set named ITEMLIST that contains the item list from the document item store.

❷ The LIST statement will list the contents of the document store. The LEVELS= and DETAILS options ensure that all the related information is listed and written to the data set ITEMLIST.

Output 7.18: ITEMLIST Data Set

	Path	Type	Size	Created	Modified	SymLink	Label
1	\Report#1	Dir	0	07NOV2015:16:45:37	07NOV2015:16:45:37		The Report Procedure
2	\Report#1\ByGroup1#1	Dir	0	07NOV2015:16:45:37	07NOV2015:16:45:37		Customer Country=Australia
3	\Report#1\ByGroup1#1\Report#1	Table	1692	07NOV2015:16:45:37	07NOV2015:16:45:37		
4	\Report#1\ByGroup2#1	Dir	0	07NOV2015:16:45:37	07NOV2015:16:45:37		Customer Country=Canada
5	\Report#1\ByGroup2#1\Report#1	Table	1714	07NOV2015:16:45:37	07NOV2015:16:45:37		
6	\Report#1\ByGroup3#1	Dir	0	07NOV2015:16:45:37	07NOV2015:16:45:37		Customer Country=Germany
7	\Report#1\ByGroup3#1\Report#1	Table	1770	07NOV2015:16:45:37	07NOV2015:16:45:37		
8	\Report#1\ByGroup4#1	Dir	0	07NOV2015:16:45:37	07NOV2015:16:45:37		Customer Country=Israel
9	\Report#1\ByGroup4#1\Report#1	Table	1666	07NOV2015:16:45:37	07NOV2015:16:45:37		
10	\Report#1\ByGroup5#1	Dir	0	07NOV2015:16:45:37	07NOV2015:16:45:37		Customer Country=Turkey
11	\Report#1\ByGroup5#1\Report#1	Table	1666	07NOV2015:16:45:37	07NOV2015:16:45:37		
12	\Report#1\ByGroup6#1	Dir	0	07NOV2015:16:45:37	07NOV2015:16:45:37		Customer Country=United States
13	\Report#1\ByGroup6#1\Report#1	Table	1696	07NOV2015:16:45:37	07NOV2015:16:45:37		
14	\Report#1\ByGroup7#1	Dir	0	07NOV2015:16:45:37	07NOV2015:16:45:37		Customer Country=South Africa
15	\Report#1\ByGroup7#1\Report#1	Table	1658	07NOV2015:16:45:37	07NOV2015:16:45:37		

Example 7.18b: Generate Macro Variables Containing Paths and Labels from ITEMLIST

```
data _null_;
  set itemlist end=last;

  if _n_ ne 1 then do; ❶
    if type not in ("Table") then do; ❷
      count1+1; ❸
      call symputx('label'||trim(left(count1)),scan(label,2,"="));  ❹
    end;
  end;

  if type in ("Table") then do; ❺
    count+1; ❻
    call symputx('path'||trim(left(count)),path);  ❼
  end;

  if last then call symputx('total',count);  ❽
run;
```

❶ The first record in the ITEMLIST data set is the main directory created by the ODS PROCLABEL. We do not want to look at or include this record.

❷ Look at all of the directory listings. One is made for each of the BY-variable values.

❸ Count the number of BY-variable items. For this example the number is seven.

❹ Create one macro variable for each BY-variable item. The values of the macro variables will be the values of the BY variable. In the data set the LABEL variable is the name of the BY variable, followed by an equal sign and then the value of the BY variable. This code strips the text down to just the value of the BY variable.

❺ Look at just the output objects, which are designated by TYPE="Table".

❻ Count the number of output objects. This should be seven as well.

❼ Create one macro variable for each table item. The values of the macro variables will be the paths of the output objects.

❽ Create a macro variable that contains the total number of output objects.

Output 7.19: Macro Variable Values

```
GLOBAL  LABEL1  Australia
GLOBAL  LABEL2  Canada
GLOBAL  LABEL3  Germany
GLOBAL  LABEL4  Israel
GLOBAL  LABEL5  Turkey
GLOBAL  LABEL6  United States
GLOBAL  LABEL7  South Africa
GLOBAL  PATH1  \Report#1\ByGroup1#1\Report#1
GLOBAL  PATH2  \Report#1\ByGroup2#1\Report#1
GLOBAL  PATH3  \Report#1\ByGroup3#1\Report#1
GLOBAL  PATH4  \Report#1\ByGroup4#1\Report#1
GLOBAL  PATH5  \Report#1\ByGroup5#1\Report#1
GLOBAL  PATH6  \Report#1\ByGroup6#1\Report#1
```

```
GLOBAL PATH7 \Report#1\ByGroup7#1\Report#1
GLOBAL TOTAL 7
```

Example 7.18c: Use Macro Code to Move Item Store Entries to a New Directory Structure

```
%macro newtoc; ❶
proc document name=temp; ❷
   make \parentchild; ❸
   setlabel \parentchild "Country Sales"; ❹

   %do i=1 %to &total; ❺
     setlabel &&path&i "&&label&i"; ❻
     copy &&path&i to \parentchild#1; ❼
   %end;
run;

ods pdf file="CountrySales.pdf"; ❽
   replay \parentchild; ❾
run;
ods pdf close;

quit;
%mend newtoc;

%newtoc
```

❶ The PROC DOCUMENT code needs to be placed inside of a macro program. The macro program, when called, will cycle through all of the BY-group (country) paths without having to write out a statement for each one.

❷ The PROC DOCUMENT statement references that document item store created in the first step.

❸ The MAKE statement creates a new directory called PARENTCHILD. The new directory will be the parent node in the final output.

❹ Set the label for the parent node. The label text will be "Country Sales".

❺ Loop through each one of the BY values, seven in total.

❻ Create a label for each one of the child nodes. The label text comes from the labelN macro variables that contain the country names.

❼ Copy the output object from their original paths (stored in the pathN macro variables) and put them in the new folder.

❽ Open the final destination that you want the output created in, in this case, ODS PDF.

❾ Use the REPLAY statement, specifying the newly created folder PARENTCHILD that contains the desired structure and node labels.

The resulting output is the same as Output 7.17.

7.7.6 Combine Multiple PROC REPORT Steps under One Node

Example 7.19, the final example in this chapter, combines the output from multiple PROC REPORT steps. The previous example created output by CUSTOMER_COUNTRY. You might have another PROC REPORT step that also creates output by CUSTOMER_COUNTRY. In the final report, you want all of the tables for one country to be grouped together, as in Output 7.20.

This example is similar to the last example, in that it uses a SETLABEL statement for each country value. There are two key differences in this example.

1. A directory needs to be created for each country. The previous example created just a label for each country.
2. A SETLABEL statement is needed for each table created by both PROC REPORT statements.

The sequence number in the path is very important in this example. Remember the sequence number in the path increments for every PROC REPORT step that is run.

Example 7.19: Create Document Item Store Containing Two PROC REPORT Outputs

```
proc sort data=orders;
   by customer_country;
run;

ods document name=temp(write);

proc report data=orders contents='';
   by customer_country;
   format customer_country $cntry.;
   column customer_country product_line quantity total_retail_price;
   define customer_country /group;
   define product_line /group;
   break before customer_country /page contents='';
run;

proc report data=orders contents='';
   by customer_country;
   format customer_country $cntry.;
   column customer_country customer_gender,n customer_age_group,n
customer_type,n;
   define customer_country /group;
   define customer_gender / across;
   define customer_age_group / across;
   define customer_type / across;
   break before customer_country /page contents='';
run;
ods document close;

proc document name=temp;
   make \multrep;
   setlabel \multrep "Sale Information by Country"; ❶
```

```
    make \multrep\cntry1; ❷
    setlabel \multrep\cntry1 "Australia"; ❸
    setlabel \Report#1\ByGroup1#1\Report#1 "Customer Sales"; ❹
    copy \Report#1\ByGroup1#1\Report#1 to \multrep\cntry1#1; ❺
    setlabel \Report#2\ByGroup1#1\Report#1 "Customer Demography"; ❻
    copy \Report#2\ByGroup1#1\Report#1 to \multrep\cntry1#1; ❼

    ❽
    make \multrep\cntry2;
    setlabel \multrep\cntry2 "Canada";
    setlabel \Report#1\ByGroup2#1\Report#1 "Customer Sales";
    copy \Report#1\ByGroup2#1\Report#1 to \multrep\cntry2#1;
    setlabel \Report#2\ByGroup2#1\Report#1 "Customer Demography";
    copy \Report#2\ByGroup2#1\Report#1 to \multrep\cntry2#1;

    make \multrep\cntry3;
    setlabel \multrep\cntry3 "Germany";
    setlabel \Report#1\ByGroup3#1\Report#1 "Customer Sales";
    copy \Report#1\ByGroup3#1\Report#1 to \multrep\cntry3#1;
    setlabel \Report#2\ByGroup3#1\Report#1 "Customer Demography";
    copy \Report#2\ByGroup3#1\Report#1 to \multrep\cntry3#1;

    make \multrep\cntry4;
    setlabel \multrep\cntry4 "Israel";
    setlabel \Report#1\ByGroup4#1\Report#1 "Customer Sales";
    copy \Report#1\ByGroup4#1\Report#1 to \multrep\cntry4#1;
    setlabel \Report#2\ByGroup4#1\Report#1 "Customer Demography";
    copy \Report#2\ByGroup4#1\Report#1 to \multrep\cntry4#1;

    make \multrep\cntry5;
    setlabel \multrep\cntry5 "Turkey";
    setlabel \Report#1\ByGroup5#1\Report#1 "Customer Sales";
    copy \Report#1\ByGroup5#1\Report#1 to \multrep\cntry5#1;
    setlabel \Report#2\ByGroup5#1\Report#1 "Customer Demography";
    copy \Report#2\ByGroup5#1\Report#1 to \multrep\cntry5#1;

    make \multrep\cntry6;
    setlabel \multrep\cntry6 "United States";
    setlabel \Report#1\ByGroup6#1\Report#1 "Customer Sales";
    copy \Report#1\ByGroup6#1\Report#1 to \multrep\cntry6#1;
    setlabel \Report#2\ByGroup6#1\Report#1 "Customer Demography";
    copy \Report#2\ByGroup6#1\Report#1 to \multrep\cntry6#1;

    make \multrep\cntry7;
    setlabel \multrep\cntry7 "South Africa";
    setlabel \Report#1\ByGroup7#1\Report#1 "Customer Sales";
    copy \Report#1\ByGroup7#1\Report#1 to \multrep\cntry7#1;
    setlabel \Report#2\ByGroup7#1\Report#1 "Customer Demography";
    copy \Report#2\ByGroup7#1\Report#1 to \multrep\cntry7#1;
run;
```

```
ods pdf file="CountrySales2.pdf" ;
   replay \multrep; ❾
run;
ods pdf close;

quit;
```

❶ Set the label for the parent node. The label text will be "Sale Information by Country".

❷ Create a subdirectory for the first country.

❸ Give the new subdirectory a label for the first country, which is Australia.

❹ Create a node label for the first PROC REPORT step. The label value is "Customer Sales".

❺ Copy the output object for the first PROC REPORT step into the country subdirectory.

❻ Create a node label for the second PROC REPORT step. The label value is "Customer Demography".

❼ Copy the output object for the second PROC REPORT step into the country subdirectory.

❽ Repeat steps 2-7 for the next six countries.

❾ Generate a new PDF document by replaying the new directory, MULTREP.

Output 7.20: Nodes for Two PROC REPORT Steps under Same Parent Node

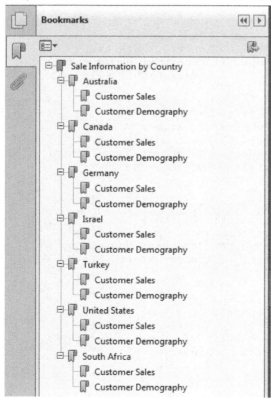

The new item store, MULTREP, restructured both the table of contents and the report table themselves. The final report starts with the first PROC REPORT table for Australia and is followed by the second PROC REPORT table for Australia.

As with the previous example, you could create a macro of this code so that you do not have to copy and paste so many MAKE, SETLABEL, and COPY statements. You should especially consider using macro code if you are combining more than two PROC REPORT steps, as the PROC DOCUMENT code will get very long.

Chapter 8: Debugging Techniques – How to Troubleshoot

8.1 Introduction

No matter how well you know your data or how careful you are when writing your PROC REPORT code, something might still go wrong. This chapter discusses errors, warnings, and notes that PROC REPORT will generate if something is wrong. It also demonstrates how you can view the value of temporary variables to ensure they contain the value that you expect. Finally, the chapter provides general debugging tips.

8.2 Errors, Warnings, and Notes in the Log

This section includes a description of various errors, warnings, and notes that PROC REPORT might generate. The focus is on PROC REPORT specific messages. Messages for global statements or common syntax errors are not discussed. Also, this is not an exhaustive list of all possible messages PROC REPORT might generate, but it does cover frequently encountered messages. The messages are categorized by which statement generates the error.

8.2.1 DEFINE Statement

The following messages are written to the log based on issues with one or more DEFINE statements.

ERROR: XXXX conflicts with earlier use of XXXX.
    PROC REPORT does not allow two different usages for the same *report-item*. For example, a variable cannot be used as both GROUP and ACROSS. This error is most often generated

when an alias is created on the COLUMN statement, but defined with another usage. An alias is most useful when you have an ANALYSIS variable that you want multiple statistics for, such as mean, minimum, maximum, or when you want to use a variable twice in the same manner but formatted two different ways.

Solution:

The workaround for this error is to create a duplicate variable on the input data set. The new variable contains the same information as the original variable but can defined with any usage in the PROC REPORT step.

ERROR: The width of XXXX is not between 1 and NNN. Adjust the column width or line size.
This error message is generated when the WIDTH= option or the length of a *report-item* is longer than the LINESIZE system option. This only affects the ODS Listing destination. If multiple destinations are open, the report will be successfully created in the other destinations.

Solution:

To avoid this error, close the ODS Listing destination if it is not needed. Otherwise, specify WIDTH= on a DEFINE statement for the *report-item* generating the error and set it to a value less than the value of LINESIZE. Also, increase the LINESIZE= system option if it is not at the highest possible value.

ERROR: There is more than one ANALYSIS usage associated with the column defined by the following elements.
A comma in the COLUMN statements means that you intend to stack columns. The error is generated when a comma is present but no variables have been defined with a usage of ACROSS.

Solution:

To eliminate the error remove the comma from the COLUMN statement or change the usage to ACROSS for one of the *report-item*s next to the comma.

ERROR: There is no statistic associated with XXXX
When there is a DISPLAY under an ACROSS, there needs to be a statistic associated with it.

Solution:

The DISPLAY usage should be changed to GROUP or the N statistic inserted after the ACROSS grouping. See Chapter 4 for a more detailed description of how to use variables under ACROSS variables.

ERROR: A DISPLAY or GROUP variable above or below an ACROSS variable requires that there be an ORDER, GROUP, or DISPLAY variable in the report that is not above or below an ACROSS variable.

As indicated by the error message, a GROUP variable needs to be in the report but not under the ACROSS when a GROUP or DISPLAY variable is under the ACROSS.

Solution:

If you do not already have a suitable variable, you need to create a grouping variable in a DATA step to place before the ACROSS variable on the COLUMN statement in your PROC REPORT step. You can define it as NOPRINT so that it will not be displayed in the table.

ERROR: An ORDER variable appears above or below other report items.

An ACROSS variable cannot share a column with an ORDER variable.

Solution:

The ORDER usage should be changed to GROUP. Please note that another GROUP variable needs to exist that is not under the ACROSS.

ERROR: XXXX is not an ORDER, GROUP, or ACROSS variable and is marked DESCENDING.

The DESCENDING option is only valid for ORDER, GROUP, or ACROSS variables. This error will be generated if the option is placed on a DEFINE statement for a DISPLAY, ANALYSIS, or COMPUTED variable.

Solution:

Remove the DESCENDING option to eliminate the error.

ERROR: You cannot have a GROUP variable stacked with an ACROSS variable when there is a DISPLAY variable by itself in a separate column.

PROC REPORT has some restrictions when an ACROSS variable is used. One such restriction is that you cannot have a DISPLAY variable that is not under the ACROSS when a GROUP variable is under the ACROSS.

Solution:

Change the DISPLAY variable to GROUP to avoid this error.

ERROR 180-322: Statement is not valid or it is used out of proper order.

This is a generic error that can be generated by a number of statements. One common reason this error might be generated inside of PROC REPORT is because an invalid style attribute is placed within the STLYE(<LOCATION(s)>)= option. This error can also be generated by a CALL DEFINE statement within a compute block.

Solution:

Check the STYLE= statement or the style specification with the CALL DEFINE statement. Make sure the statement contains a valid style attribute.

ERROR 79-322: Expecting a (.
ERROR 200-322: The symbol is not recognized and will be ignored.
ERROR 76-322: Syntax error, statement will be ignored.

Again, this error might be caused for a number of reasons. This error can also be generated by a CALL DEFINE statement within a compute block.

Solution:

When this error is generated by a style override, it is mostly likely because the attribute value is not valid for the attribute name. For example, fontstyle=bold will generate the error because 'bold' is not a valid value for fontstyle.

WARNING: XXXX is not in the report definition.

This warning is generated by a DEFINE statement that references a *report-item* that is not on the COLUMN statement.

Solution:

Be sure the *report-item* on the DEFINE statement is spelled correctly. Otherwise, add the *report-item* to the COLUMN statement or remove the offending DEFINE statement.

WARNING: The PRELOADFMT option is valid only with GROUP and ACROSS variables.
PRELOADFMT will have no effect for the variable XXXX.

As the warning indicates, the PRELOADFMT option is only valid for certain usage values. The message is generated if the DEFINE statement does not contain one of these usages.

Solution:

To eliminate the message, remove the PRELOADFMT option from the DEFINE statement or change the usage to GROUP or ACROSS.

WARNING: PRELOADFMT will have no effect on the output of variable XXXX without one of the following options: "COMPLETEROWS", "ORDER=DATA", or the define option "EXCLUSIVE".

PRELOADFMT must be used in conjunction with one of three other options. If at least one of those options is not also specified on the DEFINE statement, this warning message will be generated.

Solution:

To eliminate the message, remove the PRELOADFMT option from the DEFINE statement or add one of the other options listed in the message.

WARNING: The MLF option is valid only with GROUP and ACROSS variables. MLF will have no effect for the variable XXXX.

As the warning indicates, the MLF option is only valid for certain usage values. The message is generated if the DEFINE statement does not contain one of these usages.

Solution:

To eliminate the message, remove the MLF option from the DEFINE statement or change the usage to GROUP or ACROSS.

WARNING: A GROUP, ORDER, or ACROSS variable is missing on every observation.

PROC REPORT will issue this warning when, as it says, a GROUP/ORDER/ACROSS variable has a missing value on every observation of the input data set. PROC REPORT will issue the warning, but will not generate a table when this situation occurs.

Solution:

If a missing value is valid, then add the MISSING option to the PROC REPORT statement or the DEFINE statement for the offending grouping variable.

NOTE: Groups are not created because the usage of XXX is DISPLAY. To avoid this note, change all GROUP variables to ORDER variables.

By default, a character variable is defined as a DISPLAY. DISPLAY means that every row from the input data set will be printed. However, a GROUP variable is also defined in the PROC REPORT code. GROUP, by definition, means to consolidate the values to the lowest common level. When there is a DISPLAY and a GROUP in the code, PROC REPORT will treat GROUP as ORDER and issue this note.

Solution:

Changing the usage from GROUP to ORDER will eliminate the note.

8.2.2 BREAK Statement

These errors and warnings might be generated by the BREAK statement.

ERROR: You can only BREAK on GROUPing and ORDERing variables.

The variable listed on the BREAK statement is not defined as GROUP or ORDER.

Solution:

Remove the BREAK statement or change the usage on the DEFINE statement of that variable to GROUP or ORDER.

ERROR: The BREAK variable XXXX is not one of the GROUP or ORDER variables.
This error is generated when an alias is created on the COLUMN statement and the alias is listed on a BREAK statement. PROC REPORT cannot have multiple summary rows on the same variable or location. PROC REPORT considers the alias as the same variable that it copies.

Solution:

The workaround for this error is to create a duplicate variable on the input data set. The new variable contains the same information as the original variable, but can be used in any way in the PROC REPORT step.

WARNING: The CONTENTS option will have no effect for variable XXXX because the PAGE option is not specified.
As the warning indicates, the CONTENTS= option must be paired with the PAGE option on a BREAK statement.

Solution:

Either add the PAGE option or remove the CONTENTS= option to eliminate this warning.

8.2.3 Compute Block Statements

The messages below, as well as statements that refer to *report-item*s within the compute block, are generated by the COMPUTE statement. This section does not include all errors that could be generated by DATA step code within the compute block.

ERROR: Missing an ENDCOMP statement.
A COMPUTE statement requires an ENDCOMP statement; this message is generated if that statement is missing.

Solution:

Add an ENDCOMP statement.

ERROR: There are multiple COMPUTE statements for XXXX.
Only one compute block is allowed for each *report-item*.

Solution:

Consolidate the statements from both blocks into one.

ERROR: There are multiple COMPUTE statements for BREAK AFTER XXXX.
Only one compute block is allowed for each *location target* pair.

Solution:

Consolidate the statements from both blocks into one.

ERROR 22-322: Syntax error, expecting one of the following: a name, AFTER, BEFORE.
A COMPUTE statement contains only the compute keyword and the semicolon. It does not contain a *report-item* or a *location*.

Solution:

Add a *report-item* or a *location* to the COMPUTE statement.

ERROR: The variable type of XXXX.SUM is invalid in this context.
ERROR: Illegal reference to the array XXXX.SUM.
These two error messages generated together can be caused by three different circumstances.

1. An ANALYSIS variable under an ACROSS is referred to by compound name rather than column number, in the form _cn_.
2. An alias is referred to by compound name.
3. An ANALYSIS variable's name is spelled incorrectly on the right side of the equal sign in an assignment statement.

Solution:

Confirm the usage on the DEFINE statement for the XXXX variable and change the reference to the one that is appropriate for that usage. Also, make sure the variable name is spelled correctly.

ERROR: XXXX must use a character format
This occurs when a variable is used on a LINE statement and no format is specified after it. On a LINE statement, a format must be specified for each item (variable).

Solution:

Place a format behind the variable on the LINE statement.

ERROR 22-322: Syntax error, expecting one of the following: a name, a format name
This is a common error that can be generated for any number of reasons, especially when there is a problem with a CALL DEFINE statement.

Solution:

Check that all of the attributes are named correctly. Also, if a format has been specified within a STYLE argument in the CALL DEFINE statement, the error might be generated when a data value falls outside of the range of the format. Finally, be sure a space is placed between each attribute, especially if the statement wraps to another program line.

ERROR: PAGESIZE is too small for BREAK.

This error is generated when PROC REPORT does not have enough space to print all of the information for summary rows and LINE rows on one page. PROC REPORT must keep the LINE statements together and will not split across the page. This error is only generated when sending to the ODS Listing destination.

Solution:

To eliminate the error, close the destination or increase the PAGESIZE value.

ERROR: Invalid column specification in CALL DEFINE.

A variable is referenced in a CALL DEFINE statement that is not on the COLUMN statement. The error might also be generated if the column number used as the first argument to the CALL DEFINE statement does not exist in the table.

Solution:

The CALL DEFINE statement should be removed or the *report-item* should be added to the COLUMN statement.

ERROR: LINE statements must appear in a COMPUTE block that is associated with a location in the report.

This error message is generated if a LINE statement is inside of a compute *report-item* block. LINE statements can be used only in compute blocks associated with a *location*.

Solution:

The statement must be removed from the *report-item* block or a *location* needs to be added to the COMPUTE statement.

NOTE: Variable XXXX is uninitialized.

Variable XXXX is on the right side of the equal sign of an assignment statement, but the variable does not exist. It is not a GROUP/ORDER/DISPAY variable nor a previously defined temporary variable. This error might also be generated by ANALYSIS variables that are not properly referred to by their compound name.

Solution:

To eliminate the note, remove the offending variable, create it as a temporary variable prior to its use on an assignment statement, or change the reference to a compound name.

8.3 Temporary Variable Values

As mentioned in Chapter 2, temporary variables are created within compute blocks, but they do not exist on the input data set and are not part of the final report or the output data set. Their values are retained until overwritten with another assignment statement, but it requires extra work to see the values as PROC REPORT builds a report. You cannot use a PUT statement within a compute block. Therefore, you have to use another method to see the value of temporary variables.

There are two methods for seeing the value of a temporary variable. The method that you use depends on how often the value of the temporary variable changes. Temporary variables created in compute blocks executed at certain *location*s (that is, BEFORE or AFTER a grouping variable), usually do not change as often as temporary variables created in compute *report-item* blocks.

8.3.1 Output via a LINE Statement

The first method for seeing the temporary variable values is to use a LINE statement. This method is truly useful only for temporary variables that change as the value of a GROUP or ORDER variable changes. It works just like it would if you output a variable from the COLUMN statement. Generating the LINE statement does not have to be a permanent part of your PROC REPORT step. You can use it for troubleshooting and then remove the code. You can output the LINE statement in the block where it was created, or output it from another block referencing the other *location*.

Chapter 3 contains an example of calculating percentages for each value of CUSTOMER_COUNTRY. Recall calculating group percentages requires creating a temporary variable to hold the denominator value. Let's revisit that code to demonstrate using a LINE statement to check the value of the temporary variable.

It is often very helpful to add text in the LINE statement prior to the variable name to remind yourself what you are looking at in the final report. Also, text is helpful if you have multiple LINE statements, because it might be confusing as to which one you wrote for debugging purposes. Example 8.1 outputs a LINE statement with the value of the temporary variable and text to draw attention to that row in the final report. The result is shown in Output 8.1.

Example 8.1: Use a LINE Statement to View Temporary Variable Values

```
proc report data=orders;
   column customer_country order_type total_retail_price pct;
   define customer_country / group format=$cntry.;
   define order_type / group format=typef.;
   define total_retail_price / 'Total Retail Price';
   define pct / computed format=percent8.1 'Percent Retail Price';

   compute before customer_country;
      den = total_retail_price.sum;
   endcomp;

   compute after customer_country;
      line 'the denominator used was: ' den 8.2; ❶
   endcomp;
```

```
compute pct;
   if den > 0 then pct = total_retail_price.sum / den;
endcomp;
run;
```

❶ On the LINE statement, place helpful text along with the name of the temporary variable and an appropriate format.

Output 8.1: LINE Statement Contains Temporary Variable Values for Each Country

Customer Country	Order Type	Total Retail Price	Percent Retail Price
Australia	Catalog Sale	$1,679.40	9.7%
	Internet Sale	$613.90	3.5%
	Retail Sale	$15,028.19	86.8%
the denominator used was: 17321.49			
Canada	Catalog Sale	$5,422.38	45.4%
	Internet Sale	$6,528.70	54.6%
the denominator used was: 11951.08			
Germany	Catalog Sale	$10,034.40	65.2%
	Internet Sale	$5,360.20	34.8%
the denominator used was: 15394.60			
Israel	Catalog Sale	$1,316.10	84.4%
	Internet Sale	$243.40	15.6%
the denominator used was: 1559.50			
South Africa	Catalog Sale	$3,161.70	61.4%
	Internet Sale	$1,988.20	38.6%
the denominator used was: 5149.90			
Turkey	Catalog Sale	$4,690.20	90.6%
	Internet Sale	$485.60	9.4%
the denominator used was: 5175.80			
United States	Catalog Sale	$7,627.17	17.5%
	Internet Sale	$6,271.55	14.4%
	Retail Sale	$29,626.38	68.1%
the denominator used was: 43525.10			

8.3.2 Output via a COMPUTED Variable

The second method for seeing the values of a temporary variable is to assign them to a COMPUTED variable. This method works best if the value changes frequently, such as on every row. It is especially helpful when checking a temporary variable that is keeping a running total.

Chapter 3 contains an example of showing summary values for nested groups. The example requires temporary variables to hold a running tally of QUANTITY for each value of ORDER_TYPE. Let's revisit the example, but modify it slightly so that the temporary variables changes more frequently.

A new *report-item* has to be placed on the COLUMN statement. The best place to put the new *report-item* is at the end of the COLUMN statement so that it does not affect the creation of any of your other columns. A DEFINE statement and a compute block for this new *report-item* are needed. Again, having a COMPUTED column does not have to be a permanent part of your PROC REPORT step. You can use it for troubleshooting and then remove the column from the code or add the NOPRINT option to prevent the column from appearing in the final report. Example 8.2 and Output 8.2 demonstrate including the COMPUTED variable.

Example 8.2: Use a COMPUTED Variable to View Temporary Variable Values

```
data orders2;
   set orders;
   dummy1 = 1;
   dummy2 = 1;
   dummy3 = 1;
run;

proc report data=orders2;
   column dummy1 dummy2 dummy3  customer_group order_type
      total_retail_price quantity discount seetempvar; ❶
   define dummy1 / group noprint;
   define dummy2 / group noprint;
   define dummy3 / group noprint;
   define customer_group / group;
   define order_type / group format=typef. order=internal;
   define seetempvar / computed; ❷

   break after dummy1 /summarize;
   break after dummy2 /summarize;
   break after dummy3 /summarize;

   compute discount;
      if order_type in (1 2) then do;
         qnt1 + quantity.sum;
      end;
   endcomp;
   compute seetempvar; ❸
      seetempvar = qnt1; ❹
   endcomp;

run;
```

❶ Add SEETEMPVAR to the COLUMN statement. This *report-item* will hold the value of the temporary variable created in a compute block.

❷ Define SEETEMPVAR as COMPUTED.

❸ A compute block is needed for the COMPUTED *report-item*. This compute block will execute on every row. It executes after the block where the temporary variable is assigned a value.

❹ The SEETEMPVAR is assigned the current value of the temporary variable. Its value can now be seen in the final report.

Output 8.2: A COMPUTED Variable Contains the Value of the Temporary Variable

Customer Group Name	Order Type	Total Retail Price for This Product	Quantity Ordered	Discount in percent of Normal Total Retail Price	seetempvar
Internet/Catalog Customers	Catalog Sale	$11,216.30	99	.	99
	Internet Sale	$2,964.15	39	.	99
Orion Club Gold members	Retail Sale	$13,710.45	169	40%	268
	Catalog Sale	$6,836.47	58	.	326
	Internet Sale	$11,234.10	81	.	326
Orion Club members	Retail Sale	$30,944.12	390	30%	716
	Catalog Sale	$15,878.58	136	30%	852
	Internet Sale	$7,293.30	106	.	852
		$100,077.47	1078	100%	852
		$100,077.47	1078	100%	852
		$100,077.47	1078	100%	852

8.4 General Tips

As with SAS in general, PROC REPORT does exactly what you tell it to do. It might not do what you want it to do, but it does what you tell it to do. The following tips give guidance on how to approach generating a report with PROC REPORT and places to check if something goes wrong.

Tip #1: Know Your Data

The first tip for determining why PROC REPORT did not give you what you want is universal to programming: **know your data**.

- Check that there are no missing values. Warning messages about missing values, whether they are grouping or ANALYSIS variables, are generated because the input data set does in fact have missing values.

- Check that all of the categories that you expect are present in your data. PROC REPORT is not going to output a category that does not exist. Chapter 3 contains an example of inserting categories with no data.

- Check the length of your character variables. A text value inserted via PROC REPORT might be truncated if the length of the variable that you are inserting it into is shorter than the length of the text.

Tip #2: Plan Your Report

The next tip is to plan your report before you start to program. The plan should help you decide whether you need to create formats or whether you need to add variables to your data set for grouping or ordering purposes. Based on what you have learned about PROC REPORT from this book, planning should also help you determine whether you are going to need to pre-process your data in some way.

Tip #3: Start Small

Once you begin to program, start small and work your way up to more complicated results. Perhaps use a subset of your data when working out all of the kinks. Start with two or three variables to get the basic report and then add to it. In this way you can see how the report changes as you add more code, and it is easier to determine where something went wrong. Also, the general recommendation is to finalize the structure of the report and the numbers before adding styling attributes.

Tip #4: Check the Variable Order on the Column Statement

One of the most important things to know about PROC REPORT is that it works in a left to right direction based on the *report-items* listed on the COLUMN statement. If a column has missing values that should not be missing or a format or color is not applied, check the COMPUTE statement and the assignment statements inside of the compute blocks. Any *report-item* to the right of the one on the COMPUTE statement is not available in the compute block and will be missing.

Tip #5: Include Only One Usage Value

On the DEFINE statement, be sure to have only one usage. The usage value closest to the semicolon is the one that is used. Commonly, ORDER is placed on a DEFINE statement when the programmer wants the report to be sorted by that variable. ORDER is a usage value. It has a specific meaning to PROC REPORT. It will overwrite any other usage listed prior to it on the DEFINE statement. The ORDER= option is different from the ORDER usage, and is the one you need to use when specifying the desired sort order.

Tip #6: Take Advantage of the SHOWALL Option

The SHOWALL option, explained in Chapter 1, is very useful if you have used the NOPRINT or NOZERO options. Hidden columns affect the column numbers needed inside of compute blocks. You can use this option to confirm you are using the correct column numbers. Hidden GROUP or ORDER variables can and do effect the GROUP or ORDER variables that are seen. Use the SHOWALL option to see hidden columns without having to alter any other statements in the PROC REPORT step.

Tip #7: Use the LIST Option

As discussed in Chapter 1, the LIST option is most useful when creating output for the Listing destination, but it can be handy when you need to confirm the label, format, and width PROC REPORT is using for a variable.

Tip #8: Remove Unnecessary Options

Use only the options that you need. PROC REPORT code can become long and complicated even without unnecessary code. Including options that do not impact the output are distracting and add clutter.

References

Books

Tuchman, M. 2012. *PROC DOCUMENT by Example Using SAS®*. Cary, NC: SAS Institute Inc.

Carpenter, A. 2007. *Carpenter's Complete Guide to the SAS® REPORT Procedure*. Cary, NC: SAS Institute Inc.

Burlew, M.M. 2005. *SAS® Guide to Report Writing: Examples*. Cary, NC: SAS Institute Inc.

Conference Papers

Lawhorn, B. 2011. "Let's Give 'Em Something to TOC about: Transforming the Table of Contents of Your PDF File." *Proceedings of the SAS Global Forum 2011 Conference*. Cary, NC: SAS Institute Inc. Available http://support.sas.com/resources/papers/proceedings11/252-2011.pdf.

Booth, A.M. 2011. "Beyond the Basics: Advanced REPORT Procedure Tips and Tricks Updated for SAS® 9.2." *Proceedings of the SAS Global Forum 2011 Conference*. Cary, NC: SAS Institute Inc. Available http://support.sas.com/resources/papers/proceedings11/246-2011.pdf.

McMahill, A. 2007. "Beyond the Basics: Advanced PROC REPORT Tips and Tricks." *Proceedings of the SAS Global Forum 2007 Conference*. Cary, NC: SAS Institute Inc. Available http://support.sas.com/rnd/papers/sgf07/sgf2007-report.pdf.

Technical Paper

SAS Institute Inc. 2008. "Using Style Elements in the REPORT and TABULATE Procedures." Cary, NC: SAS Institute Inc. http://support.sas.com/resources/papers/stylesinprocs.pdf

SAS Documentation

SAS Institute Inc. 2015. *Base SAS® 9.4 Procedures Guide, Fifth Edition.* Cary, NC: SAS Institute Inc.

SAS Institute Inc. 2015. *SAS® 9.4 Macro Language: Reference, Fourth Edition.* Cary, NC: SAS Institute Inc.

SAS Institute Inc. 2015. *SAS® 9.4 Output Delivery System: User's Guide, Fourth Edition.* Cary, NC: SAS Institute Inc.

SAS Institute Inc. 2015. *SAS® 9.4 Output Delivery System: Procedures Guide, Second Edition.* Cary, NC: SAS Institute Inc.

SAS Notes

Usage Note 24182: How to remove the blue border around URL= links in an ODS PDF file
http://support.sas.com/kb/24182 http://support.sas.com/kb/24/182.html

Usage Note 24542: How to get the exact order of your input data set in PROC REPORT output when the ORDER=DATA option is specified in a DEFINE statement
http://support.sas.com/kb/24542 http://support.sas.com/kb/24/542.html

Sample 26157: Print information to the Output window if data set is empty
http://support.sas.com/kb/26157 http://support.sas.com/kb/26/157.html

Sample 37763: Conditionally print a LINE statement in PROC REPORT
http://support.sas.com/kb/37/763.html http://support.sas.com/kb/37/763.html

Index

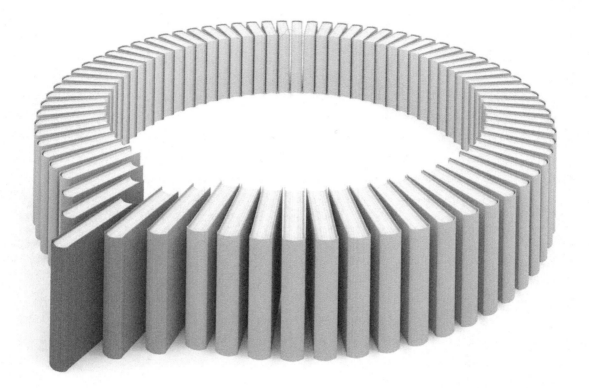

Gain Greater Insight into Your SAS® Software with SAS Books.

Discover all that you need on your journey to knowledge and empowerment.

support.sas.com/bookstore
for additional books and resources.

THE POWER TO KNOW®

Made in the USA
Monee, IL
01 November 2019